Charles Maurice Davies

Unorthodox London

Or, Phases of religious Life in the Metropolis

Charles Maurice Davies

Unorthodox London
Or, Phases of religious Life in the Metropolis

ISBN/EAN: 9783337130886

Printed in Europe, USA, Canada, Australia, Japan

Cover: Foto ©ninafisch / pixelio.de

More available books at **www.hansebooks.com**

UNORTHODOX LONDON:

OR,

PHASES OF RELIGIOUS LIFE IN THE METROPOLIS.

BY THE

REV. C. MAURICE DAVIES, D.D.

FORMERLY FELLOW OF THE UNIVERSITY OF DURHAM,

AUTHOR OF
"ORTHODOX," "HETERODOX," "MYSTIC LONDON," "LONDON SERMONS,"
ETC.

SERIES II.

SECOND EDITION.

LONDON:
TINSLEY BROTHERS, CATHERINE ST., STRAND.
1875.

LONDON:
SAVILL, EDWARDS AND CO., PRINTERS, CHANDOS STREET,
COVENT GARDEN.

CONTENTS.

	PAGE
THE STATUS QUO 1875	1
THE WESTMINSTER COUNCIL	7
THE PONTIGNY PILGRIMAGE	16
POPE PIUS'S VALENTINE	45
A "CATHOLIC" UNIVERSITY COLLEGE	59
MOODY-AND-SANKEYISM	66
A NEW ICONOCLAST	86
MR. REVELL AT LADBROKE HALL	97
A REVISED PRAYER-BOOK	101
A GREEK EASTERTIDE	122
A GOOD FRIDAY FAIR	130
A POSTMEN'S TEA PARTY	141
IN A FRENCH PASTURE	148
A PRIZE-FIGHTER'S SERMON	156
GREAT TRIBULATION	165
A LADY-PREACHER AT THE POLYTECHNIC	176
THE MERCHANTS' LECTURE	184
BRAMOISM IN LONDON	193
A MOZOOMDAR'S SERMON	203
MR. DE MORGAN ON CHRISTIANITY	211
THE JUBILEE SINGERS	224

when severe, I felt them to be just. In the case of one or two conspicuous exceptions, I could afford to smile, as I received continual calls for new editions, and meditated on Dean Swift's lines :—

> "As for his works in verse or prose,
> I own myself no judge of those;
> Nor can I tell what critics thought 'em;
> I only know *all people bought 'em*."

Adverse criticism is rather a reflection on the taste of the public than on my impertinence in answering the demand with fresh supplies.

MAURICE DAVIES.

London, June, 1875.

UNORTHODOX LONDON.

SERIES II.

THE STATUS QUO 1875.

IF it were necessary to summarize in one comprehensive expression the nature of the influences at work on the different religious bodies both within and without the pale of the Church of England as by Law Established, it would perhaps be difficult to find a more significant word than the often abused one—Revivalism. In two conspicuous examples the very term is adopted by large bodies of religionists. In other cases the thing itself is patent, though the name is repudiated.

The Roman Catholics have distinctly laid it down as their purpose to "revive" not only pilgrimages, but other similar institutions, which we practical nineteenth century people fondly thought we had left behind in the poetic Middle Ages. Paray-le-

Monial and Pontigny are *faits accomplis*. The Papal Jubilee is the appropriate climax in such a series.

At the opposite extreme, too, the impetus of Revivalism, technically so termed, long gathering strength among the Evangelical bodies within and without the Church of England, culminated in Moody-and-Sankeyism. That was but the last—if the last—link in a chain of influences which have been long since taken to represent a "great religious awakening." Noonday prayer-meetings in the heart of the City have been an outcome of this particular movement; and it was hard to criticise a method so evidently characterized by real enthusiasm, though there were times when the special intercessory prayers offered up by the "converted" for their unregenerate friends and belongings appeared to trench on the very verge of Roman direction. It seemed to be the same thing under another name; and we, whose simple mission it was to note the signs of the times, felt relieved to think our business was to describe rather than to criticise, though conscious that much of what we saw was only a novel illustration of the old proverb that extremes meet. Similar in kind, though exceeding even Moody-and-Sankeyism in degree of enthusiasm, was the effort of Mrs. Girling and her Shakers to revive in the New Forest the

Christian Communism of the Infant Church, blended, it might seem, with customs for which the only precedent available was the one of David dancing before the ark. Even the Ritualistic movement in the Church of England, and that strange development of once Presbyterian Irvingism, outside known as *the* Catholic Apostolic Church, are simply Revivals of past eras, one stopping short at Ecclesiasticism, the other assuming to reproduce in veriest literalism the apostolic age itself.

Amid these different retrogressive influences two bodies only have seemed to feel any of the reaction which is certain to accompany such an age of enthusiasm. The Broad Church party, lacking that cohesion which of necessity attaches to a theology in any degree destructive just as to political parties which are said to be "based on a negation," has made its mark rather by means of influential individuals like Dean Stanley and the late Canon Kingsley, than by force of numbers; and the Old Catholics in nature, though not in name, who were forced into existence in England as it were by way of protest against Mr. Gladstone's wholesale imputation of disloyalty to Catholics proper, can scarcely be said to have a substantive existence at all in our midst yet. But still, in the germ or full blown, all these opinions are prevalent at the moment of writing in this the world's metropolis—and it is their action and reaction one on the other that go to make up the religious status quo. To note these various influences, not in the abstract, as we are now doing, but in the concrete, as embodied in their various representative men, is still the object of the ensuing supplementary pages.

Merely to cull the clerical advertisement column from a Saturday's *Times*, or the "Preachers for to-morrow" from an evening paper, is marvellously suggestive of the exuberance of religious life in London. For instance, to take the programme of Easter Eve in this present year 1875: after the announcement of the Foundling services comes that of the Oxford Music Hall, followed by that of St. James's Hall where, after the Rev. Newman Hall in the afternoon, follows the Rev. J. B. Heard, just seceded from the Church of England, to cast in his lot with the Free Churches. Then comes St. George's Hall; then the French Protestant Church in Westbourne Grove. High Mass at the Italian Church, Hatton Garden, and the Pro-Cathedral, Kensington, succeeds the latter, including a sermon by Monsignor Capel. Mr. Spurgeon's reappearance at the Metropolitan Tabernacle curiously divides these last-mentioned from St. George's Cathedral and St.

Mary's, Moorfields. These, in turn, are followed by the French Protestant Church in St. Martin's-le-Grand, and the Catholic Apostolic Church, where an Evangelist is to preach "The Finished Work of Jesus." Next in order comes Mr. Voysey, with "The Gospel of Adversity;" and at the South Kensington Presbyterian Church somebody is going to demolish the Sacerdotalism of Romanists and Ritualists. Dr. Stoughton bids farewell to his Kensington congregation with a sermon on "The Celestial City" (misprinted in one journal, "The *Celebrated* City!") Then come Messrs. Moody and Sankey with three services at the Agricultural Hall—viz., 8 A.M., for Christian workers; at 3.30, "for women only;" and at 7 for men only; and Mr. Moncure D. Conway, at Fox's Chapel, finishes the list with a sermon on "South Kensington Museum," unless we include Prebendary Row's concluding lecture on Christian Evidences at the Polytechnic, entitled "The Historical Evidence of the Resurrection." Truly a varied bill of fare for less than a score of churches and chapels. Barren indeed must the pen be that could not, with such material, find interesting details to communicate in reference to London Orthodox and Unorthodox! I propose, therefore, once more to go over the ground in detail, but with something more of method than before, adding, at all events in the case of the more prominent religious bodies, such statistical details to the descriptive matter as shall constitute this work in some degree a book of reference. Taking one or more *coups d'œil* at the representative men in each community, I shall seek to add such particulars of minor celebrities as shall present a faithful picture of Religious London in 1875, divided still by the arbitrary line of the Establishment into Orthodox and Unorthodox. I desire emphatically to repeat, that this division is purely technical, and implies not the smallest expression of opinion as to the truth or value of any doctrine or practice. From my present standpoint as a clergyman of the Established Church, such a division naturally, almost necessarily, suggests itself; but I have never seen occasion to lay aside the excellent method prescribed by the proprietors of the journal by whose commission I first began these investigations—viz., that I should simply describe, and express no opinion pro or con.

The bulk of the papers are still reprints from the London and provincial newspapers, amplified in some instances by additional particulars, and the publication of documents *in extenso* which were originally abridged to suit the exigences of space.

THE WESTMINSTER COUNCIL.

Smoking my after-dinner cigar one summer day in 1873, I was startled from my suburban repose by the far from infrequent apparition of a Hansom cab driving up, tenanted by a rather dirty little boy, whom I at once divined to be a "devil"—I mean, of course, a printer's devil. Just such an appearance had broken in upon my serenity on a certain July evening in 1870, when a fac-simile of that boy had driven up in like manner, and ordered me off to the seat of the Franco-Prussian war. "Cross to-night"— were the laconic instructions—"Foreign Office passport enclosed. See —— in Paris, and arrange for separate routes." I wondered whither that begrimed juvenile was going to send me now. There was no war on at this time; the greatest event of the hour was the impending Roman Catholic Council at St. Edmund's College, Ware: and that academic institution was to be, I found, my destination. Armed with a letter of introduction to Monsignor Patterson, the President of the College, I was soon on my way to the Shoreditch station.

Here I found evident signs of preparation for the morrow, when the Council was to open at early morning. There were a few priests—most having already gone to Ware; and with two of these, and a gentleman whom I soon discovered to be a "converted" Anglican clergyman, I enjoyed a pleasant trip down to Ware in the soft summer evening. I was for taking up my quarters in the village; but my ex-Anglican friend assured me I should greatly offend the hospitable feelings of the College authorities if I did so. "Come up and dine in refectory," he said, though he himself had no sort of invitation; "and if they have room, I am sure they will stow you away." I need not say it was much more consonant with my tastes to accept than decline this very informal bidding; and after a most enjoyable walk across country with my new friend and two sociable priests, we entered these academic halls as though we were students in residence returning from an evening stroll.

Above the fine old College of St. Edmund's floated, as I entered, the Papal Standard; and, having gained the great hall, I found myself at once in the centre of a crowd of ecclesiastics, representing every grade of the hierarchy, and many of the orders of the Church, from the Sub-deacon up to the Archbishop of Westminster himself, whom I saw enjoying the balmy summer evening in front of the College. Here was the brown gaberdine of a Franciscan friar or Capuchin monk; here the white habit of a Dominican; here the sombre attire of a Benedictine, a Jesuit, or a Passionist Father. The bishops were distinguished by the gold chain and pectoral cross; and what struck me more than anything else was the absence of all hauteur, and appearance of universal fraternity pervading this, to me, most strange gathering. I could not help contrasting it mentally with a meeting of Protestant bishops, archbishops, and clergy—not so much, perhaps, to the disparagement of the latter as in its utter divergence from it in every possible respect. Travel-stained as we were, we sat down to dine, and I was soon quite at home with my ecclesiastical neighbours. With something of antique hospitality I was forbidden to seek the village hostelry, and was comfortably—though not, of course, luxuriously — lodged in some young student's quarters, for the alumni of St. Edmund's were then in vacation. The beautiful Benediction Office of the

Church was sung during the evening, and I had an opportunity of examining the noble chapel, one of the works of the elder Pugin. The High Altar is rich in the extreme, and at the entrance of the Sacrarium stand four huge candelabra, flanked with adoring angels. The choir is oak-stalled throughout, and divided from the ante-chapel by a rood-loft, in which is an excellent organ. There are many smaller chapels, including those of Our Lady of the Sacred Heart, St. Edmund, St. Joseph, and a beautiful mortuary chapel. Besides these each bishop had fitted up for him, in different large rooms, an altar at which to say mass on the morning of the opening of the function. The only drawback to my perfect comfort that night was that my neighbour in the next student's rooms—a worthy Franciscan friar—snored most vigorously. But the fresh air and the country walk made me pretty well proof against this; and I daresay I was soon doing the same.

At six o'clock next morning a bell was rung along the corridors, and masses began to be sung. I felt the most unconscionable heretic to be lying there under the very shadow of the crucifix, whilst all my good neighbours were getting up and going to devotions. When I emerged, I found every chapel, permanent or extemporized, occupied by a bishop or priest reciting the holy office. There were scarcely any lay visitors besides myself. Sir George Bowyer officiated as notary, vested as a Knight of Malta with a doctor's gown. Lady Herbert of Lea was also present at the function.

Directly after breakfast the procession began to form in the Studium, the archbishop and bishops coming from the further end of the corridor to vest. They were then arranged as follows:—1. Cantors; 2. Officials of the Synod; 3. Theologians of the Bishops; 4. Theologians invited by the Synod; 5. Canons of Suffragan Cathedrals; 6. Seminaries and metropolitan clergy; 7. Thurifer with thurible; 8. Sub-deacon with archiepiscopal cross, and two acolytes with lighted candles; 9. Two mitred Benedictine Abbots; 10. Metropolitan Canons, among whom were the Ministers of the Mass and Assistant Priest and Deacon; 11. Bishops, two and two, with chaplains; 12. The Metropolitan Archbishop, blessing with his right hand, and holding the pastoral staff in his left; two assistant-deacons, two masters of the ceremonies, the archbishop's assistants, train-bearers, chaplains, and gentlemen of the household (*ex familiâ nobili*); 13. Apostolical Prelates and superiors of the religious orders of the province.

Among the bishops were, besides the Metropolitan,

Dr. Brown, O.S.B., Bishop of Newport and Menevia; Dr. Ullathorne, O.S.B., of Birmingham; Dr. James Brown, of Shrewsbury; Dr. Roskell, of Nottingham; Dr. Vaughan, of Plymouth; Hon. and Rev. Dr. Clifford, of Clifton; Dr. Amherst, of Northampton; Dr. Cornthwaite, of Beverley; Dr. Chadwick, of Hexham; Dr. Danell, of Southwark; Dr. Herbert Vaughan, of Salford; and Dr. O'Reilly, of Liverpool. Besides these were the Most Rev. R. B. Vaughan, O.S.B., Archbishop of Nazianzum, and Coadjutor-Archbishop of Sydney; and Most Rev. Dr. Howard, of Neo-Cæsarea.

The mitred abbots were the Right Rev. Dr. Burchall, of St. Michael's, Hereford, and the Right Rev. Dr. Alcock, Abbot of St. Augustine's, Ramsgate; the former is President-General of English Benedictines, the latter representing those of Monte Casino.

The Secretaries of the Synod were Canon Fisher (of Liverpool), Dr. Sweeney, O.S.B. (of Bath), Father Guiron, and Rev. Father Allen; Dr. Northcott, President of Oscott; Rev. Father Eyre, S.J., President of Stonyhurst College; Father Mount (of Southampton), and Dr. Mark Oleron, V.G. (of Northampton), were among those present.

The religious orders established in England were represented by Father Galway, of the Society of

Jesus; Father Bernard, Provincial of the Passionists; Father Coffin, Provincial of the Redemptorists; Father King, of the Dominicans; Father Anselm, of the Franciscans; Father Emidius, Commissary-General of the Capuchins; Father Rinolfi, Provincial of the Order of Charity; and Father Blosio, of the Order of the Servites of Mary.

The cross-bearers were the Rev. Canon Drinkwater and Rev. Father Collingridge, parish priest of Old Hall.

The organist was Mr. Charles Cox, student of St. Edmund's College. The singing was led by Father Crookall, Vicar-General of Southwark, by whom the Plain-song of the Mass was harmonized. The Very Rev. Canon Scott, of Northampton, was also among the Cantors. The Masters of the Ceremonies were: Rev. J. Rouse, D.D., Vice-President of St. Edmund's College; Father Gadd, M.C. to the Archbishop; Rev. G. Cox, M.C. to the Sacred Ministers; Rev. John Weeks, M.C. to the Bishops; and Rev. Thomas Pearce, M.C. to the clergy.

A more magnificent *coup d'œil* can scarcely be imagined than when, having sung the first verse of the "Veni Creator," while all around knelt, the vast procession passed through the grounds to the chapel. The brilliant sun lit up the various rich vestments, and made many persons exclaim that they had never seen anything like it out of Rome; whilst, at the same time, one felt that it was not a mere pageant, but a real representative gathering of Catholic England. Each chapter sent its procurator to take part with the bishops in the deliberations of the Council. On reaching the chapel, the Archbishop passed to the chancel and vested, after which he celebrated High Mass to a plain chant. The grouping was perfect, and all went without any hitch, as smoothly as though it had all been rehearsed beforehand. After the Mass, the Litany of the Saints was sung, as is usual at high functions, and some psalms from one of the day-hours were chanted before the congregation left.

The sermon was not delivered, as usual, during the Mass, but after its conclusion, and so formed part of the proceedings of the Synod—a fact which necessitated the withdrawal of all except members of the Council. It was preached by Dr. Ullathorne, O.S.B., Bishop of Birmingham, and was a scholastic discourse addressed purely to theologians, and bearing strictly on the spiritual life.

The business of the Council was done by congregations, each consisting of three bishops, with ten or twelve members. Among the subjects set down for discussion were Liturgy, Discipline, Morals, and Education. The bishops alone voted, the other members having only a deliberative voice in the Assembly. The proceedings of the Council ranged over a fortnight, and concluded with a solemn public function similar to that at which I was present. There was, on one day, a solemn requiem mass for the souls of those prelates departed since the last Council. All this was explained by the Archbishop himself, who most courteously apologized for the exclusion of the press, as necessitated by the place which the sermon occupied in the proceedings. As one looked along the lines of bishops and clergy, whether unbending in refectory, or staid and solemn in the holy office, one could not but feel that the real power of the Catholic Church was present at the Council, or quite forbear from wondering what effect such deliberations might have on the faith of England. The immediate results were Paray-le-Monial and Pontigny. May we add *ex post facto* the Cardinalate of Archbishop Manning and the Papal Jubilee? Is not England to be converted?

THE PONTIGNY PILGRIMAGE.

IN my self-chosen capacity of ecclesiastical Ulysses, I felt it absolutely necessary that I should "follow" the Pontigny Pilgrimage of 1874. I might have my own private opinion as to whether pilgrimages in general were exactly the sort of institution adapted to the needs of the nineteenth century; and also might cherish my own ideas as to the advisability of crossing from Newhaven to Dieppe (for I may mention I am an uncommonly bad sailor); but I really felt I should be a traitor to my principles if I neglected such an opportunity of "seeing the cities of many men and learning their customs;" while, as for the contingencies of possible *mal de mer*, I was not quite so heretical as to suppose that all the ways of a pilgrimage should be ways of pleasantness or its paths peace. Quite prepared to boil my peas, I was yet aware that when I assumed the cockle-hat and sandal shoon peas of some sort would be a prerequisite.

It was, I own, with some diffidence that I applied to Monsignor Patterson, at St. Edmund's College, Ware, for a card which should prove my "good faith" to Messrs. Cook and Co., for I was well aware that, in one sense, Monsignor Patterson could not possibly endorse the quality of my faith, but I need not say that it was in a colloquial, and not an ethical sense, my faith was to be guaranteed; so I received my "Pilgrim's card" by the next post, which I duly exchanged for Messrs. Cook's coupons a week before the pilgrimage began. That preliminary week I devoted to fulfilling my baptismal vow in the way of hearing sermons, and also studying the literature of the pilgrimage; for I confess, with shame and confusion of face, I had hitherto known little of St. Edmund, and less of Pontigny. On Sunday, August 23rd, I went to the fashionable "Pro" at Kensington, and was sorry to hear the Archbishop of Westminster take the opportunity of railing at the press. It seemed to me rather a left-handed compliment to the British public when his Grace said that if the press were to represent his Holiness the Pope as having horns and hoofs (which Heaven forefend!) the community was gullible enough to believe it. I magnify mine office, of course; on the "nothing-like-leather" principle, I suppose we all do, more or less. But I don't think the press is quite so omnipotent as that comes to. When, with a touch of satire, the Archbishop divided the Established Church into two portions, one verging towards Rome, the other towards German Rationalism, I felt awfully Teutonic, and discreetly buried my face in my note-book.

On Sunday, the 30th, Monsignor Patterson preached his final sermon at the "Pro," to a not very large congregation, though the Exposition of the Blessed Sacrament, closing in the "Triduum" of observances, ought to have proved an attraction. Two *religieuses* in black habits, with white veils, were kneeling before the High Altar, on which blazed more than a hundred and fifty tapers; but these "watchers" decamped when Vespers began. The sermon was a plain and practical one, principally devoted, it appeared to me, to an apology for the sensational character of the impending pilgrimage. Monday, August 31st, however, was the real commencement of the business of the expedition, if it be allowable to apply so mundane an expression to a nineteenth century pilgrimage. Kensington, which is rapidly becoming the focus of Roman Catholic influences in London, was to be the head-quarters of the pilgrimage, of course;

and here Monsignor Patterson was to deliver his farewell address to our devoted band who were to attend Compline Service and receive Benediction at his hands.

It was still light when I sought the Pro-Cathedral and found the faithful assembled in goodly numbers; intending pilgrims being distinguished by a small red heart-shaped badge, surmounted by a cross, and also being placed in seats of honour in the church. I wore no badge; but my pilgrim's ticket procured me a front seat close to the altar. Flanking the chancel arch were white banners of the Immaculate Conception and the Blessed Sacrament, with others; and the High Altar was literally covered with tapers and floral decorations. The side altars of the Sacrament and of the Virgin were also tastefully adorned. In fact, all was *en fête* for the occasion. It is not every day an English pilgrimage sets out for a foreign shrine.

Soon after seven o'clock, the great organ pealed forth one of those magnificent voluntaries so familiar to those who frequent the "Pro;" and softly be it spoken, a great many besides the faithful do frequent it on Sunday evenings when they have got their regular church-going over. The imitation of the human voice by the *voix céleste* stop of this instrument is perfectly marvellous.

At half-past seven a large procession of clergy and assistants entered the chancel, among the former being Monsignor Capel, in purple vestments, and the Bishop of Amycla in full episcopal attire. The latter at once commenced the office of Completorium or Compline, which is the last office before bedtime, and consists of night-prayers, psalms, and hymns; among the psalms being the appropriate 91st, sung to one of the most tuneful of the Gregorian tones, and the hymn being the "Te lucis ante terminum." The office ends with the Nunc Dimittis.

At its conclusion Monsignor Patterson, entering from the sacristy, clad in purple vestments, proceeded at once to the pulpit, and gave out some notices referring to the details of the pilgrimage, emphatically urging punctuality on intending pilgrims. "And now, my brother pilgrims," he said, "though the work appears facile, those who went last year can attest that the facilities for ordinary traffic are apt to break down and interfere with comfort." His words would therefore be few, and directed to the actualities of the case. He had received expressions of warm sympathy from a dignitary of the English Church. (Who can this sympathetic dignitary be, I wonder?) This was a time, he urged, when the externation of religion was especially necessary, and the method of pilgrimage had been dictated by the circumstances of persecution in which the Church was placed. So it fell back on the ancient method of visiting the tombs of the martyrs. That was the rationale of pilgrimages. In special reference to the morrow Monsignor Patterson said we should have to suffer. Let us do so with patience. We should try to have at heart the unity of God's Church, and seek to offend no one, but rather to dissipate prejudice. The moral order of the Church was conditioned by the Prayer of Christ before His Passion. Let us pray for unity, to gain which every true Catholic heart would shed the last drop of its blood. Let it be a pilgrimage of prayer. If we went forth in the spirit of the Great Saint who once so firmly ruled England, our prayer would be heard. Let us go and show forth the beauty of God's Catholic Church, that others may be attracted to enter with us into the holy place, and so be with us in glory hereafter.

After the sermon, which was very judiciously abridged, the Benedictus was chanted, and the special prayers for the pilgrimage intoned by the Bishop of Amycla, supplication being made that "the angel Raphael might accompany us on our way, and that we may return to our homes in peace, safety, and joy." He then gave us his episcopal benediction, sprinkling us with holy water, of which, being in the front seat, I got my full share. The great altar was then lighted up to its full brilliance, and the Hymn of St. Edmund's Pilgrims sung to the particularly lively tune generally used for Faber's hymn, "The Pilgrims of the Night." The effect of this part of the service was most imposing, and the whole concluded with the benediction of the Sacrament. The great advantage of this service is that everybody knows it, and they have taken two of the best of our hymn tunes for their "O Salutaris" and "Tantum ergo;" while the Litany of Loretto is set to the most taking of measures: so we—yes, *we*—all bore part in it fullvoiced. The Litany was more ornate than usual, and the solo parts effectively rendered by a professional soprano voice.

Such was the Benediction of the Pontigny Pilgrimage—perfect as a spectacle; but whether to issue in the reconversion of England remains to be seen.

A balmy morning succeeded the stormy night, and I really began to have hopes of the day. We took in pilgrims at all the stations along the Metropolitan District Railway, and Victoria Station looked quite ornamental with its decorated *voyageurs*. Monsignor Capel was there to bid us *bon voyage*, but was not able to accompany us, being, it was whispered, subpœnaed upon a certain well-known law case. Most of our party wore their badges, and there were symptoms of impending processions in banner-poles, which had to be stowed away with difficulty along the whole length of third-class compartments. Departing amid the cheers of the crowd, we began our devotions at once, the priests reciting in a low monotone the office of the rosary. We sped quickly to Newhaven thus, alternating the scene with prayers and conversation, and so embarked on board the boat *Bordeaux*, the sea looking very white and wicked indeed. We sang—again amid the plaudits of those assembled—the perennial Hymn of the Pilgrims; but as soon as we got out of the harbour, a big wave washed over us, and *changeait tout cela*. Most of the pilgrims were speedily reduced to a recumbent position, and some of them—I was no exception—suffered severely; but in mid-channel the wind fell almost miraculously, and we entered the port of Dieppe with becoming dignity. There the Mayor boarded us forthwith, and proffered hospitality, which, I regret to say, was not accepted, for by this time we were a hungry band of pilgrims, and had to rush from boat to train without breaking fast till we came to Rouen, though we dawdled—as French trains know how to dawdle—at Dieppe.

From Dieppe to Paris, I greatly regret to state, all distinctive idea of a pilgrimage was lost. We were no longer favoured with a special train, but quartered by Messrs. Cook along with the outside world, who came by the ordinary mundane boat. This greatly exercised the souls of the faithful for a while, but some young priests accepted the situation so far as to smoke like steam-engines the whole journey. It was late—very late—when we reached Paris—after ten o'clock, in fact; and our expected arrival had not much effect on the Parisians. A few —principally priests and *dévouées*—united to welcome us at the Rue St. Lazare Station, whence omnibuses, specially chartered, conveyed us in batches of a dozen or so to our several hotels.

Strange to say, though all preparations had been made in advance, we found the worst accommodation in Paris of anywhere along the route. The host and hostess were quietly making up their accounts on the table of the salle à manger at the Hôtel Hollande, Rue Radziwill, to which I was chartered, and we were told it was "trop tard" for everything except some wretched cold meat. A Frenchman has no idea of anybody wanting anything after six o'clock dinner; though one would have thought he might make an exception in the case of a pilgrimage.

A magnificent storm of thunder and lightning, which really might have been got up for our especial benefit, was raging over Paris that Tuesday night. The flash of the lightning and the roar of the thunder were simultaneous and incessant. But we were wearied pilgrims, and it would have taken a good many storms to keep us awake. Next morning we went to Mass at Notre Dame des Victoires, which was celebrated at six or seven altars in a very gorgeous fashion indeed. Just as last night it was "trop tard," so this morning nothing was "encore prêt." The hotel accommodation in Paris was the great "hitch" of the whole affair.

However, we took expensive *voitures à remise* (the omnibuses failing to come in time), and sped to the Boulevard Mazas, passing the ruins of the Hôtel de Ville, where a special train was waiting to convey us by the Lyons Railway to St. Florentin.

Here we were thoroughly *en pelerin*, and recited endless Paternosters and Ave Marias before we came to our destination. Vines soon began to crown the slopes of the hills, and an exuberance of fruit at the wayside stations warned us that we were in sunny Burgundy. Arrived at St. Florentin, the most heterogeneous collection of vehicles waited to convey us to Pontigny; but we were pilgrims—most of us—and would do the eight kilometres of dusty road on foot, or perish in the attempt. With banners flying and surpliced priests in attendance, we set out manfully on our long walk, the Bishop of Amycla and Monsignor Patterson, each in full vestments, being amongst our party.

It was hot—very hot—and we were glad to purchase peaches and grapes from the kneeling peasants in the road. By-and-by, when we had come in sight of the fine old Cistercian Abbey Church, crowning the hill-top at Pontigny, the French pilgrimage, with the Archbishops of Westminster, Sens, and Chambéry, came out to meet us, bearing a reliquary which contained the right arm of St. Edmund, and the French ecclesiastics wailing dismally on ophicleides, euphoniums, and other brazen instruments of torture. I ran out in the middle of a field so as to get the whole thing at a *coup d'œil*, and scenically it was perfect, acoustically very much the reverse. Climbing the steep ascent into the village, we found the whole place *en fête*, and preparations for illuminating the avenue up to the abbey door were well advanced. After a very brief religious exercise in church we proceeded to the monastery, and partook of a capital cold collation in the refectory. It was open house in the fullest sense of the term, notwithstanding the melancholy fact that Père Barbier, the procurator, on whom devolved all the preparation for us at the house, had fallen dead just as the English procession came in sight. I saw him lying on his pallet bed calm in death arrayed in his simple cassock, and with the crucifix clasped in his rigid hands; a weeping brother telling us how he had only passed on at the head of the procession beyond the confines of this world to a better and more enduring one.

The church itself is a long low building, as seen from outside; but the interior is very imposing, and quite cathedral-like in extent. The nave is in the severest style of the early or transition Burgundian Gothic; and the structure, which dates from 1150, is the only perfect church of the Cistercian Order which remains. Behind the altar, in the choir, is the shrine of St. Edmund, in the style of the early part of the thirteenth century. The peculiarity of this church is that the naves run right round the transepts; and behind the choir there are seven apsidal and two rectangular chapels. The choir itself is a splendid specimen of thirteenth century work, and is to be reproduced in the new priory chapel at Downside, near Bath.

The procession passed at once into the choir, but

left after a few prayers had been said; and we then adjourned to the refectory of the monastery to tax the hospitality of the good Fathers, which we did to the fullest extent, without making any appreciable difference to them. Cold viands, ripe fruits, and capital Burgundy, were provided without limit; and when we had fed to our hearts' content we sought our baggage and lodgings, and so passed the time until vespers.

Pontifical vespers were sung in the evening; and I never heard so sonorous an effect produced by the chanting of the simple Gregorian tones as on this occasion. The whole body of the choir was appropriated to the English pilgrims; but I preferred rather to wander in the aisles which ran right round the church, transepts and all, and the severe beauty of which quite grew on one. A procession *aux cierges* ensued; and the Hymn of St. Edmund, written by the late Cardinal Wiseman, in Latin worthy of the old monastic days, haunts me still as I remember that apparently endless line that passed round the aisles and out into the illuminated avenue right into the village streets. "O beate mi Edmunde! cum Mariâ preces funde" was the burden or refrain which, set as it was to a simple processional air, it will take me a very long time to forget.

The hymn, apart from its present associations, is so characteristic and so redolent of the old monastic style, that I append an abridgment of it. We sang the whole thing diligently through, with the first stanza several times repeated by way of refrain:—

HYMNUS IN HONOREM S. P. N. EDMUNDI, ARCHI-EPISCOPI CANTUAR. ET CONFESSORIS.

Auctore Nicolao Card. Wiseman primo Archiep. Westmonast.

O Beate mi Edmunde,
  Sic pro me, ad Filium Dei,
Cum Maria, preces funde,
  Ut per vos sim placens ei.

Si Edmundi dulcis amor
Te percellat, procul clamor
  Esto ac mœstitia ;
Silens, pronus ad altare,
Ejus dotes contemplare,
  Sancta in pueritia.

In ætate juvenili,
Pollens animo virili,
  Jam insulsa despicit;
Quidquid agat, corde fixo
In te, Jesu! crucifixo,
  Deum finem respicit.

Audit inde te loquentem,
Non ex cathedra docentem,
  Scholæ in triclinio ;
Scribæ tractus non miratur,
Tuas plagas veneratur,
  In librorum minio.

Quid, quotidie visens aram,
Jesu incolatu caram?
  Vultu quam angelico,
Caput flectit, inflammatum
Cor dum levat, se cibatum
  Pane sentiens cœlico!

O quam nitens, pura, casta
Erat, his deliciis pasta,
  Anima pueruli;
Longe matris ab amplexu,
Patriæque rupto nexu,
  Nec de exilio queruli.*

Ast amore mater pulsa,
Nec a nato corde avulsa,
  Parat ei munusculum.
Ecquid erit? pulcra vestis?
An bellaria? vel qui estis
  Grati, nummi! plusculum?

---

* Parisiis, ubi studiis operam dabat.

Arculam cum recepisti,
Quid, Edmunde, invenisti?
  "Librum cum cilicio!"
Gaudet puer, mox ut videt,
Cultus mentis cui arridet,
  Carnis cum supplicio.

Tunc ad pedes non absentis
Matris, ponit innocentis
  Donum mentis, flosculum;
Manni benedicenti,
Jesu manulam tendenti,
  Frequens figit osculum.

Vitam Nazareth sic degit,
Flet, jejunat, audit, legit;
  Orat sed perpetuo.
At quam sæve in se ruat,
Culpas non commissas luat,
  Cogitare metuo.

Essem saltem mansuetus,
Simplex, humilis, quietus,
  Docilis, amabilis!
Vim, Cor! funde lacrymarum!
Nostra quam juventus parum
  Huic comparabilis!

Altiora forsan quæris
Quæ exempla imiteris?
  Sancto fruens otio,
Nostri gratias admirare,
Quibus splendet, ad altare
  Fungens sacerdotio.

Cum ad patriam revertit,
Fama illum antevertit,
  Sacræ sapientiæ:
Munus ei docendi datur;
O in me sic uniatur
  Pietas scientiæ!

Grajas affert disciplinas,[*]
Ut ancillas, ad doctrinas
  Fidei inflexibilis;
Cito tuum, Isis![†] flumen
Simile revisat lumen
  Solis invisibilis!

Sed non sufficit ardenti
Munus hoc Edmundi menti,
  Urbis spernit mœnia;
Per castella, vicos, rura,
Sparsum pecus quærens, dura
  Æque fert ac lenia.

Flagrum urens ejus, vobis
Impii! vox; solamen probis;
  Vita, lux innumeris:
Tundit pectus, edit planctus
Turba; gaudet Pastor sanctus,
  Oves tollens humeris.

En peccator stat ad latus,
Vilis, rudis, induratus;
  Gratiam Dei rejicit;
Collum curvat ei invito
Pater, quem in terram cito
  Sacer dolor dejicit.

---

  [*] Aristotelisse.
  [†] Oxonias perfluens, ubi S. Edmundus docebat.

Ut exemplar suum, Christum,
Peccatoribus immistum
   Est insontem cernere.
Heu! criminibus fœdatus,
Culpis mille maculatus,
   Audeo tales spernere!

Mœres? plorat; gaudes? gestit;
Ægros fovet, nudos vestit;
   Reficit famelicos.
Sed pusilli sunt ei flores
Suaveolentes, queis cultores
   Deus dat angelicos.

Jesum casta tenens dextra,
Ardet intus, candet extra;
   Amor flammat oculum!
Quam cœlestis, corde et ore,
Fit, divino dum cruore
   Spumans haurit poculum.

Mensæ tunc si adstitissem,
Micas gratiæ collegissem,
   Catulus sub pedibus
Nunc majora posco dona,
Sacerdotii ut corona
   Orner cœli in sedibus!

Si qui se humiliavit,
Sed quem Deus exaltavit,
   Cœlitem vis colere;
Huc ad ossa humiliata,[*]
Sursum regna ad beata,
   Veni aciem tollere.

Thomæ mitra coronatus,
Ac virtutibus ornatus,
   Ei et sorte nectitur;
Fremunt gentes, furunt reges,
Sanctum Patrem plorant greges,
   Cum exilio plectitur.

O sis domus benedicta,
Frænans (bene a Ponte dicta)[†]
   Præsulum exitium!
Præbuisti asylum Thomæ,
Nunc Edmundo paras come
   Et perenne hospitium.

Præmium sed quam reddit pulcrum!
Venerandum dat sepulcrum
   Populis gaudentibus;
Dulce simul linquens nomen,
Ut amissæ fidei omen
   Instaurandæ mentibus.[‡]

O quam suavis tui memoria
Summa circumfusi gloria,
   Dei cernentis Faciem!
Hinc flammantium radiorum,
Miti tuo reflexorum
   Vultu, lenis aciem.

Plagas tangis lætabundus,
Quas lavabas moribundus,
   Mero mixto latice:
Illas lacrymis rigare,
Ore casto delibare,
   Fac me quoque ecstatice!

---

[*] Ad reliquias, in Collegii Ecclesia servatas.

[†] Pontiniacum, nunc Pontigny, sedes Oblatorum S. Edmundi, ubi sacrum ejus corpus, magna cum populi devotione, servatur.

[‡] Sancti nostri corpus per omnes temporum, etiam teterrimorum, vicissitudines, integrum est mirabiliter asservatum.

> Salve Angliæ flos et decor!
> Sana patriam; labor, precor,
> Hœresis sit irritus!
> Tuus, in nos hic clientes,
> Et quot seminant jam flentes,
> Large fluat spiritus!

Surely in one of the queerest of Burgundian cottages did I find myself quartered that night; for we took Pontigny by storm, and only the clerical pilgrims could be accommodated in the monastery and house of the sisters. I was *not* clerical there, so had to be billeted on a villager; and very comfortably the Pontigny peasants are housed, if I may judge by my surroundings. True, the floor of my apartment was bricked, but the room was large, the bed soft and capacious, and the coverlet sufficient to smother a dozen Desdemonas at once. One's only aim on a hot September night was to cast it as far away as possible into a corner.

The Vesper Service, on Wednesday, was certainly one of the finest ever listened to, and the long *marche aux flambeaux* afterwards would have delighted the heart of a Ritualist had any been, like John Gilpin's chronicler, "there to see." From midnight, too, the shrine and chapels were occupied by priests saying Mass, and the faithful attending the same. By the way, that fact led to an interesting little episode connected with myself. I have said that I was billeted on a peasant, and I was glad enough to retire very early, for I was wearied with my day's experiences. Next door to me was quartered a Catholic gentleman, with whom I had formed an acquaintance *en route*, for the affair was like an ecclesiastical picnic in this way, everybody talked to everybody else. This excellent pilgrim felt bound in conscience to break his night's rest by attending Mass in the small hours, so did not return to his domicile until deep in the early morning. Just as I got into bed I heard his asthmatic landlady knock at the door of my domicile, and the peasant who was housing me walked unceremoniously into my chamber to ask if I knew what time the gentleman was likely to turn in. Merely saying that I had left him in church, and could not be responsible for his habits, I turned to sleep again, and should have got on very well but for a lively Burgundian baby who was sleeping in the kitchen, and seemed to be protesting in his infantile patois against the change of dormitory. At midnight, having been aroused by the wailing of this injured innocent, I heard the asthmatic old lady call again and inquire as to the probabilities of Monsieur turning up; but when my peasant looked in again to ask me I pretended to be asleep, so as to avoid the question. Next morning, as soon as I opened my eyes, I heard the old lady in the kitchen again. She was inveighing bitterly against her pilgrim, who had not turned in until two in the morning, whilst I— model that I was—had been in bed since ten. Such is the justice of the world. I, for my heretical love of bed, was credited with all the cardinal virtues, while my poor friend, pacing the weary night with unboiled peas in his boots, was set down as a roysterer.

The Low Mass at eight, celebrated by the Archbishop of Westminster, was very striking indeed, from the quietude of the ceremony and the evident earnestness of those who communicated. Thousands of French peasants and hundreds of French priests had now flocked into Pontigny, and thronged the choir, nave, and aisles of the vast Priory church. When the Mass was over the hospitable fathers again entertained us at breakfast in their refectory: and when the meal was ended I went once more, at their invitation, to see their brother who had fallen asleep so strangely just as the pilgrims, for whom he had made it his special care to provide, came in sight. He was lying on a pallet-bed clad in his simple *soutane*, and holding a crucifix in his hand, looking quite calm, and with something approaching a smile on his pale face, which was turned a little away from us towards the wall. On a table by the head of the bed stood a vessel of holy water, and one by one those who entered sprinkled a little on the cassock of the dead priest. One of the fathers still stood silently at the foot, with tears streaming down his cheeks as he gazed on the lifeless form; and in the little graveyard hard by the sexton was even then digging the grave to receive the remains.

At ten o'clock the great bell rang out for High Mass, and everybody went to church. The French priests were literally stacked behind the altar. The three Archbishops sat in the chancel. The Bishop of Amycla officiated, and we—all the rest of us *pelerins*, lay or cleric — crowded in where we could. I got distressingly near the gentlemen who played the ophicleides and euphoniums; and in my unregenerate state I thought the Gregorian cadences of the Mass excessively monotonous, and was glad when the Archbishop of Westminster began to preach. Taking his text from the words, "Where the Spirit of the Lord is there is liberty," the Archbishop said never to the latest day of his life would he forget the Pilgrims of England emerging from the wood yesterday to mingle with the Pilgrims of France. "I claim," said the Archbishop, "the same faith and jurisdiction which was bestowed on St. Edmund yonder by the Sovereign Pontiff. Those who came to meet the great Church of France were," he said, "the sons of martyrs and confessors, and, as Irenæus says, 'Ubi ecclesia ibi spiritus.' In the chapel at my right hand St. Thomas of Canterbury received a vision from Christ promising the Church should be glorified in his blood. Here St. Edmund lived the life of a saint for the liberties of the Church. There he lies still. He was truly the English saint, and therefore I speak of the liberties of the Church of England. I claim for the church of Canterbury, after St. Peter's, the glory of bearing witness to the liberties of the Church. What is the liberty of the Church? The sole and supreme authority to choose the priest and bishop. This belongs to the Church. Kings and princes can lay no hand on this Divine liberty. All liberties co-exist with this, ecclesiastical, political, and social. This our Saxon forefathers recognised. These liberties passed into the unwritten laws of England. These liberties were violated in the person of Thomas, the most glorious of all our land. But St. Edmund is in all our hearts to-day. You know why he was here. Seeing that his enemies would not receive his words, he withdrew from England, as Christ and St. Paul withdrew. With that right hand which lies here, and which we yesterday carried in procession, he blessed England, and hither he was brought six hundred and forty years ago to lie in death. No war or revolution has ever violated that shrine. It is to this hour a testimony of God's providence. Six hundred years ago a King of France was here to celebrate Edmund's translation, and since that day there never has been seen such a sight as this. This is, indeed, a day of glory to England. Would to God that all England could share it. Pray first for the unity and consolidation of France. Pray for this sanctuary of St. Edmund, and then for England—for her bishops and priests, that they may learn the sweetness of St. Edmund, the fortitude of St. Thomas; and for the people, that they may persevere in the paths of piety. Pray, too, for that England which does not belong to us. England owes a reparation to the Church. She has restored the material structure of her cathedrals. Surely this is the prelude of a better restoration—making ready the sanctuary for the Lord. Pray for the filial spirit of piety to the Mother of God, and that England may make reparation to the Vicar of Christ. If England will not do it for itself, we must do with England as those who bear the child to the font—let us stand sponsors for the future of England. Finally, pray for the world. It was never so near a crisis as now—never fallen so far from unity as now. Modern progress and civilization have drawn governments from the unity of the Church. The Church stands, and will stand. The desolations of the world will continue till the world is purified." The Archbishop concluded with a fervent appeal for the Church of St. Thomas at Rome. For my part, I sympathized much more with a subsequent announcement made by Monsignor Patterson, to the effect that a collection would be made for the expenses to which the Fathers of St. Edme had been put in entertaining us. It must have been simply ruinous; and I am quite afraid to calculate the thousands of bottles of Burgundy we must have extracted from the Priory cellars, or the depredations we must have made in the poultry-yards and fruit-trees of the community. I never found out that the proposed collection was made, or I would gladly have contributed to it, for I had lived *en prince* at Pontigny; and really the only expense I was put to was for being billeted on the good peasant woman who admired my early hours, and for that entertainment I was charged the ruinous sum of— one franc!

After High Mass we dined again in the refectory,

at least some of us who were specially invited, in company with the Archbishops and the civil authorities who came to do honour to the English. These latter included the Prefect, Sub-prefect, and Receiver-general of the department, the commandant of the military subdivision, and representatives of all the oldest families in Yonne. Such doings had never been known in Pontigny before. There was also an al fresco entertaiment in the orchard, where an altar had been erected, from which the three Archbishops eventually gave a blessing all at once—a sort of three-barrelled benediction—and then the visit to the shrine was over. We had only to make our exodus. We did make it in every kind of trap available for miles round Pontigny. Omnibuses were chartered, shanderydans rigged up, and peasants' carts impressed. I travelled in the last, wedged in between two remarkably well-fed priests, who would have been invaluable in case of a "spill." None such occurred, however. The road was lined with people; and the Archbishop of Westminster went out some way in procession, and stood by the roadside to give us his final benediction. "Vive l'Angleterre!" "Vive la France Catholique!" were the cries that echoed along the whole of that now populous road. The Bishop of Amycla and Monsignor Patterson passed me in a market cart precisely similar to the one I occupied, and in due time we got to our special train, which left St. Florentin at 4.30.

I must not omit to mention that in the final procession we sang the proscribed hymn which gave some offence to neighbouring powers at Paray-le-Monial as having an occult political reference; and I am afraid we all thought it the nicer because a little naughty. The objectionable refrain was, it may be remembered—

> "Pitié nom Dieu, c'est pour notre patrie,
> Sauvez Rome et la France,
> Au nom du Sacré Cœur."

And so the pilgrimage was over. I came to Paris with as "jolly" a party as ever it was my good fortune to meet. In our carriage were a Benedictine friar and two fathers of that order, a Dominican Italian priest, a young secular priest, two Catholic laymen, and my exceedingly heretical self. We passed on to Dieppe the same night, leaving most of the rest to follow in the morning; and after an exceedingly disagreeable passage to Newhaven, which literally prostrated us all, and was about the only trying portion of the pilgrimage, we sped on by special train to London, and so ended our very pleasant outing, where we had begun it on Tuesday, upon the platform of the Victoria Station.

As a numerical success, Pontigny did not equal Paray, and is even said to have resulted in a pecuniary loss to Monsignor Patterson. But though the number of pilgrims was smaller, the devotees will not allow that the prestige of pilgrimages is on the wane. It was perfectly natural, they say, that the Sacré Cœur itself should draw better than a saint, however eminent and respectable. The number of English pilgrims was disappointingly small; but what was wanting in mere bulk was amply made up in enthusiasm. It was, no doubt, a most enjoyable outing—brief, but delightful. The only incident which threw any gloom over the excursion was the death of Procurator Père Barbier. It was a gloomy episode enough; but it is only fair to say that its occurrence did not damp the ardour or diminish the hospitality of the good Pères de St. Edme. How many bottles of wine must have been extracted from the monastic cellars, or how many chickens met with premature ends among the ecclesiastical homesteads, it would be difficult to calculate. The fathers made up their minds to do the thing well, and they spared no expense. The old virtue of hospitality certainly came into full relief during the few days spent by the pilgrims at Pontigny. The modern science of political economy has thrown some discredit on the antique almsgiving of the convent gate, which, it holds, encouraged vagrancy and mendicancy; but this affair at Pontigny was exceptional. Like Christmas —or like the ecclesiastical picnic it has been christened—it comes but once a year, and should certainly bring good cheer when it does arrive. It was literally a big Cook's Excursion, and the catering would have done credit even to the hotel coupons of that enterprising firm. Then, again, on the score of æsthetic effect, there was a good deal to be said in the way of praise. There were incongruities, as a matter of course, for the ideas of the Middle Ages were being grafted on the nineteenth century. Monsignor Patterson in his purple vestments looked oddly enough, scrambling to catch a train ; and more than once the Itinerarium was broken in upon by an irreverent guard appearing at the carriage window when the train was in full motion and crying out, "Vos billets, messieurs," or interrupting the five-and-fortieth Ave Maria in the Joyful Mysteries of the Rosary by throwing wide the door and shouting, "Melun! Vingt minutes d'arrêt." The meeting of the French and English processions at the foot of the hill whereon the magnificent Cistercian Abbey stands *ought* to have been a climax, and would have been, had not the Hymn of St. Edmund's Pilgrims been taken up in two utterly different times and tunes at the opposite ends of the procession, while the active ecclesiastics in the centre with ophicleides and euphoniums nearly blew themselves into fits by starting the tune in a third key to set the other two straight. Each pursued the anything but even tenor of his way, innocent of what the others were doing; but the effect from the middle of a field skirting the line of procession was distressingly discordant. The Vesper-service and procession *aux cierges* of Wednesday evening were perfect. Never did Gregorians come forth with so sonorous an unison; never wax chandlery was indulged in with so unsparing a hand. At the Low Mass on Thursday, as during all the small hours that succeeded midnight on Wednesday, the quiet business of the visit to the shrine was being done. The pilgrims confessed and communicated at the High Altar or in one of the many chapels that star it round, while an incessant single file passed up the narrow stairway to gaze on the features of the Archbishop some seven centuries dead, and who lay there in his glass case looking so ludicrously like a pickled prelate. But the faithful could not see it so. They reverently placed their chaplets on the shrine to be blessed by the dead man, or bent to kiss the step of the tiny chapel where a

Divine apparition warned St. Thomas à Becket of his impending martyrdom. It was a night to be much remembered by Pontigny; and when the eight o'clock bell rang for the Bishop of Amycla's Mass in the morning, they went at it again as though nothing had happened. Mr. Ravenstein, in his "Statistics of Religious Denominations," calculated that, under ordinary circumstances, one Dissenter did as much church-going—or rather chapel-going—work as ten Churchmen. It would be satisfactory to know how far the Romanist or the Methodist exceeds the normal average when the religious pulse is at fever-heat in the thick of a Revival or a Pilgrimage.

POPE PIUS'S VALENTINE.

The Festival of St. Valentine in the year of grace 1875 was cut in two, as it were, by the circumstance of its occurring on a Sunday; and, as far as the metropolis was concerned, the weary postmen rested from their annual task on the Feast itself, doing half the work on the vigil, and the other—probably the larger—half on the morrow of the Festival. Well indeed may the jaded letter-carriers address ardent lovers in the words of the frog in the fable, who assured the pelting boys that what was sport to them was death to the frogs.

In the intervals between the frequent visits of the postmen on Saturday evening, one of which caused a stampede to the door on the part of all my female household, from the plain cook down to my three-year-old daughter, I managed to get a furtive peep at the *Times*, and there saw it announced that Archbishop Manning would read the Pope's Encyclical Letter announcing the Jubilee of 1875, in the Pro-Cathedral, on Sunday morning, the 14th. Incongruous ideas as to the connexion between the Papal letter and the *billets doux* about which I had of late been hearing so much at once crossed my mind, not, however, that there is any incongruity necessarily involved. St. Valentine was, I believe, a holy priest, who was "martyrized with divers torments" somewhere back in the dear dark Middle Ages, so that if we could at all succeed in realizing the present position of the venerable gentleman at the Vatican, there might be some colour for calling the Pope's Letter a "Valentine" after all. No doubt somewhere in the mysterious abysses of the Mass for the morning of the 14th there would be enshrined some collect or other memorial of the "martyrized" saint, if I could only discover it; at all events, I would go and try. I had never heard an Encyclical read. That in itself would be a novel sensation.

Very chastened and beautiful was the appearance of the sanctuary at the Pro-Cathedral that Lenten Sunday morning. The altar was vested, and the whole chancel draped in the penitential purple; and on the former, in place of the accustomed vases of flowers and multitudinous candles, were only six tall tapers flanking the central crucifix. To our prim "Protestant" minds, as they are called (though I protest against nobody), there is something far more imposing in these chastened adornments than in all the profuse decoration of Easter-tide; but then the transition is telling too. The Archbishop's crozier was poised artistically against the throne; and the silent choristers who occupied the stalls looked like a veritable lot of little porphyrogeniti. Presently a small procession filed west, and waited at the great western door of the church for the Archbishop's arrival.

Dispensing his archiepiscopal blessing to the kneeling congregation, Dr. Manning soon passed into the sacrarium, the organist now playing a subdued voluntary. The Archbishop vested at his throne; the celebrant and his assistants, clad in brightest purple, took their places at the altar; fragrant clouds of incense rose; sensuous music alternated with the constant "Dominus vobiscum" or "In sæcula sæculorum," which to an outsider seem to constitute so large a portion of the Mass. Then a young man entered the pulpit, and told the faithful under what circumstances they might or might not eat flesh meat, announced the events of the coming week (including a Requiem Mass for the late Cardinal

Wiseman, the anniversary of whose death occurred on the Wednesday), read the Epistle and Gospel for the day in English, and then made room for the Archbishop, who ascended the pulpit with mitre and crozier, supported by Lord Douglas and another chaplain, and in his clear, silvery voice read, for twenty mortal minutes, the utterances of the Vatican Valentine.

The title of the document—every word of which was given as faithfully as though it had been the Gospel itself, or an Apostolic Epistle at least, ran as follows :—

ENCYCLICAL LETTER OF HIS HOLINESS BY DIVINE
PROVIDENCE POPE PIUS IX.

TO

ALL PATRIARCHS, PRIMATES, ARCHBISHOPS, BISHOPS, AND OTHER
LOCAL ORDINARIES, IN GRACE AND COMMUNION
WITH THE APOSTOLIC SEE,

AND TO

ALL THE FAITHFUL OF CHRIST,

ON THE

GREAT JUBILEE
OF 1875.

On the fly-leaf of the copy, which was politely handed to me by Father Foley after the reading, I found the following note, which was of great service to me, and may possibly be the same to my readers, who may have to be informed as to jubilees, just as, a year or two since, we had to get up pilgrimages :—

" A jubilee is a solemn plenary indulgence, given

by the Sovereign Pontiff to the faithful on condition of their performing certain works of piety, and with special power to confessors to absolve from reserved sins and censures, and to commute certain vows for other good works. It differs from an ordinary plenary indulgence by reason of its solemnity, and of the privileges attached to it; and also by reason of the abundant and extraordinary graces which God bestows. The first jubilee was celebrated in the year 1300, in the Pontificate of Pope Boniface VIII., who fixed every hundredth year for its recurrence. But the next was celebrated in 1350 under Clement VI., who appointed for its recurrence every fiftieth year; in 1389 Urban VI. reduced the period to thirty-three years; and in 1470 it was reduced by Paul II. to twenty-five years. Jubilees are of several kinds: 1. The greater, or great jubilee, occurring regularly every twenty-fifth year, and lasting a year; which year is called the holy year; and this jubilee, by reason of its occurrence at fixed periods, is also called the ordinary jubilee. 2. The lesser jubilee, usually granted by each Pope on his elevation to the Sovereign Pontificate, and granted also on other special occasions; and this is called an extraordinary jubilee. 3. A general, or universal jubilee, which is granted to the whole world; as is always the great jubilee, and sometimes also the lesser jubilee. 4. A particular, or partial jubilee, which is granted to a particular country, city, or place. The conditions of the Great Jubilee for 1875, as prescribed in the following Encyclical Letter, are:—True repentance with Confession and Holy Communion; also a visit, to be devoutly made on each of fifteen days, to four churches appointed for that purpose, with earnest prayer to be offered at each visit for certain specified holy objects. Provision, however, is made in the Encyclical for the gaining of the jubilee by children who have not made their First Communion, and by persons who are unable to make the prescribed visits to the churches."

To my uninitiated mind the terms of " gaining the Jubilee" I confess seemed easy enough; and I fear I was almost tempted to smile at the legal tone of the terms employed, as also at the dolorous character of the preamble. It ran thus :—

"VENERABLE BRETHREN AND BELOVED CHILDREN, HEALTH AND APOSTOLIC BENEDICTION.

" Moved by the grave calamities of the Church and of this age, and by the necessity of imploring the Divine Protection, We have never during our Pontificate omitted to arouse the people of Christendom earnestly to endeavour to appease the Majesty of God, and by holy habits of life, by works of penance, and by pious supplications, to merit the Divine clemency. To this end We have, with Apostolic liberality, several times opened to the faithful of Christ the spiritual treasures of Indulgences, in order that, animated thereby to true penance, and cleansed by the sacrament of reconciliation from the stains of sin, they might approach more confidently the Throne of Grace, and be worthy that God should graciously receive their prayres. And this, as at other times, so especially on the occasion of the sacred Œcumenical Vatican Council We thought it our duty to do, in order that the very grave work which had been undertaken for the benefit of the Universal Church might by the prayers likewise of the whole Church, be helped before God; and although, through the calamities of the times, the celebration of the Council was suspended, We nevertheless, for the good of the faithful, declared and decreed that the Indulgence, to be obtained in form of Jubilee, which had been promulgated on that occasion, should remain, as it still remains, in its force, and firmness, and vigour. But the course of these sorrowful times still continuing, we are now entering upon the year one thousand eight hundred and seventy-five—the year, that is to say, which marks that sacred space of time, which by the holy custom of our forefathers, and by the decrees of our predecessors the Roman Pontiffs, has been consecrated to the solemn celebration of the Universal Jubilee. With what veneration and religious devotion the year of the Jubilee was observed when the tranquil times of the Church permitted its due celebration, both ancient and more recent monuments of history bear witness : for it was regarded always as a year of salutary expiation for the whole Christian people, a year of redemption and of grace, of forgiveness and of Indulgence; a year in which people came together from all parts of the world to this our city, and the See of Peter—in which the faithful were aroused to the duties of piety, and had every help of reconciliation and of grace offered to them all, in great abundance, for the salvation of their souls. What a pious and holy solemnity was seen even in this our century, when Leo XII., of happy memory, our predecessor, having proclaimed the Jubilee of 1825, this benefit was received by the Christian people with so much fervour that the Pontiff could rejoice at an uninterrupted concourse of pilgrims to this city during the whole year, and at the splendour here wonderfully manifested, of religion, piety, faith, charity, and all virtues. O that such were to-day our condition, and the condition of civil and sacred things, as to permit us, now at least, happily to celebrate, according to the ancient rite and custom of our forefathers, that solemnity of the Great Jubilee, which, occurring in the year 1850 of this century, We had by reason of the mournful circumstances of the times to omit. But the grave difficulties which at that time prevented Us from proclaiming the Jubilee, so far from being removed, have rather, God so permitting, daily increased. Nevertheless, pondering in our heart the many evils which afflict the Church, the many efforts of her enemies to pluck out the faith of Christ from souls, to corrupt sound doctrine, and to propagate the poison of impiety; and pondering also the many scandals which are everywhere put before believers in Christ, the widespread corruption of morals, and the shameful overthrow of rights, both Divine and human, which is so extensive and so ruinous, and which tends to destroy all sense of rectitude in the minds of men,—We feel that, in so great an accumulation of evils, We are bound by the duty of our Apostolic office more than ever to take care that faith, religion, and piety may be protected and may flourish, that the spirit of prayer may be cherished and may increase, that the fallen may be raised up to repentance of heart and reformation of life, and that the sins which have deserved the anger of God may be redeemed by holy works. And, as these are the objects to which the celebration of the Great Jubilee is principally directed, We have thought it our duty not to suffer the Christian people to be deprived of this salutary benefit, in such form as the circumstances of the times permit, so that, strengthened in spirit, they may walk daily with more alacrity in the ways of righteousness, and, having expiated their sins, may more easily and more abundantly merit the Divine propitiation and forgiveness. May therefore the whole Church Militant of Christ receive our words, by which, for His exaltation, for the sanctification of the Christian people, and for the glory of God, We proclaim, announce, and promulgate, a Universal and Great Jubilee, to last for the whole of the coming year 1875. And by reason, and in consideration of this Jubilee, suspending and declaring now suspended, during our pleasure, and that of this Apostolic See, the Indulgence above mentioned, which was granted in form of Jubilee on the occasion of the Vatican Council, We now lay open in all its amplitude that heavenly treasure which, acquired by the merits, and sufferings, and virtues of Christ our Lord, and of His

Virgin Mother and all the Saints, was entrusted to our dispensation by the Author of the salvation of mankind."

Then came the terms of " gaining Jubilee :"—

" Relying on the mercy of God and on the authority of His blessed Apostles Peter and Paul, by virtue of the supreme power of binding and loosing which God has conferred upon Us, though unworthy —to all and each one of the faithful of Christ—both to those living in our city or coming to it, and to all those outside the city in whatsoever part of the world, and remaining in the grace of, and in obedience to the Apostolic See,—We mercifully concede and grant in the Lord that, once in the above-named year, they may gain the full Jubilee indulgence, remission, and pardon of all their sins,— provided that, being truly repentant, they confess their sins and receive the Holy Communion; and provided also that for fifteen consecutive or separate days, either natural, or ecclesiastical (computed, that is, from the first vespers of one day until the full evening twilight of the following), they shall at least once in the day have devoutly visited, if living in *or coming to* Rome, the Basilicas of SS. Peter and Paul, of St. John Lateran, and St. Mary Major,—or, if out of Rome, the cathedral or principal church, and three other churches of the same city or place, or in its suburbs, to be designated, after the receipt of these Letters, by the Ordinaries, or by their Vicars, or by their order,—and that they shall there have prayed piously to God for the prosperity and exaltation of the Catholic Church and of this Apostolic See, for the extirpation of heresies and the conversion of all who are in error, for the peace and unity of the whole Christian people, and according to our intention: and We grant moreover that this Indulgence may be applied by way of suffrage to the souls that have departed this life, united to God in charity.

"To travellers by sea or by land who, having returned to their homes, or reached any other resting-place, shall fulfil what is above written, and shall visit for the said number of times the cathedral or principal, or parochial, church of their place of domicile or stoppage, We grant that they may obtain the same indulgence. . . . .

"If any persons, having, with the intention of gaining the Jubilee, begun the fulfilment of the prescribed works, shall be overtaken by death, and be unable to accomplish the fixed number of visits, desiring graciously to favour their pious and ready intention, We will that the said persons, provided that, with true repentance, they confess and receive the Holy Communion, shall participate in the aforesaid indulgence and remission, in the same manner as if they had, on the prescribed days, really visited the aforesaid churches. . . . . Therefore your chief care, Venerable Brethren, after you have publicly implored the Divine Clemency to fill the minds and hearts of all with His light and grace, will be, by means of suitable instruction and admonition, to see that the Christian people understand the fruits of the Jubilee; and that they accurately know what is the force and the nature, for the profit and advantage of souls, of a Christian Jubilee, in which, in a spiritual manner, are abundantly fulfilled by virtue of Christ our Lord, those benefits which were given to the Jewish people every fiftieth year by the Old Law, the messenger of the things that were to come; and that at the same time they are fitly instructed with regard to the effect of indulgences, and with regard to all those things which they have to perform for the fruitful confession of their sins and for receiving worthily the Sacrament of the Eucharist."

The familiar feeling of a "Special Correspondent" came upon me as I read the words I have italicized; and it was all I could do to prevent myself writing off forthwith and placing my services at the disposal of some journal, should the Papal Jubilee not interfere with the revival meetings of Messrs. Moody and Sankey, for which I was specially retained.

There was a pathetic tone of sadness traceable throughout the Letter; which, by the way, was considerably too long, and spun out towards its conclusion like the sermon of a young curate, who feels bound to exhaust the orthodox twenty minutes, or perish in the attempt. The Archbishop, in consideration, no doubt, of the length and homiletic character of the Letter, added no words of his own. I should greatly have preferred to have heard an abridgment of the document, and a recommendation of the contents by so able and eloquent an advocate. That, no doubt, is a treat in store for us.

Surely enough the very next morning—the morrow of St. Valentine, when the tender missives came more thickly than on the vigil, and all was excitement "from garret to basement," from the nursery to the kitchen—I snatched another glance at my *Times*, and there read, as I had expected, the announcement, by a well-known entrepreneur, of the inevitable personally-conducted tour " to arrive in Rome at Easter."

Little did I then think that, before Eastertide was well out that same year, the Archbishop himself would have assumed the red hat, and that rumour would busily associate his name with the Popedom at its next avoidance!

A "CATHOLIC" UNIVERSITY COLLEGE.

THIS institution, which had been opened for the reception of students for some time, was, shortly after his elevation to the Sacred College, formally opened by Cardinal Manning in presence of most of the bishops and a large number of the Roman Catholic nobility, including, amongst others, the Duke of Norfolk, the Earl of Denbigh, Lord Ripon, &c. &c.

Proceedings commenced soon after half-past three o'clock in the temporary chapel attached to the College, when a procession passed from the College consisting of choir, acolytes, and clergy, Cardinal Manning, and the following bishops, the latter habited mostly in purple dress, with gold pectoral cross :—Dr. Brown, Bishop of Newport and Menevia; Dr. Vaughan, of Plymouth; Dr. Vaughan, of Salford; Dr. Cornthwaite, of Beverley; Dr. Amherst, of Northampton; Dr. Bagshawe, of Nottingham;

Dr. O'Reilly, of Liverpool; Dr. Danell, of Southwark; Dr. Clifford, of Clifton; the Coadjutor Bishop of Amycla; and the Mitred Abbot of Ramsgate. The Cardinal was habited in scarlet cassock and biretta, his train being borne by two priests.

Passing to the extreme east end of the chapel, which was crowded to the doors, the Cardinal knelt before the altar while the choir chanted the "Veni Creator Spiritus," the students, who were seated in the centre and habited in the ordinary undergraduate gown, bearing their full share. This was followed by a sermon, delivered from the top step of the altar by Monsignor Capel. He eloquently compared the position of the Catholics in founding their College to that of St. Mark at Alexandria, and then passed on to notice the curious coincidence between the mission of St. Augustine by Pope Gregory and the fact that his Eminence Cardinal Manning had newly come invested with his recent dignity, as it were, under the auspices of St. Gregory himself, whose title he bore in the Sacred College. He dwelt forcibly on the liberality displayed by the Catholic laity in founding the College, saying that in seven months they had contributed more than 5000*l*. He congratulated himself on the staff of professors he had been able to gather round him—men of eminence in the universities of Oxford, Cambridge, Dublin, and London, many of whom had, he said, in a true Catholic spirit, given up lucrative posts of honour to cast in their lots with him. He concluded with an eloquent tribute to the conduct and diligence of the students.

At the conclusion of his sermon, Monsignor Capel passed to the Rector's chair, amid the Professors, who were habited in their gowns and academical hoods; and the Benediction Service was then celebrated by the Cardinal. When this was over an adjournment was made to the Lecture Theatre of the College, where the Cardinal occupied the centre of the platform, with the bishops ranged round him, and two little boys in scarlet cassocks and surplices at his feet; the Rector and Professors occupying the front ranks of seats beneath.

An address was then read by Monsignor Capel from the Rector, Professors, and Students, to which Cardinal Manning replied.

If, he said, he regarded that high office to which he had been promoted simply as a dignity, he should fear it. Honours were often real dangers to those who received them. He prayed, therefore, that he might not look upon his elevation as a mere honour or dignity—though it was both—and that they might never perceive any change in his life or spirit in consequence. He looked upon it rather in the light of a commission to carry on a warfare. He believed the Holy See was approaching the greatest crisis through which it had gone for three hundred years; and he hoped he should not be found wanting. In this hope lay his greatest consolation.

The preacher had said that he came direct from the source of English Christianity. "Ten years ago," he said, "when I knelt to receive the pallium first worn by St. Augustine, the Holy Father turned and said to me in an undertone, 'I am not Gregory, but I have the same faculties.' This was his testimony to the imperishable identity of the Church." To-day the restored hierarchy in England did its first collective act in founding an institution which was to be the common property of the Province of Westminster and the thirteen Bishops of England. It was *not* an University, but University College, so called because it was the first of the kind, and intended hereafter to form part of a confederated University. It was not designed—at least not now—that there should be one common centre, as in the ancient universities. The six or seven colleges scattered over England would form, if he might so say, a dispersed university, which would be more suited to the present exigences of England. It was better that the Higher Education should not be concentrated, but that the centres should be multiplied. It would be like opening up so many separate fountains of learning to irrigate the country around each. He was not only content with such an arrangement, but he preferred it for two reasons. 1. The History of the Middle Ages, when knowledge was thus concentrated, was one of perpetual conflict and controversy. 2. The Universities of Italy and Germany even now generated intellectual aberration, which was dangerous to the Church. At Bologna, Paris, Padua, and Pavia, intellectual errors had arisen; and he thought the separate system more healthful. Each College, therefore, of which this was one, along with Ushaw, Stonyhurst, Oscott, Downside, Prior Park, and others, would preserve perfect autonomy.

It was the object of the Holy See and the Council in establishing this College to carry out the commission *Euntes docete omnes gentes*, not only by teaching the Catechism, but by insuring the highest culture of the intellect. It was desired to secure union between all branches of intellectual culture, revealed and scientific. They were indivisible; distinguishable, but not to be divided. Lastly, it was desired to perpetuate the Catholic method. A great authority had said that in the Catholic system there could be no Higher Education. "I commend this to the Rector and Professors," said the Cardinal with a smile. A Catholic University, added this authority, there could not be, because the Catholic method could not embrace science and philosophy. It was the un-Catholic method which made havoc of the world. He concluded by bearing testimony to Monsignor Capel's untiring industry in this institution, at a time when there was only a horizon of poverty before him; and announced that the donors of 500*l.* would have the privilege of nominating for life one student exempt from all fees.

Monsignor Capel described the building and its educational apparatus. Already they have had two donations of 500 and 300 volumes to the library, and he had purchased a collection of 10,000 more with a herbarium. Professor Mivart had acquired a good geological collection, and founded a museum; and Professor Barth had a laboratory where twenty-five students could be taught at a time. There was also a Student's Club in the College. He hoped one day to build round the ground, on which the present building stood, three sides of a quadrangle, with accommodation for eight hundred or nine hundred students.

The Cardinal and Rector then conducted the

visitors over the building and grounds; and the effect of the varied costumes of His Eminence and the Bishops and Priests in the latter was quite picturesque, so much so as to startle the Old Court Suburb out of its serenity, when the company withdrew for refreshment to Monsignor Capel's house, opposite the College gates.

MOODY-AND-SANKEYISM.

WHILE the American Evangelists were working in the great provincial towns of England and Scotland previously to their London visit, the outer circle, so to say, of the influence they were exerting elsewhere seemed to extend to the metropolis; and what was publicly announced as a "Great Spiritual Awakening" seemed to be taking place, as if in anticipation of their advent. Daily prayer meetings, held at noontide in the very heart of the City, were among the machinery used to promote this influence: and at one of these I made it my business to be present.

There are few more suggestive sights than the frequent City churches, which, even in these days of demolition, still "point with taper spire to heaven," among the multitudinous shops and warehouses: few more significant sounds than the far from frequent bell pealing out from such spires, and calling men to worship. But when it does so sound, and one enters the sacred edifice, the contrast of the quiet service within, and the din and noise without, is, indeed, perfect. It was such an experience I sought one Monday, when, having read the announcement that intercessory prayer for London would be offered at midday in the Moorgate Hall, and continued every day at the same hour, I sped on the wings of the Underground to Moorgate Street, at the intersection of which thoroughfare by London Wall the hall in question stands.

It is among the busiest of our London streets at noontide; and a curious crowd was gathering outside the chapel—for it was so called until the present—to see what in the world people could be thinking of to seek a place of worship on a Monday at noontide. So it was, however, they were seeking it, and in goodly numbers too. By the time I got in, the body of the hall was full, and stragglers had begun to drift into the galleries—a large portion, of course, women, but with a goodly sprinkling of men, most of them evidently devoting their dinner hour to this religious service, and not a few of the genuine working class, with the signs of labour on their brawny hands. They were already singing the opening hymn by the time I arrived, for time pressed, and there was no need to wait for a congregation; and they sang it full-voiced from the collection of Ira D. Sankey, the recent revivalist. To this succeeded an opening address, read from MS., by a soft-spoken old minister, who entirely failed to make us hear, and who grievously scandalized a working man, boxed up in the same pew with me, because he read instead of spouting. He was a tall, venerable man, this old minister, and stood erect as an arrow, with his spectacles hoisted on to his forehead, and I afterwards learnt he was Mr. Mannering, late of Bishopsgate Chapel. During his ten minutes of dumb show I had leisure to take stock of the surroundings.

The Hon. Captain Moreton, R.N., occupied the chair, and around him were some twelve or fourteen gentlemen and ministers, elderly, substantial-looking men, and all evidently brimful of the most intense earnestness. The chapel itself was ugly enough to bear out any of Mr. Gladstone's assertions in the *Contemporary* as to the unæsthetic character of the English people; but the congregation was a sight to see. By the time Mr. Mannering got to the end of his tether he elevated his voice a little, and I could just gather that the gist of his address was the excellent advice, "In essentials unity; in non-essentials charity."

At the conclusion of the address—which I fear cast rather a damp on the proceedings—the chairman asked us to engage for a few minutes in silent prayer, and read several "requests for prayer," which had been sent to him. A congregation at Bexley Heath requested our prayers; another in Dublin, and yet another at some place in Cumberland, each specifying its peculiar needs with some minuteness. A widow would have us pray for the conversion of her daughter: and a working man who had been through the Crimean War, wished to believe, but felt that the door was shut against him. We were asked to pray for God's blessing on a little book which had been given to him, called "The Open Door." After a very brief pause, Captain Moreton offered a prayer with much gesticulation, and which sounded to an outsider rather like a sermon in disguise. It was accompanied all the way through by those peculiar groan-like ejaculations on the part of the hearers which are common in such gatherings. The burden of the prayer was that London might be stirred up; while outside one heard the din of Moorgate Street, and inside the response, continued in a strong crescendo, made the strangest medley of sounds; but the effect was very striking. A sonorous "Amen" concluded this portion of the devotions. At its conclusion the chairman stated the order of proceedings, and made an earnest request for brevity on the part of " brothers" who should take part in them. After the hymn he was going to give out, "the meeting would be open." But no brother would be "allowed" to take two exercises or on any account to give out a hymn. The one selected by Captain Moreton to be as it were the line of demarcation between the " close" and " open" part of the proceedings, was taken from Mr. Ira D. Sankey's " Sacred Songs and Solos," and was set to a very lively tune indeed, as were most of those sung on the occasion. It is so characteristic as to be worth quoting :—

"MORE TO FOLLOW.

" Have you on the Lord believed ?
Still there's more to follow;
Of His grace have you received ?
Still there's more to follow;
Oh, the grace the Father shows!
Still there's more to follow;
Freely He His grace bestows,
Still there's more to follow.

Chorus.

More and more, more and more, always more to follow;
Oh, His matchless, boundless love! Still there's more to follow.

" Have you felt the Saviour near?
Still there's more to follow;
Does His blessed presence cheer?
Still there's more to follow;

"Oh, the love that Jesus shows!
 Still there's more to follow;
Freely He His love bestows,
 Still there's more to follow.

"Have you felt the Spirit's power?
 Still there's more to follow;
Falling like the gentle shower?
 Still there's more to follow;

"Oh, the power the Spirit shows!
 Still there's more to follow;
Freely He His power bestows,
 Still there's more to follow."

An aged minister on the platform followed with an eloquent prayer for more power of the Spirit on "the masses." Might it be outpoured on every family where there was an unconverted child or servant. "Shake this great city," he prayed, with an earnestness that provoked an audible response. It was the great wish of all those who prayed that day—that London might be "shaken." Another prayer was offered by a person in a pew, the chairman making a particular request that the brothers who were moved to pray would stand up, and not put their hands before their mouths, because the congregation were straining their ears to hear them. "No bellowing or bawling, only speak out." Then followed another hymn, the opening verse of which combined the strangest collection of metaphors :—

> "Let us gather up the *sunbeams*,
>   Lying all around our path;
> Let us keep the *wheat and roses*,
>   Casting out the *thorns and chaff*;
> Let us find our sweetest comfort
>   In the blessings of to-day,
> With a patient hand removing
>   All the briars from the way.
>
> Then scatter seeds of kindness, then scatter seeds of kindness,
> Then scatter seeds of kindness, for our reaping by-and-by;"

and another person far up in a cavernous gallery prayed again that London might be shaken. There was no holding back among the brethren. Sometimes two rose together; but there was no confusion. One readily gave way; and it was still a prayer for shaking. "If the Cross of Christ could not *shake London*, the case of London was hopeless."

Yet another prayer followed, this time by a man with a thin inaudible voice (at which the chairman looked annoyed, almost cross), and while he was praying that London might be shaken I had time to take stock of the occupants of my pew. There were two ladies—one of whom was much affected and in tears most of the time—two working men, evidently fresh from their labour, and obliged to return to it before the meeting was quite over, a young man of a superior class in society, and myself. The quaint Old Testament phraseology of the prayers and address fell strangely on the ears of one accustomed to a different cultus; but the earnestness of the whole proceedings could not fail to strike the most casual observer. A young man stood up and read a few verses from his well-thumbed Bible: then another —quite a lad—stood as he was in the passage, between the pews, and offered a prayer, fervent though grotesque, and once more, finally, the strange hymn-book was laid under contribution. The singing was even more spirited and vigorous than the prayers— very much more so than the addresses. This time the hymn was :—

"THE LORD WILL PROVIDE.

' In some way or other the Lord will provide:
It may not be *my* way,
It may not be *thy* way;
And yet, in His *own* way,
' The Lord will provide.'

CHORUS.

Then we'll trust in the Lord, and He will provide;
Yes, we'll trust in the Lord, and He will provide.

"At some time or other the Lord will provide:
It may not be *my* time,
It may not be *thy* time,
And yet, in His *own* time,
' The Lord will provide.'

" Despond then no longer; the Lord will provide;
And this be the token—
No word He hath spoken
Was ever yet broken:
' The Lord will provide.'

"March on then right boldly, the sea shall divide;
　The pathway made glorious
　With shoutings victorious,
　We'll join in the chorus,
　'The Lord will provide.'"

The hour was now up, but one more "request" was read by the chairman. It was for a blessing on a medical consultation then taking place in a case of a child suffering from gastric fever—a blessing whether in life or death. With this special supplication the meeting ended. The clock struck one; and we passed out into the bustle of Moorgate Street once more.

After undergoing a long period of waiting and probation, almost like the Lenten vigil of the more orthodox of her inhabitants, London at length received the visit of the American Evangelists, as it had become customary to call them, though the term Apostle might seem almost a fitter one to convey an idea of the influence these gentlemen had been exerting elsewhere. England had become for them, so to say, another Decapolis, and it was, indeed, an interesting problem whether the vast effects they have produced elsewhere were destined to be reproduced in the metropolis, or whether it should be as of old when Galilee was receptive but Jerusalem remained obdurate. For more than a week previously preparatory services had been held in the Agricultural Hall and other places, while an experiment—which turned out abortive through causes unconnected with the Evangelists or their friends—was made to compass a tabernacle service in Messrs. Edgington's mammoth pavilion at the Kennington Oval. On the Sunday before their arrival, too, the burden of many sermons among their more immediate sympathizers was "How shall we receive them?" But in truth the actual, though not the nominal, preparations for Messrs. Moody and Sankey stretched much further back, and long antedated the announcement of their arrival. For a considerable period the noontide prayer meetings alluded to above had been held in the heart of the City daily—a marvellous parenthesis in the whirl of business—where the hymns of Ira D. Sankey had become familiar in men's mouths. This had been a movement outside the Establishment, but the influence which radiated from these Evangelists as a centre seemed to have crossed the frontier line of the Church of England herself. On all sides there had been what might be claimed to be a "great spiritual awakening." The employment of lay agency in the Church had also received an immense impetus of late. It is not only—if at all—that there has been a dearth of clergy, but it has been ascertained that there are depths which can better be sounded by lay than clerical instrumentality, and this fact had certainly paved the way towards that climax of lay evangelism at which we had now arrived, even if their work elsewhere did not suggest or sanction the idea.

A preliminary prayer meeting was held at Exeter Hall, and was fairly attended, though neither of the Evangelists was present. Lord Radstock presided, and the Rev. Mr. Chapman, chaplain of the Lock Hospital, delivered a suitable address. The number of ministers, clergy, and laymen on the platform was very large, and the singing of Mr. Sankey's beautiful hymns was admirably conducted by Miss Bonar and a choir of ladies. Those selected were, first the 100th Psalm, which was given full-voiced and formed a most appropriate commencement; then "Rejoice in the Lord," with its refrain, "Sound his praises, tell the story;" then "I hear the Saviour say, thy strength, indeed, is small;" and finally, "Hallelujah, thine the glory, revive us again." It was in every respect a real revival service. The " requests for prayer " were numerous and significant.

At the Agricultural Hall, in the evening, the gathering was all that could possibly be desired; every inch of the vast building was filled with a congregation numbering probably 15,000, representing all sections of the population of London. During the hour of waiting some of the best known of Mr. Sankey's hymns were sung by an excellent choir, especially the beautiful one, "Tell me the old, old story." The pianissimo rendering of some of the passages in this was exceedingly telling, and could be heard distinctly over the whole building; for example, the touching stanza—

> "Tell me the story softly,
> That I may take it in,
> That wonderful redemption,
> God's remedy for sin."

With admirable punctuality, Mr. Moody made his appearance on the platform exactly at half-past seven, by which time the whole of the hall was filled. With some abruptness, and in a decidedly provincial accent, he gave out the verse, "Praise God, from whom all blessings flow;" adding, "All sing; let's praise God for what He's going to do." The congregation responded heartily, every man and woman appearing to join full-voiced in the doxology. Then followed a brief prayer, after which Mr. Moody gave out the 100th Psalm, again adding, "Let all the people sing," and certainly all the people did. It was a fine sight to see that vast assemblage rise, and a treat to hear their powerful unison. After a brief silent prayer, Mr. Moody offered a special supplication for London. It was a great city, he said, but God was a great God. "Thou God of Pentecost," he said, "give us a Pentecostal blessing here in London."

Then followed a solo by Mr. Sankey, "Jesus of Nazareth passeth by," and for the first time was heard the clear notes of that rich voice ringing through the recesses of that spacious building. One excitable gentleman caused a little contretemps by proposing a chorus, evidently not wishing that Mr. Sankey should have it quite to himself, but Mr. Moody was an admirable manager, and easily restrained the interrupter's unseasonable zeal. After "Rock of Ages" had been sung to the tune of "Rousseau's Dream," the climax of the evening was reached. Mr. Moody read a passage from 1 Cor. i. 17, with following verses, and commenced his address. God's people, he said, had generally been looked upon as the greatest fools in their respective times. Moses was not the sort of person we should have selected to save three millions of people, and when he asked who he should say had sent him, God "drew him a blank cheque, and told him to fill it in with the name of Jah whenever necessary. Samson slew his enemies with what? The jawbone of an ass. Be always ready to grab up the first jawbone of an ass you come to, and let the world laugh as much as it likes." London, he said, was a big city, but there were people enough in that hall then to save London. Amongst other unlikely people whom God had chosen to subserve his ends, he instanced "The little tent-maker of Tarsus," and "The Bedfordshire Tinker who wrote the 'Pilgrim's Progress.'" His great fear, he said, in coming to London was lest the people should trust in man and forget God. The very teaching of the text was that God was everything and man nothing. There were hundreds of better preachers in London than himself, and yet he specially asked the aid of ministers in the metropolis, because he was not coming to undo their work, but simply to supplement it. He asked the aid of parents, too, and concluded an impressive and captivating address, comprised within most modest limits, by telling a story of a poor mother who had come to him in Liverpool to tell him how she had lost her son, a fine lad of seventeen, whom she believed to be in London. "Perhaps the lad is before me now," he said; "if so, let me tell him his mother loves him still, and so too, like that poor mother, God loves us all." On this he based a very fervent appeal for unity, and suddenly broke off as if inspired by the occasion, calling on Mr. Sankey to sing the appropriate hymn, "Hold the Fort."

It was impossible to imagine a more signal success than that which attended this opening meeting. There was nothing sensational in the address, though there were several outbursts of genuine eloquence, agreeably varied with quaint touches of humour that provoked a smile, while they conveyed truths which one felt would go straight home to the hearts of the hearers. The proceedings terminated with the benediction, which was pronounced by the Rev. Dr. Allon, of Islington.

I purposely avoided "following" Messrs. Moody and Sankey in their work at the Agricultural Hall in the same way as some correspondents had done, because I wanted to see whether the work really would prove ephemeral, as its detractors predicted, and also because it seemed slightly uninteresting, and not a little unfair withal to report addresses every day, which must in the nature of things involve considerable repetition. I waited with considerable curiosity to see first whether the interest would continue at the North of London, and what probabilities there seemed to be of its being reproduced in other districts, especially at the West End. One day a circular letter was addressed by Mr. Moody to the clergy and ministers of the fashionable West End, inviting them to attend a meeting at the Opera House, Haymarket, on a Wednesday morning at ten o'clock, in anticipation of commencing work there the next week. I made a point of being present at that meeting, which consisted of about a hundred and fifty individuals, mostly clerical, but including a few well-known laymen; among others, the Earl of Shaftesbury, Sir Harry Verney, Mr. Samuel Morley, M.P., Mr. S. Blackwood, &c. As I passed up the familiar staircase, and peeped through the box-doors into the house, I found extensive preparations being made, and everything smelling of fresh-planed deal. The pit was boarded over, and looked like the arena of a large circus, while the stage resembled the seats in an infant school, rising tier above tier. On all sides were heard the sounds of axes and hammers, and with one hasty glance I sped towards the place of conclave. In the chair was the Rev. C. D. Marston, vicar of St. Paul's, Brompton, where he succeeded the Rev. Capel Molyneux; and on his right hand was seated Mr. Moody in lay attire, and seeming to take little interest in a somewhat warm discussion which was going on around him. He toyed with his umbrella after the manner of a man who had made up his mind and was not to be moved from his purpose, and my subsequent experiences proved that I read his physiognomy aright. The point in debate was this—a large building had been erected at Bow for East London, and the Victoria Theatre was shortly to be secured for the South. The North had already been provided for at the Agricultural Hall, and Mr. Moody was so elated with his success there that he could not entertain any proposal to abandon it entirely. In fact he had but one answer (like Wordsworth's little girl) to all questions, and it was "I wun't." The original scheme was, it appears, that one month should be given to each London district. That period had now expired at Islington, though the tenure of the hall still continued. Mr. Moody averred that the month at the Agricultural Hall ought to be considered one of six weeks, for it had taken him a fortnight to feel the people's pulse, and now his success was most marked. He tested it by the inquiry-room. "I could not," he said, "with a clear conscience leave 10,000 people at Islington to speak to 3000 at the Opera House." In reply to those who suggested that a different class would be reached there, he said the poor man's soul was as valuable as the rich man's, and seemed to imply that his own mission was rather to the lower and middle than to the upper classes. To this the Earl of Shaftesbury replied that though it was quite true that the poor man's soul was worth as much as the rich man's, yet Mr. Moody must remember that when one of the upper ten thousand was converted his wealth and influence were turned into a right channel, and so he became the means of doing more good. He believed that the simple Gospel preaching of Mr. Moody was just what was wanted to win these people, and suggested that he should make the experiment for a week; but Mr. Moody played with his umbrella, and looked, though he did not say, "I wun't." When, however, Mr. Marston leant over to him and suggested that he should leave himself in the hands of the meeting, then he not only looked, but said in an extremely audible stage whisper, "I wun't leave myself in the hands of no meeting nor no committee." "'Twas throwing words away," as Wordsworth said of the immovable little girl above mentioned, and gradually the meeting accommodated itself to this view of things. Mr. Morley pleaded, and minister after minister pleaded, that the West should not be neglected. Mr. Moody did not think they were being neglected. He thought if he stirred the people up at the morning and afternoon services they would listen to another minister at night. On this the assembly was divided. Some thought that the evening service had better be given up altogether if Mr. Moody would not come. Others said that would be a confession of failure. Local ministers urged that there was a vast poor population as well as rich around the Opera House; that Westminster and Chelsea would send their contingents to swell the evening congregations. "Try it for a week," again suggested Lord Shaftesbury; "and if you can't get on with us immovable people, turn to the Gentiles." But Moody was adamant. He smiled, but his heart was with his Islington Gentiles. A young minister in the back benches timidly said that if Mr. Moody could not come Mr. Sankey might; but the reply was still, "No, Sankey wun't." I never in all my life saw a man so thoroughly impenetrable to all suggestions as this American Evangelist. I have no doubt he owes his success greatly to this, and the meeting evidently thought so too. They accepted what they might fairly have considered discourtesy in another person as a sign that Mr. Moody was overruled to do the work in his own way.

Eventually it came to a show of hands. Formal resolutions were framed—(1) That the morning prayer meeting and afternoon Bible class should commence on the following Tuesday, under the personal superintendence of Messrs. Moody and Sankey; and (2) that the evening meeting should be held without him whilst he divided his attention between Bow and Islington. This was to be tried for a week, and it was suggested that the meeting should choose a superintendent for the evenings; but no, again the inflexible Mr. Moody must name the man, and he named him in two syllables—"Blackwood." About this there was no difficulty. The meeting had in fact already named Mr. Stephenson Blackwood, who accepted the office, and all was pleasantly settled.

This nearer view of Mr. Moody gave me, as I have said, a very probable clue to his marvellous influence. He was what the Spiritualists call "positive" to a degree I had never witnessed before. I am quite sure if Mr. Moody sat at a séance and wished no manifestations to take place, none would. His manner was brusque to a degree that was ludicrous. He always referred to a speaker as "that man." "That man has made my speech for me," he said of somebody with whom he agreed. "He's said just what I was a-going to say." It seemed a marvellous instance of history repeating itself—the herdsman of Tekoa, without man's qualifications, carrying point after point against the Amaziahs, who had all external advantages to command—if mortals ever could command —success.

A NEW ICONOCLAST.

THERE is little doubt that the effect of the Public Worship Bill, giving as it does almost unlimited power to the Bishop *in camerá*, will have the effect of greatly augmenting the Free Churches outside the pale of the Establishment; and already, at the time of writing these chapters, a preliminary and almost prophetic activity seemed to have taken possession of those unorthodox bodies. Several of these I hope forthwith to examine in detail; but before doing so there is one gentleman who, as I write, is in that interesting transition state wherein we are fortunate to catch a convert; while a second, whom I noticed in such a transition state in the first series of these papers, has now found temporary resting for the sole of his foot.

"Eikonoklastes" wrote John Milton, with correct classical spelling, in his celebrated answer to the

Eikon Basilike, "the famous surname of many Greek Emperors who, in their zeal to the command of God, after long tradition of idolatry in the Church, took courage, and broke all superstitious images to pieces;" and, somehow or other, the massive periods of the sturdy old Puritan would come ringing into my mind as I paced breathlessly up the lofty staircases of the Memorial Hall, in Farringdon Street, to hear a clergyman of the Church of England lead off a series of lectures on Disestablishment, to be delivered under the auspices of the Liberation Society. It seemed but a little while ago I had been present at the laying of the foundation stone of this fine building; and here it was now in working order, and already forming the head-quarters of our modern iconoclasts! Surely there is no new thing under the sun. Taking its rise with literal image-smashing in the times of the Eastern Emperors, that term had been but slightly metamorphosed under the Stuarts and Commonwealth so as to include the breaking down of the Monarchy and Episcopacy; and here it was, two centuries afterwards, still alive in Farringdon Street, no longer concerned with such trifles as the Exeter reredos, and certainly with no disloyal ideas of "putting down" Queen Victoria, but simply bent on dissolving what it no doubt conscientiously believes to be the unhallowed union of Church and State. It was surely well to hear what a clergyman newly emerged from the Church of England—if indeed yet passed from that chrysalis condition—had to say in favour of this panacea for all the ills the Church is heir to.

The Memorial Hall, which is at the top of an apparently interminable flight of stone steps, is a handsome Gothic building, so very correct that one really looked round in half dismay lest it should not be iconoclastic after all, and one would have lost the advantage of a good euphonious title which would not be "understanded" of the common people at first. The "storied windows" were indeed filled with the figures of the old Puritan divines; and one exceedingly sarcastic lady behind me said, in reference to the handsomely-decorated platform with brass lectern for the lecturer and elaborate chair for the president, that it was the "High Altar." It will answer that purpose admirably if the "Catholic" party do one of these days get the upper hand, and there be another Nonconformist stampede from Blackfriars.

Six or seven rows of the front seats were labelled "Reserved," and I noticed the ministers and their ladies pass to these. For myself, not being "liberated," I sat humbly down on a back seat, though I had my white tie on just as though I had been a "minister," too. I got there very early; and when the gas was turned on to the full in the beautiful *coronæ*, I thought I had never seen a more ornate rendezvous for avowed iconoclasts. During the always irksome period of waiting for proceedings to commence, I listened to a lively discussion going on behind me between two old gentlemen, one I presume an iconoclast, and the other an Eikon-Basilike man. The Church of England, said the latter, was a tower of strength against Romanism: while the other avowed she was nothing better than a buttress of Rome. "What do you say of Romanizers in the Church?" asked this one. "Are there no Socinians among Dissenters?" rejoined the other; and either that or the entry of the lecturer and presidents shut up the Liberationist.

The chairman—a member of Parliament—referring to the memories of the place in which they were assembled, and even pointing to the figures in the windows, which we could not see, as it was dark outside, stated that the policy adopted there would be the same as that of Mr. Miall elsewhere. By the same faith and courage they were resolved to succeed. The question then and there to be agitated might not come home to an Englishman in the same way that questions of free trade and finance did, but it appealed to every thoughtful and educated Englishman with a power for good as remarkable and as far-reaching as those questions had done. It concerned not the mere physical condition of the subjects, but aimed to release them from the mental and moral trammels which were only to be thought of to be realized. The lecturer appeared as one lately a minister of the Church of England, and he deserved their hearty thanks for the course he had adopted. It showed that there were plenty of men in the Church ready to join those outside. He said he could understand the feelings of those inside the Church, as he was bound to it by very tender ties, but he could not approve of the shocking union between the Church and the State, and he desired for it the spiritual life of truth, that perfect toleration might exist, and that no particular creed should be set up above another. They could understand how a Churchman, if he could step down from his lofty height and meet his fellow men in preaching the Gospel, would breathe more freely. They mourned over the sale of livings, and the struggle about education, which would all be reduced to nothing when one creed was not allowed the advantage over others. Men were now divided because of the tone of domination assumed by Churchmen through the union of Church and State. When men began to think on that question they will see the vast amount of power which is wasted through that union, and would then devote themselves to spreading those principles until right should be done. It was said that the enterprise was vast, and so it was, but it was because of its effect upon the mental and moral development of the country that they engaged in it. Englishmen were naturally Conservative, and would not advance in the path of progress until their minds were convinced, and that was the work the Liberation Society was engaged in doing, with a full apprehension of its difficulty, but undaunted by the prospect before them. But vast as it was, it was not more so than those conflicts which had been fought out in times past, and they must not forget the moral force which could be brought to bear on the subject. There was a public opinion which could not be put down, and even those who based the existence of the Church of England upon the argument that it was God's truth were now obliged to give their reasons for the assertion. If they came to argument, it would be their duty to show their fallacies, and he believed that ultimately victory would crown their cause.

Not being at first aware of the senatorial dignity of this gentleman, I began to feel almost aggrieved at his much speaking, and wondered whether he was going to introduce the lecturer at all or give the lecture himself. At length, however, he announced the Rev. Mr. Heard, late of All Saints', Pinner, and a tall, bearded gentleman, with an evangelic expanse of shirt-front, advanced to the brass desk and read his lecture from manuscript.

In commencing his address, Mr. Heard said he was but a young recruit, and might be compared to the Uhlan officer who crossed the frontier and fired the first shot in the war of invasion in France. The battle of religious liberty was fought in the seventeenth century when the Toleration Act passed, but the campaign for religious equality was only now opening. To use those dangerous watch-words, " Liberty, Equality, Fraternity," it appeared to him that they marked the three acts of the drama of Disestablishment. Liberty was the cry of the seventeenth century. Equality was that of the nineteenth, and when they had reached that, Fraternity and the free intercommunion of the Churches would come of itself, perhaps in the twentieth century.

At this point, a working man at the back of the hall, who, I fear, did not lean to teetotal principles, rose to address the meeting, and had to be summarily expelled. He covered his retreat with some remarks not at all complimentary to the lecturer, the audience, or the cause commemorated in that Memorial Hall.

I could not help thinking what a pity it was that theological working men could not reserve their potations until after they have been to controversial lectures. Both beer and theology are so apt to get into the heads of excitable people.

Having borne very good-humouredly this interruption, the lecturer returned to the subject of Disestablishment. To attain that they must not "rest and be thankful," but follow in the steps of their predecessors. He should treat his subject that evening less on the ground of abstract principle than on that of the special difficulties of Churchmen, arising from anxiety as to the future of the Church when its connexion with the State was dissolved. After pointing out the fallacies involved in the idea that it is the duty of the State to maintain and establish the Church, the lecturer stated the case of those who held the principle of Establishments on other grounds. It was said that the alliance was more for the benefit of the State than the Church. As that was a political difficulty it might be left to the State to answer for itself. Another supposed difficulty was the impossibility of keeping Church parties together without the cohesive clamp of the Establishment, a difficulty which the Church had created for itself by its own Act of Uniformity, and which would disappear with that Act. A third difficulty was thought to be that of dealing with country parishes without a scheme of endowment. But he thought that a sentimental difficulty appalling only to those who were ignorant of the power of Voluntaryism. It was ordained that those who preached the Gospel should live of the Gospel, and their best security was in relying on the promise of their Lord. The last difficulty he should mention was the argument that the State never formally established the Church or endowed it, and therefore had no right to disestablish or disendow it. They replied to that by saying that a Church which was nationalized to some extent under Henry VIII. by the deprivation of the Romish hierarchy, may be nationalized still further under Victoria by the deprivation of an exclusive clerical corporation, and the throwing open the Church to the use of the various denominations under the control of a board of public worship.

Coming at last—and quite modestly at the end of a long lecture—to personal matters, Mr. Heard said he had arrived at the conclusion that an Established Church *must* be exclusive; and therefore he left the Establishment, and cast in his lot with the Free Churches—a statement which I need not say was received with vehement cheers. Twice lately he had been taken to task by the Bishop of London—and here the cheers were exchanged for hisses—simply for doing what Mr. Fremantle had endeavoured to do at the City Temple. (Here again there were loud cries of "Shame!") He felt therefore that the time had come for him to claim his freedom. We had had enough of ecclesiastical prosecutions, and therefore he had simply enclosed his licence to the Bishop of London.

There was some more speechifying from the ministers and laymen present; but the great attraction was over when Mr. Heard thus announced himself a Coriolanus in the Volscian camp. I was literally inundated with papers of the Liberation Society as I came out; and found the list of episcopal salaries look not so large as usual side by side with Messrs. Moody and Sankey's figures. However, the battle of Iconoclasm has begun in real earnest; and there is no disguising the fact that Mr. Heard's lecture was a very telling, because a very temperate, discourse; quite different from this which was handed to me by an exceedingly juvenile Iconoclast as I came out—it forms part of "The Age of Disestablishment":—
" Who believes that England alone will resist the universal tide of religious equality? She will not—

she must not—she cannot. The shadow is turning upon the dial towards the hour when this nation will decree that thenceforth all religions shall stand upon the foundation of their own faith and liberality, and that hour will witness the downfall of that highest barrier which has for ages prevented the fusion of our nation into one harmonious and organic whole. Fictitious and usurped supremacies are inconsistent with the unity of any people, and it is vain to expect that the Nonconformists of England will rest for one moment until every man, whatever be his creed, stands on the same level, without favour or disparagement, in the eye of law. To accomplish this is our purpose, which we believe to be in accordance with the will of God, the claims of justice, and the highest interests of the nation and of the world."

Eikonoklastes the First never wrote anything like that!

MR. REVELL AT LADBROKE HALL.

The other Iconoclast to whom I referred is Mr. Revell, recently a Nonconformist minister, who made his *début* at Mr. Conway's chapel, and is now holding Sunday Evening Services at Ladbroke Hall. To this place I paid a visit.

For a long time after I got there I thought I was going to be the congregation. A lady was playing sacred music on a grand pianoforte on the stage; and two boys were playing hide-and-seek in and out of the stage doors on either side of the proscenium, in the intervals of brushing the green baize which covered the desk in the centre. There was, in fact, a good deal more hide-and-seek than brushing going on. However, the congregation dropped in by small driblets, and by-and-by Mr. Revell made his appearance on the stage, dressed in the attire of every-day life. There was a sober scene "set," but the whole arrangement looked rather theatrical. There strikes me as always something more or less dissipated about the appearance of a grand piano, and of course the stage accessories did not help to tone this down.

The services commenced with a hymn nicely sung by a young lady who had joined the pianiste. We bore our part but mildly and timorously, for there were not enough of us to embolden one another; but we all had hymn-books given us, and I found they were selections from Mr. Conway's volume used at South Place Chapel. Then there was a reading on the subject of "Beauty," from some secular work, the name of which I did not catch. Another hymn followed by way of canticle; this was Tennyson's stanzas from "In Memoriam," commencing "Strong Son of God, immortal Love!" but slightly altered. Then came a second reading from Carlyle; and at the conclusion of each Mr. Revell said, "Here end-*eth* the reading"—an archaic form of diction I should have expected him to have out-grown. Another hymn closed the brief and simple service; and then he delivered his lecture, the title of which had been advertised as "Philosopher and Poet."

It was a learned discourse; too learned, if one may express an opinion, for the majority of those to whom it was addressed. It traced a similarity between

Science and Poetry, from the fact of their each dealing with ideal creations—the one of the intellect, the other of the emotions. He contrasted them by viewing each as dealing with the subject of human love, for instance. Herbert Spencer described it as due to molecular motion, but Shakspeare represented it to us in a Romeo or a Juliet. The physicist described Mont Blanc to us scientifically; but Shelley placed it before our eyes in the well-known poem which Mr. Revell read. The aim of the one was Truth, of the other Beauty; and yet there was not, of necessity, any antagonism between the two.

The orthodox churches, he went on to say, were wanting in a scientific habit of mind; while, on the other side, those who had separated from them were often deficient in the cultivation of the emotions. This was the great mission of poetry. If we neglected this, life was shorn of half its beauty. Rather than confine one's self to a mechanical philosophy, it would be better to go back to the old religions. Many of the highest models were to be found in the old poetry. We wanted a moral inspiration; and there was great moral inspiration in the Christian idea. So as to the work of the world. Philosophy gave the direction, but Poetry gave the motive power. Philosophy left us still in face of the mystery of the Unknown and the Unknowable. Poetry and Religion lifted us to ideal constructions of the highest kind. There was a truth in beauty, he concluded, but the whole truth was comprised in the world of intellect and the world of poetry. But art, including poetry and music, was greater than mechanical science.

The service and sermon—or lecture—were a strange instance of the speaker's own proposition—beautiful and able, but cold and unemotional. I am sure there would have been a larger gathering if Mr. Revell had carried out in practice his own excellent theory.

A REVISED PRAYER-BOOK.

THERE is, perhaps, no man who occupies a more thoroughly unique position in the ecclesiastical world than the Rev. Charles Voysey, who may be described as formerly vicar of Healaugh, Yorkshire, and now of St. George's Hall, Langham Place. Though deprived of his benefice for unsound teaching, he still claims to belong to the Church of England; and has elaborated at St. George's Hall a form of theistic worship which would, indeed, bespeak the Anglican Communion comprehensive could she be proved elastic enough to contain it. Such is his attitude, however; he declines to join any of the existing religious bodies, and especially eschews the name of Unitarian, though, of course, holding the doctrines of that communion. He waits, in fact, until the Church of England is "broad" enough to welcome him back, like a theological Prodigal, to her maternal arms.

One of Mr. Voysey's first acts when, having made his *début* at the Free Christian Church, Croydon, he proceeded to elaborate the St. George's cultus, was to compile a liturgy. In doing this he adhered pretty closely to the letter of the Book of Common Prayer, excising all that militated against a theistic creed. He speaks thus of his attempt in the preface to the first edition :—

" This Prayer-Book was compiled under the conviction of the editor's inability to adopt the old Nonconformist worship, with its long extempore prayer, even had it been preferred by the congregation. He believed however that, as some form must be used, the form most likely to find acceptance would be one which was already partly familiar to English ears, and yet stripped of all that has become obsolete and out of harmony with a pure Theism."

After using this manual of devotion for three years, Mr. Voysey or his congregation, or probably both, felt that they had outgrown it; and the result has been the revision of this volume and the adoption of another, which he still speaks of as a *modest attempt to adapt the Liturgy of the venerable Church of England to a purely theistic worship.*

On a recent Sunday this book was to be used for the first time, and Mr. Voysey was advertised to preach a sermon on "The Reasonableness of Worship." Now I own to some difficulty in realizing the theistic position in reference to worship, and went, in real curiosity, to see what I could gather from observation as to the genius and essence of this studiously nondescript body of religionists.

I found the hall well filled; or at least there were cards on a very large proportion of the seats showing that they were let, and most of these were occupied during the morning. Mr. Voysey himself, with a blue pilot coat surmounting an intensely clerical dress, as though to signify a compromise between the Church and the world, was conversing with little knots of his paulopost congregation, and by him I was ushered courteously into a private box. It sounds grotesque to say this; and there was a feeling of something like dissipation in entering that *loge au premier* for Divine worship; but one soon got reconciled to that. Indeed, it was not the first occasion by very many on which I had worshipped at the shrine of St. George and the Dragon; and I have long since learned to get readily acclimatized to unfamiliar ecclesiastical surroundings in the course of my varied peregrinations. The "use" of St. George's Hall is curious enough to warrant a description in detail.

The service opened with a selection from an entirely

new set of Scriptural sentences, of which Mr. Voysey read four. Indeed, generally speaking, the service had rather a tendency to err on the side of length as compared with the orthodox one; at least, such was my impression. A new exhortation of great length followed and a quasi-confession, each much longer than the Church of England forms. I was surprised to notice this after reading the following passage in the preface:—

"The most striking change will be found, perhaps, in the introductory portion of the service. Not ourselves alone, but a large portion of conforming members of the Church of England also, have completely outgrown the taste for the old 'Dearly Beloved,' 'The General Confession,' and 'The Absolution.' A clergyman, who was and is perfectly orthodox, confessed to me that these were quite out of place in a mixed assembly, and as an introduction to worship. Centuries ago the service began at the Lord's Prayer, and a little later Psalms and Introits of praise were sung as an opening; a much more fitting prelude to devotion than the miserable whining introspection and confession of sin, the exaggerated terms of which stamp them with insincerity.

"It is quite possible for rare occasions to arise when such confession would be true and appropriate, but equally impossible for numbers of well-conducted happy people to use them with anything like sincerity every week at a certain hour."

Now, however, I came upon the most complete alteration of all. Mr. Voysey had revised the Lord's Prayer! Two of its clauses were changed so as to stand thus: "Forgive us our trespasses as *we should* forgive them that trespass against us; and *leave us not* in temptation."

The First and Second Lessons, which were separated by an abbreviated Te Deum, were read from an article in the *Boston Index* on the subject of "Worship in the Nineteenth Century."

First Lesson.

Worship is the expression, or an expression, of the religious sentiment. The worship has not created the sentiment, but the sentiment has created the worship. The worship, whatever form it has taken, has been the natural language of the sentiment. And so now or in the future, whatever form of utterance the religious sentiment may adopt as its natural language, that will be worship; if it adopt the same for a number of people, then common, or public, worship is the result. The question, then, at the root is the permanence of the religious sentiment. And when I look back upon the history of the human race, and see how vast a part the religious sentiment has played in human history, how active and constant and fertile it has been from the very rudest beginnings of man's career, how large a share it has had in his interests and how mightily it has affected his destiny, how it has built up some nations and destroyed others, pervaded the affairs of all; how it has inspired art and created literatures, and shaped thought and determined private conduct, and built up gigantic and peculiar institutions of its own, and moved great masses of men with a common enthusiasm and purpose,—when I look back upon all this, and see what a power the religious sentiment has been, it does not seem to me at all probable that this power has all been a mistake, that it has all rested on a mere superstition, on a false conception of things, and that under the increasing knowledge and culture of modern times, it is now near the end of its career. I see, indeed, that the religious sentiment has made mistakes, some of them grievous and great; I see that for want of knowledge it has allied itself often to superstition, and for want of humanity to bigotry. I see and admit the alleged evils and corruptions that have sprung from dogmatism, sectarianism, ecclesiasticism, idolatry,—they are indeed, from my habit of thought, almost too constantly before my eyes; and yet, in spite of all, the religious faculty is to me the noblest endowment of the human mind,—the crown, so to speak, of the long struggle of the "Cosmical Life" to develop a finite being of reflective intelligence and volition. And this sentiment seems to me as ineradicable from human nature as it has been the constant accompaniment of human nature's historic career. The consciousness of relation to the power whence he has sprung, once having been developed in man and making an integral part of his nature, it is indeed impossible to conceive of its being extinguished while man remains. Not by culture, scientific or other, is this sense of relationship to the inscrutable creative energy of the universe—call it, with Tyndall, "Cosmical Life," or call it "Deity"—to be lessened. Rather by every day's fresh intelligence will our sense of the mysterious relationship be deepened and broadened and brought more into accordance with facts, while from the very nature of the case something of the infinite mystery must for ever remain concealed, enticing the mind upwards to boundless search.

But let me add that, in saying that the religious sentiment is the natural and ineradicable root of worship and of all historical religions, I do not use the word sentiment as synonymous merely with feeling or emotion. I do not believe that the religious sentiment would have been so powerful in history, if it had been only an emotion. But I use the word sentiment as involving both perception (or an intellectual act) and feeling; as including also the sense of moral obligation. I use it as denoting the entire disposition or tendency or faculty of the human mind which has resulted in religion.

Historically, this disposition or tendency has always been of a complex nature. There has been the feeling of wonder, of awe, of reverence, or it may be of fear, aroused by some remarkable scene or occurrence; and accompanying it, some mental judgment or conception concerning the phenomenon, referring it to a more than human power; and also an impulse to some line of conduct for effecting conformity with the power. Or the mental perception of human relation to some superhuman power may have come first, and often, I believe, did, and the emotion was subordinate to it. All that I wish now to say on the point is, that I use the term religious sentiment as including all these phases of mental action, and that historically all these elements have been present to make religion the great power it has been.

But though man's nature and history would seem to prove the permanence of the religious sentiment and of some form of worship as the expression of it, the question still remains whether the institution of a Sunday service like this is a kind of expression that best meets the demands of the cultivated religious sentiment of the present age. In other words, can we show the present utility of this service—utility in the fine sense of enlarging and feeding man's higher nature? The question of what may come in the future when the "coming man," with the garnered wisdom of all centuries added to his own inspiration, shall appear on this planet, we may dismiss as little concerning us who are on the planet to-day and responsible to some extent for its condition. Admitting that the religious sentiment is the creator of its forms of worship, and that with increasing light and culture it transforms old forms and creates new ones, we may have to admit our ignorance as to what kind of worship the future may bring, but may also safely leave the problem for the future to solve. But for the present, and so far as seems probable from man's present condition, for many a year and generation to come, I for one cannot doubt the utility of a specific organization for the promotion of religious culture and life, and of a specific religious service set apart in place and time like this.

Here we are, on this earth, immersed for the most

part in material pursuits, more or less gross, in buying and selling and getting gain, in taking care of our bodies or our estates, in the drudging toil of shops, or farm, or counting-room, or household, in eating and drinking, and providing the wherewithal to be clothed; and day after day this immersion goes on, absorbing our faculties, using up our energies, and draining off our vitality. And yet we all confess that there are parts of our natures—aspirations, desires, capacities for thought and action—that this daily routine of material pursuit, whether it be necessary or voluntary, does not satisfy. Nor is it the office of the Sunday service to meet these higher demands of human nature : to feed these better aspirations, hopes, impulses of the human mind, to cultivate just that side of life which is admitted to be the nobler side, and which yet is left to so large an extent uncultivated by the hard necessities or customs of daily toil amid lower interests. The Sunday service is intended to appeal to the moral and spiritual nature of man in distinction from the physical, to his rational nature as having the rightful supremacy over carnal appetite and passion. It aims, or should aim, to rouse the better motives, to quicken conscience, to stir generous impulses into activity, and to plant them where they are wanting; to awaken a stronger love and admiration for goodness; to open, purify, and cultivate the best affections of the heart. It seeks to make men more zealous for the truth, and more heroic in the defence of it; less selfish and more self-sacrificing, more kind, more benevolent, better citizens. It finds them fallen and vicious, and it strives to utter some word that shall renew their courage, and help them to restoration. It finds them in despair, and it speaks and pleads for hope in darkness, and it endeavours to show the dawning light. It finds them amid trials and under crushing burdens, and it strives to show how obstacles may be surmounted by the brave soul, and made into steps of ascent to power and virtue. It finds them sitting in the valley of the shadow of death, and it points them to the old hope of the Hereafter, or to the new doctrine that death is but a phase in the eternal process of life.

Second Lesson.

Thus the Sunday service, for two or three hours one day in the seven, comes into our busy life as a quickener of moral effort and of spiritual aspiration, to the end of lifting the whole of our life to a higher level. In the midst of our material cares and callings, our moral struggles and failures, it holds before us the noble aim of Ideal Excellence. And even those of us who may not be so wholly engaged in material callings, but whose pursuits may be more mental and literary, or even philanthropic, may find it no small benefit to have the routine of our pursuits thus regularly interrupted, and our thoughts and feelings turned to other channels, in a common religious service with our fellow-men. For the advantage comes in part from the social communion as well as from the uplifted individual aspiration. In a word, if the phrase spiritual nature of man, including his higher mental and moral nature as distinguished from the lower motives to which the ordinary pursuits and occupations and customs of life appeal, has any meaning, if there be any such higher part of our natures, any possible higher life than that with which our days are now most familiar, anything above these absorbing cares and tempting passions of the flesh, then the specific religious service which appeals to these higher motives, and aims to strengthen and develop this higher life of man, is amply vindicated as having a right to be, and may be expected to survive so long as it shall answer such high ends. And as helps to this aim let us have all the accessories that are within our reach from art and culture. Worship may be very real, and attain for some hearts its ends, in a meeting-house of Quaker plainness and under conditions of whatever extemporaneous speech may chance to arise from the congregation, or of silence, which is often better than speech. But there is danger of spiritual inertness under such conditions. Most of us are in need of such appliances as appeal to the eye and the ear, and to the cultivated reason, to stir our spiritual thoughts and emotions to activity. Music often touches with uplifting power places in the heart where the word of the preacher fails to penetrate. Forms of beauty in architecture and colour lend also their gracious influence in awakening the emotions of reverence and aspiration.

But all such accessories appeal chiefly to the religious emotion, and a church cannot live on emotions. There must be living thought in the pews, and the living word in the pulpit; thought and word abreast with the time, and palpitating with the spirit of divine life that is freshly flowing in the world to-day. I have already said that in the history of religion, emotion and mental perception, feeling and thought, have been the constant factors in all healthy, normal, and powerful religious development. And so it must be to-day, if religion is to preserve its ancient prestige and power. And this is a point on which I should take decided issue with a portion of Professor Tyndall's late address, if I rightly understand it.

He speaks of giving up to religion the region of the emotions, while he would have it abandon the province of thought on the great problems of existence, and thus he apparently encourages the notion, popular among certain classes of theologians, that religion and science are of incompatible temperament, and must be divorced; though, at the very close of the address, there are some words of a different tenour, and, as a whole, it seems to me most admirable. But against the statement above alluded to, in the name of religion itself, considered in its nature and its history, and in behalf of the dignity of my office as a religious teacher, I would enter a protest. I would make the protest, too, in behalf of the present and future interests of religion and of mankind. The weakness of religion to-day, the very reason why it is losing its hold upon so many thoughtful and cultivated people—and people that, though not much cultured, are full of the thought of the age that is in the air—is because this very divorce has to a considerable extent taken place, and religion is already too much given up to feeding the emotions. A religion that is wholly absorbed in the region of the emotions cannot, I believe, long survive among an enlightened people. Emotion has its proper office, and it is a very important one; but it is thought that guides the emotions, and, in the long run, safely moves the world. A religion without thought is emasculated, and must dwindle to decay. And if, under the emotional influences of this place, if amid these surroundings of art and beauty and elegant comfort, this society or its minister should ever become enervated in thought, and forget their obligations to ideas, and sink into mental stagnation, then I pray that some old iconoclast may rise from the grave, some Luther, or George Fox, or George Whitfield, and raise the trumpet-voice of reform, and sweep from these walls all their beauty, and silence the music, and leave the congregation in a plain meeting-house, or drive it into a hall or a barn, or into the open air, where it may hear with undistracted mental ear the living voice of truth. For better unadorned and desolate walls, with living and earnest thought within, than all possible elegance and beauty of an emotional religion with mental death.

And if the Sunday service of religion, while it kindles the emotions of the spiritual nature, must at the same time aim to awaken thought, and to keep pace with its progress, much more must it serve to sustain and to strengthen the natural principles of morality. This, the final point, is also in its practical aspects the chief point. Matthew Arnold has defined religion as "morality suffused with emotion." Philosophically this may hardly pass as a complete definition. But practically the definition is excellent, because it lays the emphasis where, in the common affairs of life, it most needs to be laid. Taking mankind in general, the emotional nature in religion does not need so much to be aroused as it needs to be guided by a wise knowledge and a true moral culture. And one sees sometimes such lamentable illustrations of an intense emotional piety combined with a feeble moral sense, and even with positive immorality, that one is tempted to exclaim, " Emotion is nothing—morality is everything." And certainly, if religious emotion does not issue in good works, it proves itself of little worth; and to many souls it doubtless operates as a delusion and a snare. They mistake an inflated currency of feeling for the solid coin of virtue. The emphasis, then, must be placed on moral conduct, and all religious feeling brought to that clear test. We may say of emotion that it is desirable, but of morality that it is a necessity. Given two persons, one of whom shall be emotionally religious, even to a high degree, fluent in prayer-meeting, zealous for his church, ready at any time to speak of his conscious relation to God, but weak in morals; and the other shall be simply upright, vigorously honest, pure, generous, merely a moral man, as the saying is, but shall have never known what it is to be thrilled with a sense of the Divine Presence; and I am sure that the latter will go into heaven before the former. I would rather anywhere take the chances of the merely moral man than of the merely pious man. The merely pious man, by his aspiration, his feeling, his sentiment, is reaching upward through the air to get his hold on God. The moral man, though he may be utterly unable to say what the phrase "presence of God" means, and has no consciousness of it, yet actually dwells nearer to it; for that line of strict integrity which marks his daily conduct is the identical pathway where the Divine Presence walks.

And at this day, so rife in public and private corruption, when we hear and see so much of self-seeking intrigue in politics, of dishonesty in trade, of embezzlement and swindling in financial institutions, of mercenariness in public men, of loose licence in domestic relations, of portentous evils menacing the sacredness of marriage and the stability of the family, surely the Church has a special call, as it has in the Sunday service a grand opportunity to proclaim, with all the emphasis at its command, the primal obligation and sanctity of the moral law. Whatever it may do or neglect to do for the culture of the religious emotions, it has a solemn duty in upholding public and private morality, which it cannot evade without peril to itself and society. Whatever be the means this must be the end. Whatever else may come into religion to give it grace and symmetry, this must come as its abiding substance. For the old prophet-voiced words have lost none of their truth, and need to be uttered to-day with fresh energy: "Who shall abide in thy tabernacle? Who shall dwell in thy holy hill? He that walketh uprightly, and worketh righteousness, and speaketh the truth in his heart. He that slandereth not with his tongue, nor doeth evil to his neighbour. He that sweareth to his own hurt, and changeth not. He that doeth these things shall never be moved."

It certainly was something novel to see a clergyman in full canonicals reading the Lessons from a newspaper instead of a Bible! The Jubilate was sung to a "service" as it would be called in a cathedral—an elaborate composition like an anthem, and then followed a long series of collects, each concluding with a choral "Amen" from an unseen choir hidden behind the red drapery which swathed the act-drop. What with a Glastonbury chair and crimson baize over the rostrum (which in its nude state on a Sunday afternoon looks like a gallows or incipient guillotine) St. George and the Dragon appeared more ecclesiastical than could have been expected under the circumstances.

When the ordinary Morning Prayer was ended, and a hymn had been sung—the music, by the way, being particularly good—Mr. Voysey proceeded to the "Service of Praise and Thanksgiving," which, commencing with a choral "Sanctus," consisted of a number of suffrages to which the choir and congregation responded melodiously, "We thank Thee, O Father, Lord of Heaven and Earth." An interval of silent prayer followed; and the whole concluded with the Epilogus to F. W. Newman's "Theism," sung as an anthem. The final clauses of this composition, and one passage in the Prayer for the Church Militant (revised), were the only ones I noticed where reference was made to a future state; and these did not enable me to grasp any very clear conceptions as to the opinions held by Mr. Voysey and his followers on this subject. Of course where no formal creed exists, one can only infer the belief from passages in the liturgy. The former, from the Epilogus, was—

"So shall we love thee while we live, and partake of thy joy,
And triumph over sorrow, and fulfil thy work,
And be numbered with thy saints, and *die on thy bosom.*"

The second substituted for the ordinary clause in the prayer for the Church Militant the following words:— "We also bless Thy holy Name for all Thy servants departed this life *into Thy home above;* beseeching Thee to give us grace to follow *all* good examples, that with them we may be partakers of Thy heavenly kingdom."

Previously to the sermon, Mr. Voysey made a statement as to the expenses of his services, for which there was to be a special collection. They cost, he said, a hundred pounds a month. This sum was not met by the seats which were let; and the weekly offertory was only intended to give strangers an opportunity of contributing. He might, he added, double or treble the amount if he adopted the plan of handing the plate to each person individually; but he would rather have no money at all than make their contributions compulsory. Hospital Sunday showed that there was no need of such "extortion;" but still he could not disguise the fact that the general fund was not in a satisfactory condition. Eight hundred pounds had just been carried over to the General Building Fund; but, unless there should be permanent resources, a building fund would be of no avail. He exhorted the congregation to bring their friends or themselves to make donations. If one-fifth or one-sixth of the congregation would subscribe ten pounds a year each, all would be well. He was not in straits, but he wanted to be secure against anxiety.

Among the occasional offices in this book, is one for the Burial "or Cremation" of the dead, which again throws some light on the doctrine of a future state :— (Here the body is to be committed to the furnace) "In faith and hope, then, we commit unto the flames the body of our dear brother here departed, in sure and certain hope that his soul hath ascended into the rest of God, and is at peace in our Heavenly Father's home; believing that we, too, shall soon be numbered among the happy throng, and meet again in everlasting joy."

Such, surely, is one of the strangest ecclesiastical experiments of the day. There must be a certain amount of fascination in such a position. Mr. Voysey is as purely his own master as Pope Pius himself. In leaving the Church of England for any other body a clergyman exchanges one service for another, or at most can be only said to compass quite a limited authority; but here is an autocracy beside which that of the most despotic civil ruler or infallible spiritual guide sinks almost into insignificance. He may parody some historic words, and say, "L'Eglise, c'est moi."

A GREEK EASTERTIDE.

THERE is a rumour—only a faint, vague, and far-off one at present, but still a rumour—that we are likely to have, ere long, an English-speaking congregation of the Holy Eastern Church in London. Charmed, perhaps, by the adopted title of Orthodox, and the claim put in by the Greek Church to be based on a purely apostolic model, several converts, some of high position, have recently passed from the Anglican to the Greek communion. I could mention names; but do not quite know whether it would be proper for me to do so, as the matter is scarcely public property at present. Hitherto, however, there have been only two Greek churches in London; one, the well-known church in London Wall, described in the first series of these papers, where the Rev. N. Morphinos is the priest; and the other, the chapel of the Russian Embassy at 32, Welbeck Street, served by the Rev. E.

Popoff. In the former the service is performed in modern Greek or Romaic, at the latter in Russ; but there has been up to this time no church or chapel in London with the service in the vernacular.

Sunday, April 25, 1875 (our fourth Sunday after Easter), was, according to the Eastern calendar, Easter Sunday, and I took the opportunity to renew my acquaintance with the Greek ritual, which is exceedingly imposing. I know not why, but though it is ornate in the extreme, it seems much more like one's own Eucharistic service than the Romish Mass, at least to me. I have carefully studied the two services under the guidance of a priest in each denomination respectively; and, I must confess, I seemed, apart from all prejudice, able to enter much more readily into the spirit of the Greek than the Roman ritual. This may be simply an idiosyncrasy of my own, and need imply no judgment as to their relative intrinsic merits.

The liturgy used at the church in London Wall is that of St. John Chrysostom, which can be purchased in a small volume, with the English translation arranged in parallel columns with the Greek; and a visit to the Strangers' Gallery in that church on any ordinary Sunday will quite repay the trouble of a journey to the uttermost ends of London for any one who is interested in studying a foreign and highly ancient ritual.

Late in the evening of the Vigil of Easter I presented myself at 32, Welbeck Street, and found a most intelligent and courteous attendant airing himself on the doorstep. The service, he informed me, would be at eleven, but no stranger could by any possibility be admitted. On my telling him who I was, and my purpose in being present, he relaxed his rule in my favour. I really had some most interesting conversation with this man, who was thoroughly posted up in his subject. (It was not, by the way, from him that the rumour of an English Church of the Greek Communion reached me.) In the Oriental Church I was vastly interested; but unfortunately there was an Oriental wind blowing at the same time, which made the doorstep rather a more airy situation than I should have selected had I been free to act; but the man's post was there, and he stuck to it like a sentinel on duty. The great merit of the Greek Communion, according to him, was that there was no Pope in its economy. The churches and sees were virtually independent, he said; thus confirming what I had already gathered in my previous study of the subject as to the perfect elasticity of system pertaining to the Holy Eastern Church. I had some preliminary difficulty next morning in obtaining entrance to the church in London Wall; but was again rescued by a civil attendant—this time from the opposing arms of a rigid City policeman. The Strangers' Gallery was generally reserved on this day, and was, he believed, at that time quite full; but I could mount and try. I did so, and found myself among a motley group of all nations, many being Greek sailors carrying lighted tapers in their tattooed hands. Several of those present had quite a Jewish cast of features, and there were a few English, evidently lost in bewilderment. Two young men, who looked very like University men, were sharing a Liturgy of St. John Chrysostom, and gave me an occasional peep at it. They were hunting hopelessly amid its pages as I entered, and I was just able to tell them that the introductory portion of the service was special to Easter. I recognised, in fact, a beautiful Troparion, as it is termed, which the choir was singing as I entered, and which Dr. Littledale thus translates:—

> "Christ hath risen from the dead,
> Death by death down doth He tread,
> And on those within the tomb
> He bestoweth life."

This was repeated at frequent intervals throughout the whole Eucharistic Service, and the melody was most delightful. The choir sings without accompaniment, and is of rare excellence. I could just see, by craning my neck over the heads of people in front of me, that the whole church was ablaze with the light of tapers carried by all the male portion of the congregation, while huge clusters of candles burnt before the screen that hides the altar, and the candelabra and sanctuary lamps were all lighted in honour of Easter morn. As new arrivals kept dropping in, there was hearty hand-shaking and exchange of greetings, quite putting one in mind of the old Christian salutation on that same morning, "The Lord hath risen." The Greek ritual seemed to realize as intensely the joy of the Resurrection as the English does that of the Nativity at Christmastide.

When the special service was over, the Liturgy of St. John began, and continued for about two hours. A foreign priest, with long black beard and olive complexion, assisted Mr. Morphinos, and the vestments of each were of rich white satin. The acolytes wear an English-shaped surplice, with a light blue cross embroidered upon it. The Liturgy, which really divides at the Sursum Corda, consists of two portions —the Prothesis and the Anaphora; and the two most striking hymns are the Cherubic Hymn and the

Trisagion. The canon of the Mass is gone through with the veil drawn between the sanctuary and congregation, but the greater portion of it is chanted aloud, the congregation and choir bearing their part, and only a certain portion being said in secret by the priest and deacons. The celebrant in the Greek Church consecrates five small loaves, each of which is stamped with letters signifying, "Jesus Christ conquers." These he divides with what is called the holy spear, and sets aside portions for the Holy Lamb, for St. Mary, for nine prophets, apostles, and martyrs, together with a portion for the living and another for the dead. After consecration the elements are brought forward, veiled, in front of the altar screen, and elevated before the people, but there was no communion. A very beautiful prayer, too, is that called the Prayer of the Entrance, which I would translate freely thus :—

"O Lord our God, who hast appointed in the heavens troops and armies of Angels and Archangels for the service of Thy Glory, let there be, with our Entrance, an entrance of Holy Angels, worshipping with us, and joining us to glorify Thy goodness. For to Thee belongs all glory, honour, and worship, to the Father, Son, and Holy Spirit, now and ever, and to eternal ages. Amen."

At one period in the service, the foreign priest in his magnificent robes stood fronting the congregation, and held the silver-bound Gospel for them to kiss. All advanced, one by one, grey-headed men and tiny children, kneeling reverently as they kissed the sacred volume. I could not help noticing throughout the service that, though the doctrine of the Real Presence was prominent, it never merged in transubstantiation; and also, while special honour was paid to the Virgin Mary, there was nothing that could be construed into Mariolatry. I fancy the Eastern Church has never been a missionary or propagandist body to the same extent as the Western; but I cannot help thinking that, to persons who left the Anglican Communion in search of more advanced doctrine and ritual, there would be less violence in the transition to the Greek than to the Romish Church. But this is foreign to my purpose. Whatever else the Greek Church may be, and whether, as the late Dr. Neale thought, she s to form the future basis of reunion in Christendom, we can, at all events, concede to him that she presents "the phenomenon of a permanent Christian society and doctrine external to the Roman obedience." The Patriarchates still occupy what were the great centres in the generations immediately succeeding the Apostles; and though I could scarcely go so far as my communicative doorkeeper in Welbeck Street, who opined that the ritual then and there to be carried out by Mr. Popoff was identical with that of the Apostles themselves, still the very names of the Liturgies— those of St. James, St. Mark, St. John Chrysostom, and St. Basil—attest their great antiquity, and make us feel that in the orthodox Greek Church we have a curious link binding us to the very earliest ages of our faith. Dr. Neale, in his "History of the Holy Eastern Church," speaks of her as already "extending herself from the Sea of Okotsk to the palaces of Venice, from the ice-fields that grind against the Solevetsky monastery to the burning jungles of Malabar, embracing a thousand languages and tongues, that bind them together in the golden link of the same faith, offer the tremendous sacrifice in a hundred liturgies, but offer it to the same God, and with the same rites, fixing her patriarchal thrones in the same cities as when the disciples were called Christians first at Antioch."

A GOOD FRIDAY FAIR.

YEAR by year our great annual Spring Fast culminates in the solemn observance of Good Friday; and while the tendency is gradually to lose sight of the merely ecclesiastical discipline of Lent, the bias is quite in an opposite direction with regard to Good Friday itself. This is perfectly comprehensible. In proportion as merely human deductions from the Sacred Biography sink into desuetude, the great facts of that Life of Lives assume the importance which intrinsically belongs to them. Christmas, Good Friday, and Easter would, in all probability, be more universally and decorously observed, just as the apparatus of vigils, Saints' Days, and other minor observances came to be discarded. It is so with the emblem of the cross itself. When it is not gifted with materialistic adjuncts by being turned into a crucifix it is sublime, and speaks to the heart as the symbol of self-denial; but when multiplied, as it too often is, and put in every possible position, the symbolism is frittered away. In fact, the Ritualists themselves have protested against this unintentional desecration of the sacred emblem by thoughtless devotees, and speak of it strongly as "The Cross in the Mire." The event of Calvary will gradually take its true position as the sublimest in the world's history just in proportion as it is allowed to assume its due prominence, and the attention of those who contemplate it is not distracted either by minor ecclesiastical observances or human dogmas as to its import.

But when it is said that the event of Good Friday is thus gaining in general acceptance one would not for a moment aver that this is true in what may be called a theological sense. Perhaps, again, in proportion as men think more about the great event they will be less demonstrative in their observance of it. We can instance this from commonest experience. The childish, immature grief for the loss of a beloved one is often noisy and uncontrolled; but the same feeling as years pass by is deepened in the adult into " the quiet sense of something lost." More frequent reference to the departed in secret thought, perhaps a glance at old-faded letters or a furtive visit to the grave—this is all; and those who know us best see no difference from our every-day demeanour. Nay, we are even bold to say that, could He of whose Death we think on Good Friday Himself prescribe the mode of its observance, we cannot, with the Sermon on the Mount before us, believe that He would sanction the "sad countenance." Even the holiday-making, the sight-seeing, the country excursion which, as a fact, we know to be associated with Good Friday in general, appear no sort of desecration when looked at from the high standpoint of Him who would not have His disciples to be taken out of the world, but to be kept from its evil. In this sense, and this only, do we believe that the great facts of Christianity—the fact of Calvary among them—are being more thoroughly taken to heart just in proportion as the technical theology is ignored; and the substitution of the substance for the shadow is a matter for warm and unqualified congratulation.

If it be true that one-half the world does not know how the other half lives, in the sense of supporting that material existence which is more or less a struggle to all of us, still less does the one moiety of the community comprehend how the other passes its daily life, what are its occupations, and especially what are its amusements. The upper sections of society are as ignorant of the lower in this respect as though they belonged to two different orders of creation; and never, perhaps, is this fact more prominent than at that season of which we have just spoken. Good Friday to the one is, however, free from anything like formal observances, a period of serious thought; while to the other it is the recognised commencement of the holiday season. Even if only in deference to others who think differently from themselves, the former, without any deep interest in the grand event commemorated, will forego some of the ordinary amusements of life, while the latter, without the slightest idea of irreverence or disrespect, look on Good Friday simply as the first holiday of the year. Christmas is the domestic festival, and is observed almost perforce at home; but Good Friday is the day for outings and jollity in general. Protestant England, as far as the lower middle class is concerned, seems to turn Lent upside down, and keep carnival at the end, as a sort of prelude to Easter. It is idle to shrug the shoulders and say this should not be so, or contrast the attitude of the French bourgeoisie on Vendredi Saint, prone though they be to mirth far beyond any Cockney capacity, with the behaviour of the corresponding class in English, and especially in London society. They simply have not been educated to it. They are unæsthetic to a degree; and to expect them to keep Good Friday as we, perhaps, keep it, would be only to invite them to a round of formal observances which would be meaningless, because not the expression of their own genuine emotions.

Now it has so happened that my own avocations, clerical or journalistic, have generally kept me pretty much within the circle of influences which the more serious portion of the populace bring to bear on the Great Annual Fast. I have been aware of the fact, of course, that Good Friday was the day for excursions, raree-shows, cricketing, and what not; a heavy day at the Crystal Palace, and a profitable one for all entertainments that the law allowed to be opened during Passion week—as the week before Easter is popularly termed; but I had never seen the people doing their pleasuring on that particular day. I resolved I would do so, and the opportunity presented itself withal, compelling me quite to forego those observances which are deemed appropriate to this very solemn occasion. For some time before Passiontide our suburb had been liberally placarded with pictorial announcements of Messrs. Sangers' Circus, which was to open on Wormwood Scrubs on Good Friday; and one young lady, a happy exception to the strong-minded "Higher Education" order of female now prevalent, actually paid me a visit to inquire what a

Hippodrome was. On the gaudily-coloured posters were represented steeple-chases with all their accustomed adventures—leaps over hedges and ditches, and falls into running streams. The young lady in her simplicity, deeming the picture a faithful representation of the coming reality, asked where they would get their brooklet on Wormwood Scrubs, and I could not pacify her until I suggested that the Grand Junction Canal might be equal to the emergency. However, I made up my mind to visit Messrs. Sanger on the occasion.

Wood Lane, which leads to the Scrubs from Shepherd's Bush Green, was about equal in point of passenger traffic to Fleet Street at midday; and when I arrived at the scene of action, an amusing episode had just occurred. Whether the quiet and orderly portion of the community living in Wood Lane or near the Scrubs had interfered or not I cannot say, but the Lord Chamberlain had put his veto on the performances, when, on measurement, it was found that the field where the so-called circus was established was *five yards outside* the radius whereto that functionary's jurisdiction extends: a circumstance which aspirants to suburban quietude will do well to take into consideration before settling on a house; for certainly the four days over which Messrs. Sangers' entertainment extended must have been anything but peaceful to the denizens of Wood Lane. The circus was simply a revival of the old suburban fair with a difference, and the populace soon recognised the fact by speaking of it as the fair, not as the circus at all. The old glories of Bartlemy and Greenwich were to be revived on the very outskirts of one of our most fashionable suburbs! A large field skirting the North-Western Railway, near Wormwood Scrubs Station, was fenced off with canvas walls, and inside the spacious *enceinte* were gathered all the shows, knock-em-downs, shooting-galleries, and skittle-alleys that seemed to have lain dormant since the days of old Greenwich, to be revived for the behoof of Shepherd's Bush and Wood Lane. Here were wax-work shows, outside one of which was a cruel German band, and on the platform of the other a fearful wind instrument played by turning a handle, and called, I believe, an Apollonicon, alongside which a youth nearly blew himself into an apoplexy by way of punishing a cracked trombone, on which he played the same melodies as the ventose instrument beside him, and two bedizened children danced stiffly at intervals. Here was the wonderful baby a yard high, and weighing eighteen stone: here the fat lady and the skeleton man. The mammoth horse, twenty-one hands high, and weighing I do not know how many tons, divided honours with the Wizard of the East, and every alternate booth seemed to be devoted to shooting at little mimic birds, which worked on a wheel, and flew within a few feet of the Cockney sportsmen's guns. The skittles too were nothing like those one sees in a cozy alley at the back of some country "public." The bowlers seemed almost to touch the pins with the ball, and the wonder was how they missed making a clearance every time.

The prime joke of this fair, however, was squirting. Little bottles of soft metal with a minute orifice, supposed by courtesy to contain scent, were sold at a penny each; and the holiday-makers enjoyed themselves consumedly by squirting this nauseous liquid over each other or chance passers-by. Then there was the roundabout, worked by steam, and with a depressing grinding-organ in the middle, where infatuated people, and these by no means the younger portion only, courted nausea at the expense of a penny; or, for twice that amount, they were wafted into ether and down again in those horrible machines that are always so much in favour on such occasions.

There was the commencement of a very neat little shindy just as I passed one of the booths where some reputed wild Indians were to be seen. Not finding the pictures outside the show a sufficient "draw," some of them came to the front, and were immediately squirted at by a facetious youth; whereupon these wild sons of the desert treated us to some strong expressions so very much in the vernacular, that I was fain to move out of earshot.

Every now and again there was a feeble attempt at a race in the stadium, and for that while the attention of the thousands present would be drawn thereto; but they were soon back at the booths again. The shilling entrance money, be it observed, covered none of these extra exhibitions. It simply took you inside the canvas screen, and then you had to pay for your amusements according as your proclivities lay in the way of squirting, wax-work, wild Indians, or an emetic on a roundabout or in a swing. In fact, as far as the circus proper went, the economical people outside who saved their shillings and stood on a dust-heap, could see what there was to be seen just as well as we.

In the course of the hour or so I spent here a balloon went up, with two mistaken individuals in a sort of clothes-basket; and it struck me we were wrong in discrediting stories of the Chinese estimating life so cheaply, when two sane men could be induced to venture their necks in such a machine—to make a London holiday! However, the crowds

A Good Friday Fair. 139

cheered them vociferously, and off they went on their aërial voyage.

I took one more turn just to analyse the vast masses of people who could afford to pay their shilling entrance money, and afterwards invest largely in knock-em-downs, shows, nausea, and the different attractions. One would scarcely have thought they had so much money to spare. Some of them were substantial tradesmen, with their missises in holiday attire of many hues, and these just looked on in a dignified way, without joining in the diversions to any great extent. But the lads seemed to place no limit to their acquisition of squirts or exercitations with the fowling-piece. Respectable-looking girls, who appeared like domestic servants, passed a period of real Lenten mortification on roundabout and swing, and stared open-mouthed at the wax-work until they must have known them by heart. It was, of course, early when I was there, and I did not stop an hour, but I saw no symptoms of drunkenness, and nothing offensive in any other way; only a dull, heavy, phlegmatic kind of business-like enjoyment. It was the *mode*, as much a matter of fashion, and expected of persons in that grade of life as the barouche and opera-box are artificial necessities in a higher stratum of society.

I could not help mentally contrasting the Parisian

bourgeois in pretty suburban Asnières, the family parties in the Salle Valentino, or the rollicking students in the Closerie des Lilas; and as I passed beneath the canvas fence, and was grimly informed by the Cerberus that there was no re-admission—which Heaven forfend!—I found myself realizing, as I never realized before, that we English did do our pleasuring sadly.

It is true that at Hammersmith Police Court an aggrieved costermonger named Hobbins was brought up for gambling, and naïvely remarked that he had paid five shillings for his stand, and if it was illegal, he did not see why Mr. Sanger should have permitted it; and the magistrate did not seem to see either, since he remanded Mr. Hobbins for inquiries.

Another idea crossed my mind, and that was that if I was the occupier of one of the pretty houses in Wood Lane, I would agitate for an extension of the Lord Chamberlain's jurisdiction another five yards, and hold monster demonstrations in Hyde Park until I got it, or let my residence at a very low rate every year from Maundy Thursday to the corresponding day in the Easter week, if a *soi-disant* "circus" was likely to squat annually in the neighbourhood.

A POSTMEN'S TEA PARTY.

The existence of a Special Correspondent seems gradually to resolve itself into an effort after ubiquity. To be in two or three places, if not exactly at the same time, yet at times so nearly coincident as to tax to the utmost the powers of locomotives and hansom-cab horses, is among the primary requirements of his position. There is no rest but the grave for the collector of news.

There is, however, one consolation; it is that such a state of things as this only comes spasmodically. Occasionally there is a lull in events as marked as that which becomes chronic in the silly season, when only a shower-driven frog or a gigantic gooseberry interposes to mar the tranquillity of that blissful period. So too, in like manner, this bustle and drive is not the normal condition even of the Special Correspondent. He has green oases in the sandy desert of life; but when the attacks do come on, he has them, as a rule, badly. Unless he be of a very philosophical turn of mind indeed (and he must be or he would not survive) he will be haunted by an insane desire to anatomize himself so as to be in several places simultaneously.

I am thinking of a recent experience especially which, in truth, comes once every year, but seemed, for some reason or other, to be rather worse this year than usual. I again allude to Good Friday. Eastertide and Christmas, when other folks make holiday, are about the hardest working times for him who would faithfully portray the manners and customs of this great metropolis, as I have for a long time made it my mission to do. And Good Friday is a sort of prelude to Easter in this respect. Having gone to, I will not say how many churches, personally or by deputy (Specials have even to go to church by proxy!), in the morning, I ate my salt fish—of which I am particularly fond—like the most devout of Lenten observers, and then, in the intervals of editing a local journal, sallied forth to the "Fair" as described in the last chapter. This did not tempt me to stay long; so after a brief recurrence to editorial work, and having seen a nice damp specimen of my morrow's broadsheet, I hurried off eastwards to the distant region where the London Postmen had elected to drink tea this

Good Friday. I had quaffed the bowl that cheers but not inebriates with them last year, when they held their festival in the school-rooms under Mr. Lewis's Chapel in Westbourne Grove, but these were by no means adequate to their requirements, and soon became like the Black Hole of Calcutta; an adjournment to the chapel being resisted on account of the secular nature of the proceedings. This year they selected the East London Tabernacle, Burdett Road, E., a building which was estimated to hold four thousand people; and here I am sorry—or ought to be sorry—to say I quite forfeited any good character I might have earned through my previous diet of salt fish by partaking of a meal which was only called tea by courtesy, and was a good deal more like dinner. . But the postmen were hospitable and I unromantically hungry, the viands of the best, and *voilà tout!*—my fast was over.

It is a dreadful thing to say of one whose salt you have eaten, but I generally look back upon a letter-carrier in the light of a personal enemy, because he brings me letters which I know will require answers; but on this occasion I sat down with him as my own particular friend. I saw him in his domestic aspect without the accompaniment of that double-rap and bundle of epistles. I realized that he had a wife and multitudinous babies. This made the most charming feature of the feast, the domestic adjuncts of Mrs. Postman and the baby-postmen.

When tea was finished—and it had to be done in three acts, like a sensation drama—the cheery minister of the Tabernacle, Mr. Archibald Browne, made a capital speech, welcoming the postmen to his oriental tent, and justifying the festival being held on Good Friday, upon the thoroughly comprehensible grounds that it was the postmen's one holiday in the year. Another minister followed, and won golden opinions by one little joke he made when he expressed his pleasure at meeting the present company because they were "men of letters." Then there came music by the Borough Tonic Sol-fa Choral Society; and they performed their parts very creditably; but the chefs-d'œuvre of the evening we did for ourselves, the Sol-fa folks being quite in the minority, as far as numbers were concerned. I allude to two hymns with which we divided the first and second parts of the concert. First of all we sang—didn't we sing? babies and all; those too young to sing cried— Sankey's song that all the little boys in the street are whistling, "Hold the Fort." This is the first verse—

"Ho, my comrades! see the signal
Waving in the sky!
Reinforcements now appearing,
Victory is nigh!

CHORUS.

Hold the fort, for I am coming, Jesus signals still
Wave the answer back to heaven, 'by Thy grace we will.'"

As I am not writing a report so much as sketching my own experience, I pass over the performance of the Tonic Sol-fa people with simply a respectful allusion, because I think our part of the proceedings was much more characteristic—more in keeping with the colossal chapel where we were gathered. Our second hymn was the familiar one, "Shall we meet beyond the river?"

"Shall we meet beyond the river,
 Where the surges cease to roll?
Where in all the bright for ever,
 Sorrow ne'er shall press the soul?

CHORUS.

"Shall we meet? Shall we meet?
 Shall we meet? Shall we meet?
Shall we meet beyond the river,
 Where the surges cease to roll?

"Shall we meet in that blest harbour,
 When our stormy voyage is o'er?
Shall we meet and cast the anchor
 By the fair celestial shore?

"Where the music of the ransomed
 Rolls its harmony around,
And creation swells the chorus
 With its sweet melodious sound?

"Shall we meet with many a loved one,
 That was torn from our embrace?
Shall we listen to their voices,
 And behold them face to face?

> "Shall we meet with Christ our Saviour,
> When He comes to claim His own ?
> Shall we know His blessed favour,
> And sit down upon His throne ?"

Then came more speechifying. Mr. Binder, the active secretary of the Association, frankly confessed that there had been a want of unanimity on the present occasion; and I was almost disposed to think such division of opinion had been fortunate, for if all the London postmen had come *en masse* with their wives—and their multitudinous babies—there would have been nothing for it but an adjournment to Hackney Fields forthwith. The men of the W. and W.C. districts had stood aloof, perhaps not deeming an East London Tabernacle "genteel;" and applications had even been made to the Post Office authorities to stop the proceedings. Thereupon Mr. Binder proposed to take a show of hands as to whether the Festival should continue in future years; and if a show of hands means anything at all certainly that Festival should be sempiternal. I never saw a clearer case of unanimity. The very babies held up their hands, I believe. In a short and telling speech, Mr. Oetzmann, who was present as a visitor, stated that his firm received and despatched about ninety thousand letters in the year, and instances of miscarriage were extremely rare. He also thought it was a wise rule which forbade all discussion of postmen's grievances at these social meetings, and hoped the time would come when there would be no postmen's grievances at all to discuss. An interesting feature of the gathering was the presentation of fifteen hundred Testaments sent by Lady Cairns along with tracts, numbers of the *British Workman*, &c., for gratuitous distribution. Even with these liberal numbers I am afraid a good many of the party were minus their literature. I am, as Shakspeare says, "ill at numbers," but I should think the Tabernacle limits must very nearly have been reached. I heard that eleven hundred of us sat down in one batch to tea. The consumption of viands must have been terrific; but I am unable to give details, as, this year, the matter was in the hands of a local contractor, Mr. Earll, of Hackney Road, who certainly catered on a liberal scale.

So, then, in singing and speechifying the time passed pleasantly enough. It flew swiftly, too, withal: for just as I seemed to be getting into the swing of the thing, I received a secret intimation that "supper was ready;" and in quiet, with a few select spirits, I put the climax to my heretical proceedings by coquetting with a dainty little *souper* and drinking success to the next Postmen's Festival.

IN A FRENCH PASTURE.

THERE are few phases of social life more curiously noteworthy than the eagerness with which people in a foreign country combine to celebrate the customs of the Fatherland. From the captive Jews singing their Hebrew melodies on the banks of Euphrates down to Englishmen eating rosbif *bien sanglant* and slabby plum-*bodeng* in the Rue de la Madeleine in Paris, and deluding themselves that they are keeping Christmas à l'Anglaise, the illustration holds good; and it was prettily exemplified, too, at a little chapel in the Monmouth Road, Bayswater, whereinto I strayed one Sunday. As Melancholy did with the youth in Gray's Elegy, so had I often in the course of my devious wanderings marked this place of worship for my own. The pastor, the Rev. Jules Marc Henri du Pontet de la Harpe, is a man of many advertisements, who does not hide his light under a bushel; but wisely, in these days of keen competition, lets the London public know what he is doing. Consequently it was from no lack of previous invitation that I had not gone thither before.

The Eglise Evangélique Française, in Monmouth Road, is the tiniest of buildings, unpretending without, and coloured within, as to its bare walls, a delicate French grey, so that it is national to its very whitewash, if it be not Hibernian to say so. It wanted a quarter to eleven when I got there, and eight little children were being catechized by a French schoolmaster and mistress in the front seats around the pulpit. I was accompanied by my little daughter, and great was her astonishment to hear such young children able to speak French so fluently, her own dialect of that language being at present somewhat of the Stratford-atte-Bow order. They repeated a prayer all together, and ended by singing a little French hymn which sounded quite in the style of the Waters of Babylon.

While this was going on, a female verger was engaged in arranging the pulpit cushions, putting a glass of water within easy reach of the preacher, and also laying the little table with its fair white cloth, simple communion plate, and huge pile of bread for the Lord's Supper. I was again unfortunate in my experiences with this lady, though the way she treated my request for a seat was quite characteristic of the *locale*. She did not fly at me snappishly, as a good lady in a chapel had done the week before, but assured me with the most effusive politeness that she would put us in a seat immediately; but left us all the morning to cool on one side with the draught from the adjacent door, and on the other to bake by the aid of a fierce little French stove, about the size and shape of a sugar-loaf, hard by. It was an exact illustration of the opposite courses adopted in the allegory of the Two Sons who were told to go into the vineyard. One said, " I will not;" but afterwards repented and went. That was the truculent Methodist abovementioned, who eventually relented so far as to send me upstairs. The other said, "I go, sir, and went not." That represented the suave lady of the Eglise Evangélique Française. I fancy she was pressed for room, however. The chapel was homœopathic in its dimensions; and the female congregation large. There were not a dozen men; and at least half of those seemed to be officially engaged for the impending collection. The other six were youths. There are no such things as French boys.

When the catechizing was over and the congregation had settled, and while my own hopes of a seat were growing fainter and fainter, a nasal little harmonium somewhere in an upper gallery struck up, as if in derision, " I waited for the Lord," and the false and flattering pew-opener handed me a torn copy of the Cantiques, or Hymn Book. I then saw she did not mean to move us to more eligible quarters. What business had we, I daresay she thought, by the Waters of Babylon?

Presently the Pastor entered, down centre, as they would say on the stage. He was a handsome blackhaired and whiskered gentleman, coiffé quite after the English fashion, and wearing the costume now obsolete in the Establishment, of Geneva gown and extensive bands. It was the quondam attire of the pet parson revived; and in some respects, if he will excuse my saying so, M. du Pontet de la Harpe revived the manner, too. After a few appropriate words, he gave out a hymn, which was sung to a thoroughly French melody, with the accompaniment of the harmonium. All the hymns were strikingly characteristic, and exceedingly well sung. I transcribe two stanzas from this one—

> " O Dieu de vérité, pour qui seul je soupire,
> Unis mon cœur à toi par de forts et doux nœuds,
> Je me lasse d'ouïr, je me lasse de lire,
> Mais non pas de te dire,
> C'est toi seul que je veux.

> "Parle seul à mon âme, et que nulle science,
> Que nul auteur, docteur, ne m'explique tes lois,
> Que toute créature en ta sainte présence
>   S'impose le silence
>   Et laisse agir ta voix."

A lesson from the Prophets was then read, without any attempt at elocution, but in a simple unaffected style, so that every syllable reached even my dull Britannic ears, to which the sounds of the French language had long been unfamiliar. This was followed by a rather long extempore prayer, in which the Deity was addressed by the name of "Eternel," and great stress was laid on the natural depravity of man. It was followed by another hymn, which bore reference to the approaching Fête de Noël:—

> "Ouvrez-vous, portes des cieux,
> Tressaillez, célestes lieux,
> D'une allégresse nouvelle!"

Then—strangely enough, and not without semblance of repetition—came another lesson, Psalm cvii., and another extempore prayer, followed by a third hymn. I am afraid this repetition made me inattentive. I looked round at my neighbours, most of whom were, as I said, of the female sex; and all those in the same seat, which was at the very back of the chapel, seemed to be servants. The physiognomies were plainly Celtic, and the women had put on their little bits of English finery quite French-wise. What is the occult law, I wonder, which makes a French *modiste*, like a French cook, able to make so much more of slender materials than our English "artists?" I also noticed that the Pastor had in his Bible quite a High Church-looking marker of coloured ribbon, with I.H.S. emblazoned upon it; and I trembled with fear lest anything in the shape of Ritualism should insidiously have crept like a wolf into that little French pasture. The second prayer was rather a strange combination; at one time quite conversational, at another breathing such a tone of mystic devotion as suggested the Brahminical Nirwana, or absorption of the devotee in the deity. The succeeding *cantique* was set to the tune of "Adeste Fideles," and bore on the subject of the Communion that was to follow—

> "Célébrons son amour,
> Louons sa mémoire,
> Et dans la foi combattons chaque jour,
> Sainte victoire!
> Eternelle gloire!
> Seigneur, qu'avec les Anges
> Nous chantons tes louanges
> A ton banquet au céleste séjour."

After a brief extempore prayer, occupying the place of our pulpit collect, M. du Pontet de la Harpe gave out as his text St. Matthew iii. 8, 9, and commenced his sermon. It was a skilful and eloquent analysis of Repentance, blended all along with fierce invectives against external and ceremonial religion. Building on this ceremonial religion the Jew, in the time of John Baptist, said he had no need of repentance, he was of the seed of Abraham. So, too, Christians said they went to Church, they were " en règle avec Dieu " without repentance; and these two were reminded that God could of the very stones beneath their feet raise up children unto Abraham. The expression did not refer to actual stones—" C'est absurde." It related to nominal Christians whose hearts, prior to repentance, were hard as stones.

It was not a matter of sentiment or ceremony, no; —*that* was absurd too—a blasphemy. You feel it is impossible to be a matter of ceremony. " Vous sentez," he kept repeating with much gesticulation, " c'est dégrader Dieu — homme — religion ! " In Abraham all the nations of the earth were blessed; and so, among Christians, there was neither Jew nor Greek, barbarian nor Scythian, bond nor free. All were the " sainte famille de Dieu," not according to the flesh which was sinful, but by the regimen of repentance that sin was done away, as it was expressed in " ce chapitre superbe " he had read from the prophet, where they were told how their sins, though red like crimson, should be made white as snow. Then another final diatribe against ceremonialism. It was not by " actes du culte " but by the " actes de la vie, tous les jours, tous les instants," that this was to be effected. " Vous avez compris ?" he kept asking. The one was the condition of the stones " point de foi, d'amour, de zèle," the other that of the " enfants d'Abraham." "C'est par la prédication de l'Evangile qu'il faut espérer faire des pierres les enfants d'Abraham." The sermon eventually merged into a prayer, and the service concluded with a very comprehensive form, which embraced petitions for all sorts and conditions of men ; for the Queen and Royal Family; for the sick and the poor—" pour tous ceux qui pleurent—le nombre en est si grand," it was touchingly said. It also embraced the Lord's Prayer and the Apostles' Creed, and finished with the old Jewish benediction pronounced with extended hands.

Very few communicants seemed to remain, and all who had voices were invited to come and join a practice of Christmas hymns on the ensuing Wednesday evening.

A PRIZE-FIGHTER'S SERMON.

It would really seem, in these wonderful days on which we have lighted, as though the situation of Horace's First Satire were realized, and fate had said to some of us "mutatis discedite sortibus"—"Your lots are changed, be off!" Only the merchant does not become a soldier, or the lawyer a sailor, but the fashion seems to be for everybody to turn parson. We have had converted thieves, and regenerated colliers; and at the time of which I write the last lion of the theological world was Bendigo, the converted prize-fighter. Rumours of strange doings at the Cabmen's Mission Hall, King's Cross Circus, attracted me strongly in that direction; and the contemporaneous occurrence of a clerical throat rendering me *hors de combat* on Sunday morning, I took the opportunity of presenting myself at this new shrine of my devotions. I got there, as usual, a good deal too early, and found the Mission Hall proper closed; but went on a tour of inspection amongst all the different doors, and at length found one that yielded to my efforts. This was on the basement, the hall itself being on the first floor. I entered, and found myself at Sunday-school. Judging from the small numbers assembled, I should say either that the cabmen are not a prolific race, or else that they do not appreciate the value of religious education. There were only six girls and three boys present, with six teachers to attend to them, three male and three female. Happily the proceedings were brief, for it was nearly eleven o'clock, consisting only of a hymn and the Lord's Prayer. In the former it seemed as though the author or compiler had chosen lines with as many aspirated syllables as possible, all of which, I need scarcely say, were studiously omitted by the singers. The tune of the hymn was "Home, sweet home;" and after the last verse a little gentleman among the congregation would insist upon appending the ordinary refrain from the song. I say "the congregation," for everybody as they came did as I myself had done, and we were requested to wait there until the room upstairs was opened; so we really did form a select little congregation. An old gentleman in a clerical hat and white beard sat reading the *Church Times.* I thought it was well for him that nobody knew what he was about.

In due course we were ushered upstairs; but even then had a quarter of an hour to wait before proceedings commenced. The interval was devoted to moral talk on the part of the adults; while the three schoolboys, who were placed in front under the pulpit and facing the six school-girls, amused themselves with shooting light missiles into the young ladies' faces. At 11.15 there was a suppressed exclamation from three awakened cabmen behind me, "Here's Ben," and I saw a tall man pass into the small vestry in the corner, which looked scarcely big enough to hold him. The hall itself was a neat building with a double gallery, and the usual arrangement of pulpit and benches, all in clean stained wood.

In a few minutes the minister, who announced himself on the bills as the Rev. Mr. Dupee, entered in violently clerical costume, with Bendigo in lay attire on his right hand in the rostrum; while a timid tenor in the gallery sang "I will arise," to a harmonium accompaniment. I saw from the hymn-books that this Rev. Mr. Dupee had been the organizer of the "Hallelujah Band"—whatever that might be—at Wolverhampton.

We began with the hymn "Before Jehovah's awful throne," and then the Rev. Mr. Dupee engaged in prayer, with frequent and loud ejaculations from his congregation. Among the clauses of his prayer was one that Brother Bendigo, having been engaged for many years in fighting *his country's battles*, might now fight as valiantly for Christ. He also besought in a stentorian voice, and amid much interjectional applause, that Infidelity, Ritualism, and Popery might be put away (the old gentleman had hidden his *Church Times*), and that Her Majesty might be converted! There were also special suffrages for lunatics, cabmen, and prisoners!

Then we had another hymn from the Hallelujah book—
"How happy every child of grace
Who knows his sins forgiven!"

the conclusion of which was a hope that we might, in the curious phraseology of this school of religionists—
"Greet the blood-besprinkled bands
Upon the eternal shore!"

Thereupon followed a Scripture lesson, Acts ii., in which I was surprised to hear the reader trip over what I thought was a favourite and comforting word, Mesopotamia. He called it Mesopotonia, and also leaned to long penultimates in Phrygia and Libya.

He concluded by saying, "Here ends this *encouraging* portion of Holy Scripture."

Then there was another hymn to the Tantum Ergo tune, and I found my three Sunday-school lads, with the versatility of boyhood, amusing themselves by trying the effect of stopping and unstopping their ears throughout its progress.

During all this time Bendigo stood, old man though he was, erect as an arrow on the right hand of the sleek parson. He was a slender, clean-limbed personage, and I should never have suspected his former occupation from his appearance; but there was considerable hardness about his wrinkled face, and his eye was bright and clear as an eagle's. I could quite believe that in his earlier days it would have been difficult for an antagonist to catch that eye napping. I saw that the third finger of his left hand had been broken, I presume during some of "his country's battles."

Before Bendigo's address we had one from a brother of the presiding minister, who—the Rev. Mr. Dupee informed us—used to go to fights with Bendigo. "We are all of one town," he added, "and I used, when a boy, to follow that man, and pray that he might be converted."

This Dupee the un-reverend was a capital old

fellow, and told first-rate stories of adventures he had had when selling Bibles at fairs. First of all he gave us, in good North-country dialect, a homely exposition of the Exodus—his text or motto being "Go forward," though he apologized for never having been "'prenticed to parsoning." I liked him all the better because he had not. He gave a long account of an altercation he had with a man at a fair, who told him he had no right to be selling Bibles there; but he overcame him with a text, and "went off singing Hallelujah." Hallelujah seemed to run in the Dupee family, both lay and reverend. There was also another excellent story of his being taken up by a policeman for the same offence, and going off with the constable singing a hymn to the tune of "Pretty Polly Hopkins." He sang two verses of it, and marched dramatically up and down the rostrum, the congregation joining in with him full-voiced, and beating time with their feet. "Christ for me - e, Christ for me," was the refrain, which was lustily taken up by all except the apathetic Sunday-school children; but he was a rare old ranter was this un-reverend Dupee.

Another hymn followed, and it was about half-past twelve before time was called for Bendigo, and then the Rev. Mr. Dupee brought him in with a slight sermonette on his own account, as if he did not like the laity to have all the talk. For thirty years, he said, he had been trying to get "Bendy," and now he had got him. Ben had been beside himself for sixty years, but for the last two had been in his right mind, preaching Christ. In his wild times he had been a brave fellow. He had fought twenty-one prize-fights; and when he was going to fight Ben Caunt, he was offered 1000*l.* to lose, an offer which he acknowledged by pitching into the street the man who made it. He could not read from the book, but he could do that which was better still, read his title clear to mansions in the skies; and with that remark he gave him a sounding pat on the back and yielded place to him in the pulpit.

Bendy's address was very brief, and uttered in a rapid nervous manner, which—besides the loss of his teeth—made it difficult to follow him. When he began to be good, he said, his friends gave him a fortnight, and said he would be locked up again by that time. The tagrag and bobtail, when he did *not* get locked up, began to say, "If God can save Bendy, He can save me!" He compared himself graphically enough to the dying thief, and told us how he had got his little "country seat" and 1*l.* a week for the rest of his life—so strangely did the material and spiritual blend in this exceptional sermon. It was fifty-five years ago, he said, that he first came up to town to fight Burke, and all through that time, though he was making so much money, he never had a penny to bless himself. It was Dick Weaver who converted him. The most amusing part of his address was his account of the ministrations of the prison chaplain. He was particularly interested in the combat of little David and big Goliath, so much so that, when the chaplain was telling him, he anticipated the result by saying, " I do hope the little 'un will lick the big 'un !" Even in his " wild state" he used to like to hear preaching, but got snubbed when he tried to go to church. Now people said, " Bendy's making a good thing of it." " Bendy's togs are better than they used to be." You're right, he continued; at sixty-three years of age, and after fighting twenty-one prize-fights, I feel like a boy. Champion of England is a big title, but took a deal of trouble to get, and was no good when I got it. Now I'm struggling hard for another crown."

He sat down long before we expected or wished; and the Rev. Mr. Dupee took up his proverb again. That man, he said, was a miracle. We might not have been able to follow, he thought, because all his teeth had been knocked out. He was one of twenty-one children, and the youngest of three at a birth. His parents, brothers and sisters, were all dead, and so was every man he ever fought with !

On the following Sunday Bendy would be at the Hall again. There would be three services at 11, 2.30, and 6.30. At the last Bendy would receive the Lord's Supper. He had not done so hitherto because, being a teetotaller, he had scruples as to the wine; but the cup on this occasion would be filled with unfermented juice of the grape, so that any Good Templar or teetotaller might partake with Bendy.

It is the fashion nowadays to disbelieve conversions, from that of Constantine downwards; but whatever we might think of the method, there could be no doubt that Bendy's conversion had landed him on a better life than his old one. A single fact like that ex-champion of England, I could not help thinking, was, after all, worth a hundred theories.

GREAT TRIBULATION.

It is remarkable to what an extent those sects which are one degree elevated above the vulgar denunciations of the conventicle, fall back on the Great Tribulation as a sort of make-weight. We are all familiar, of course, with the mild joke appertaining to Crown-court, "The Great Tribulation—Cumming upon Earth;" but it is really strange to find how much stock, so to speak, is made out of this apparently unprolific article of theological produce. I was attracted one Tuesday evening to the cathedral-like structure of the Catholic Apostle Church in Gordon Square by seeing that this same Great Tribulation was to form the first in a series of sermons; and it struck me at once that I should find an old friend with a new face, so I girded up my loins and set out for a new ecclesiastical "experience."

As I passed from the unfragrant mews in Torrington Place, under the portal of this splendid church, I was greeted with the welcome odour of incense. The nave was lighted, but the choir in gloom, the three lancet windows of the Lady Chapel beyond just showing their rich tints against the evening sky; and the organ was being played softly as the congregation assembled. Courteous attendants, some in cassocks, others in the garb of ordinary existence, handed hymn-books to each stranger as he entered, passing them on to the seats, all of which were free. Two gentlemen in surplices and red stoles—"ribbons," as the Primate once termed them—entered and took seats near the choir steps: and an excellent mixed choir in one of the aisles commenced the service by singing a hymn.

Thereupon followed what was in some respects an abridgment of the Church of England service. There was, first of all, an exhortation, which I should think was original: then followed the Confession, nearly as it stands in our service-book, with just a few verbal alterations. The Absolution was the same as that of the Church of England, and was followed by the Collect for the Second Sunday in Advent, "Blessed Lord," &c. Then a lesson was read from Isaiah xiii., commencing at verse 6, followed by portions of the Prayer for the Church Militant, all reference to

Bishops being studiously avoided. The second and third Collects for Evening Prayer were added: and the General Thanksgiving brought to its close about as heterogeneous a service as one could well listen to. Another hymn was sung, and then the younger-looking of the two clergymen ascended the pulpit for the Great Tribulation.

He looked as little like a man who had ever seen trouble or tribulation as any one could well imagine. A fresh, hale, clean-shaven face was his in all parts (as Cæsar says) except the upper lip, which bore a cavalry moustache. High shirt collars, which a less reverent writer than myself would term "gills," stood bluff above his stole, and looked incongruous enough in his exceedingly clerical attire. Now that he was closer I could see that his stole was fastened with a gold cord in front with two bright tassels. His face struck me as a sort of compromise between Monsignor Capel and Mr. Edmund Yates.

After a preliminary Collect and Paternoster, he stood surveying his congregation just as Mr. Bellew used to do at his readings, gazed severely at somebody who moved out or in, and then, without enunciating any text, plunged boldly into the middle of the Great Tribulation.

The French Revolution, in the last century, he

said, marked an epoch in the history of Christian people. The altars were desecrated, and the Churches turned into Temples of Reason. Religion was clean swept away; and not only the laws of God but the laws of man—international law itself, amongst others, were forgotten. Mob law prevailed.

The influence of this state of things was not transient but permanent, and extended to succeeding generations. Christian men and Christian nations were not the same since as they had been before. That particular nation was a warning to us, if, after we had been redeemed, we did not "take care what we were about."

A similar state of things obtained in 1852; but it was put down with a strong hand. So, again, under the Commune, the Reign of Terror would have been reproduced if men had been strong enough to do it. It was not the will but the power that was wanting. So, too, it spread once more to other nations in the shape of international Societies and Leagues. The object was to bring about a state of anarchy. The principles of the first French Revolution were still spreading, not only abroad—in Paris, Vienna, and St. Petersburg—but in England. Look, he said, at the state of English society. Vice was kept out of the wide street, but only to lurk in by-ways. We were in the midst of a season gayer than we had had for many years. What was there behind it all? Lawlessness and vice. Strong police and military forces were necessary; for society was being disintegrated, especially among the lower orders. Servants set themselves against their masters; working men and agricultural labourers against their employers. There was a handsome veneer, but society itself was rotten. There was nothing good in it except the varnish with which it was overlaid.

Pausing awhile in his catalogue of woes, he proceeded to say—Look at the political world. Sovereigns were visiting one another and exchanging congratulations; they were crying peace, and simultaneously arming to the teeth. They were building forts and ironclads, and making endless experiments in the art of destruction. Famine was desolating India; and yet we were told that all was well.

If we looked from a religious point of view, we still saw restlessness. Rome was rent and torn; in Germany the religious question was likely to undo all the boasted unity. At home the great question of the Session was a religious one. It was an endeavour to restrain the lawlessness of the clergy. The Press—the greatest power of all—was simply bent on setting parties at variance one with the other.

Scepticism was giving it out on all hands that the Church was merely a worldly institution. Men sought other means of regenerating the world—such as Temperance Societies, Benefit Societies, and what not. Virtue and morality were to be put in place of God. So, too, God's day was desecrated. Sunday was made a public holiday, a day for taking trips, going to see one's friends, or going on excursions.

There was another power of evil abroad too—a spiritual power. Even the clergy sought evil spirits (I felt sure the preacher had been reading *Mystic London*). They had left off going to God in order to *go to the Devil*.

All this, he held, was the outcome of the French Revolution; but what did it mean? We had only to turn to God's Word, and we should find our answer at once. We had come to the last days; and these things were precursors of the Great Tribulation, and the reign of Antichrist. We could see this in the revelations of the Hebrew Prophets, in the words of Christ and His Apostles, and, lastly, in the Apocalypse. He here quoted largely from each source, scarcely ever needing to refer to his Bible, and reciting long texts with wonderful facility. I employed my time while I had not to write in taking stock of the congregation, which was mostly composed of heavy old ladies and unintellectual-looking men. Paul, he continued, described a state of society at Corinth really very little worse than any at the present time—not one that was utterly irreligious, but that had a form of godliness without the power thereof.

But we had not got to the worst yet. There were still the Seven Trumpets to be blown and the Seven Vials to be poured out, and then King Antichrist was to rise. Then the Lord would come and destroy Antichrist. That was to be the order of events—the Great Tribulation, the Reign of Antichrist, and the Victory of Christ.

It might be said—why draw this gloomy picture? That was just the point. Why? See your position, he said. You are in covenant with God—a covenant to defy the Devil. That was the vow of our baptism. All these nations of which he had been speaking were God's people. A way and means of grace were given to all in the fourfold ministry. The covenant of the Spirit made at Pentecost included that ministry. We vowed to follow Christ, and we had not. We had pampered the flesh instead. Look at the civilization around. It resolved itself into luxury, amusements, dress. Was this keeping the flesh in death? And yet we were in covenant with God. God did not love this world, and we did. That was God's controversy with us. We had despised the ministry He ordained. We said it was only meant to last for a time; that Apostles were only necessary to launch the Church, and then she might be left to get to heaven as she could. So said not the Scriptures. These Ministries were to continue till we all came to perfection.

Then again he bade us remember — this stern preacher, whose outward man seemed almost to belie the tremendous doctrines he was enunciating—how all previous dispensations had ended in judgment. The days of Noe issued in the Flood. The Jewish Dispensation beginning with Abraham ended in the ruin of Jerusalem, and in the name of a Jew being a reproach and a taunt. Now we were standing in the same critical position. God let that French Revolution come as the first shock of the earthquake. It did startle men. It made them look into their Bibles. This was why he was speaking to us of these things. We had been breaking the covenant for ages, and generations, and God had sent what we read of in the daily press, and in the history of the last century.

But we might still ask, who are you? You are no better than we, it might be said. No; and the prophets of old were no better than their brethren;

but God called them—called Noah, Lot, Isaiah. We come, because we are sent to tell you that God has restored the Ministers of His Church. We are sent by the Apostles, and the Apostles by Christ (?). This is our testimony.

It was announced on the handbills of the sermons that opportunity would be given after each, for persons to make inquiries of the minister in the Church; and there (where I have printed a query), was my great difficulty with the Catholic Apostolic Church. I could get no historic account of the revival of the Apostolate. I would ask that night, if I found a "likely" minister.

All we say is, he concluded, read the signs of the times. Be warned; or else you will find yourselves under the reign of Antichrist before you know it. With the Mission of Judgment was a Mission of Mercy bound up; and that would be the subject on Tuesday next. It was particularly hard to alarm Englishmen with a sense of danger; but now God would have us tremble. Don't let all pass like water from a duck's back. Amen.

There was considerable power, intellectual and physical, in the sermon, which was succeeded by another hymn and the Apostolic benediction, the latter pronounced with outstretched arms. I saw my "likely" minister; indeed he did not wait for me to see him. He saw me and made up to me, as they always do at Gordon Square. He was, however, a feeble man, the very antipodes of the preacher, with whom I would far rather have exchanged words. The preacher's name, he informed me, was Wells. He held no position of eminence, being simply "one of the priests of the Church." As to how the Apostolate was restored, it was, he told me, by the voice of prophecy—"the only way it could be." The ranks of the Apostles were thinned by death; indeed there were only three alive, and they did not much expect that the ranks would be filled up, because they felt the work was done. There might be another call, but they did not look for it.

The voice of prophecy was still, he said, heard among them—mostly in the exposition of Scripture by the prophet in the public services of the Church, sometimes, but rarely, among the congregation. I could not help thinking how the *charismata* of the early Church had passed through the same ordeal of organizing and methodizing until they seemed to be lost altogether.

There are few more interesting phenomena than this same Catholic Apostolic Church. All looked so correct that one scarcely dared at first to include it in the ranks of Unorthodox London. It need scarcely be said that I do it without the slightest inclination to offence, and in the technical meaning of the term only. It has changed vastly since the days of Edward Irving; but is now pushing to the front with the new energy of the phœnix. Who shall forecast its effect on our day and generation?

A LADY-PREACHER AT THE POLYTECHNIC.

AMONG the various offices which the exuberant ambition of advanced ladies claims nowadays as their own, the pulpit has not yet asserted itself as much as might have been expected; in fact, of the three learned professions, medicine is that which has been specially patronized by the fair sex. That the law has not been so attractive we can well understand, for the female mind is the reverse of legal, and an unromantic judicial bench would, it is to be feared, oppose the "call" of any modern Portia. But that the pulpit should remain unscaled by feminine ambition is remarkable. If, however, the actual pulpit is not occupied by ladies, the platform, which may be regarded as a kind of outwork leading to the citadel, has been successfully carried; and from Mrs. Girling, the Suffolk peasant who represents the Jumpers, up to the aristocratic lady of whom I propose to speak in this paper, we have a whole series of aspirants to platform celebrity. The present position, however, and the well-known antecedents of Mrs. Thistlethwayte made me more curious to hear her utterances than those of the various speakers, spiritualistic, scientific, or strong-minded who lure us from time to time to sit at their feet; and I readily repaired to the Polytechnic on a recent Sunday, having received two ten-shilling tickets for reserved seats; such being the somewhat high tariff at which this lady rated her attractions. The admission was free, but the reserved seats cost half-a-sovereign. The occasion, however, was a charitable one; and it was, I suppose, considered that those who were inclined to contribute would do so in the way of paying a high sum for seats. Be that as it might, I found the Great Theatre of the Polytechnic full, galleries, unreserved seats, reserved stalls, and all. The vast assemblage was singing the familiar hymn, "Ashamed of Jesus, can it be?" to the tune which usually accompanies the "O Salutaris Hostia" in the Roman Benediction service. There was a harmonium on the platform played by a young man; and three ladies in sober, almost Quakerish attire, were leading the voices, but the hymn was well taken up by all present, rich and poor, and there were a great many of the latter—a remarkable number of aged women, I noticed, as I gazed around while they were singing.

On the platform were five persons; three ladies, young but demure—almost sad-looking, one elderly gentleman, and a second, a tall, handsome, soldierly man, whom I inferred to be Mrs. Thistlethwayte's husband. She herself stood behind a baize table and lecture-desk in the centre, habited in solemn black.

It was something like a quarter of a century since I had seen that face—then, perhaps, the loveliest in London. There it was again—the same face, but toned and chastened by lapse of years and changed experiences. The eyes retained much of their former expression—I noticed it especially when the preacher, in the course of her address, warmed into more than usual eloquence—but the mouth was sad, and the whole face like that of a Mater Dolorosa.

When the hymn was finished, Mrs. Thistlethwayte uttered a brief invocation, and then engaged in prayer; eloquently enough, but it struck me that her manner was a little *distrait*. I noticed, too, that her white hands were covered with rings. I know not why, but I had expected to see more outward and visible signs of asceticism than I found present. It is so one always sketches ideal pictures, and is half disappointed, though without the slightest occasion or excuse, to find them not realized.

Prayer over, the preacher told us that she had come forward to aid in the establishment of a school church for the children of miners in Gloucestershire, where they might be taught the truths of the Blessed Book she held in her jewelled hand—the best antidote, in her opinion, to Unions and Communes. She bade us, from what we knew of the Commune in Paris, picture the horrors of a Commune in England—a Commune in London! The everlasting truths of that Book taught them what to be ashamed of—taught us of the upper classes as well as the poor. To be ashamed of what? Poverty? No; but to be ashamed of sin, ashamed of rejecting the Saviour. She then spoke of her last week's sermon and collection for the same object, and told how the tears rolled down her cheeks when she saw among the collection the numerous pence of the poor. "All I have myself," she said, "I give away, and in asking your alms for this purpose I am not, therefore, telling you to do what I do not do myself."

She then went on to the sermon proper, and was glad to notice that so many had their Bibles with them. She chose her text from St. John xi. 19-21, which she read with much emphasis, though I could not help thinking I detected a provincial accent in her speech. Did this raising up of Christ's body herein predicted take place? She would read another passage from the 20th chapter of the same Gospel, which was the narrative of Mary Magdalene's visit to the Holy Sepulchre. Mary Magdalene was therein bidden go to Christ's brethren and announce Him risen; so was she herself sent to us. Referring to 1 Cor. xv. and Rom. vi., as further announcing the grand truth of a risen Christ, she exclaimed, "Why, it's great! Why, it's magnificent! Whoever confesses this truth shall be confessed before the angels in Heaven. There may be here some poor crossing-sweeper who shall be thus confessed before archangels. God has said it. How cold we are, then, to be ashamed of Him!"

An old Scotch divine had said that this first witness of the Resurrection, Mary Magdalene, was one whose name was worthy of the deepest reverence. She was not—and I was surprised, almost again disappointed to find Mrs. Thistlethwayte taking this line—she was not the "Sinner of the City," as some thought. St. Luke, chap. viii., militated against this view; and she could, she said, weep when she found this woman placed in a wrong position. She had met women of every grade, but she had never met one who was worthy to be called Magdalene. Her theory was that by the expulsion of the seven devils it was simply meant that this woman had been cured of insanity by Christ. Her gratitude to Him was for "reason restored upon an abdicated throne." Henceforth life was given up to Him. She went to Jerusalem with Him when He went up thither to die, though it was not the custom for Jewish women to "go up;" but what cared she for custom? Real love forgets self. Perhaps it was Mary's first sight of Jerusalem—and here the preacher drew a glowing picture of her own first sight of the Holy City. She stood by the cross to witness the greatest drama the world had ever seen. The sun was ashamed to look on it; but this woman feared not. She remained last at the cross: and then she was first at the tomb. She found it empty, but she waited. It was the grand May morning of our holy religion. She went and told His brethren that Christ had risen.

She stood alone weeping—the *pose* with which these words were delivered was perfect—and then took place that meeting; write it, God, on every heart here! He was victor over death for you. He conquered death and hell for you and yours. Be in earnest, my sisters, like her. Hers was the grandest embassage ever given. Go tell my brethren I am risen. It was given, not to a Church, not to a man, but to a woman. Dear, precious people, she burst forth, I stand here not in my own power, but, God helping me, in gratitude to Him who shed His Blood that I might be washed pure and white. I would lay down my life that you may have hope!

To each sister I would say, Are you a believer? Then go and call a brother. We women were first in the fall, let us be the first in the New Creation!

Men, do you believe? Then you are risen with God's Son. You are kings and priests, though none may see your crown. Be good soldiers, and then, when death comes, you shall know in whom you have believed. Be faithful. We women need your strength. Be our best friends. Out of Jesus we are nothing, in Him we are everything.

It had been, she said, in a glowing peroration, the dream of her girlhood to see the Mount of Olives, the one place that had not been tampered with in succeeding ages. She stood there where Mary mistook for the gardener Him who was the gardener of every blade of grass and every flower in the wide world, who had created the rose of Sharon, and the vines on the hill-side. She looked out over the land of Moab, and as she did so, there came into her mind Mrs. Alexander's beautiful lines on the Burial of Moses, with which she closed her address by reciting from memory.

The above are but fragments of a long sermon, not, it maybe, logical, or even always coherent, but evidently sincere, and full of deep significance to those present (and I fancy there were many such), who could remember the preacher more than twenty years ago.

THE MERCHANTS' LECTURE.

For those in search of the sensational in religious matters, I still must think there is nothing more effective than the contrast of the great busy City of London at midday during the week, and those few churches and chapels which open their doors charily to worshippers, whether in public or private devotion. Though one cannot guess why such should be the case, it would seem as though it were foreign in some way or other to the genius of the English Church to make any provision for private devotion in church for her members. It is done in some churches, I know; but these are so exceptional as to prove the rule; that rule being far too generally that they are rigidly shut, except at service time on Sundays, when the gorgeous beadle, so graphically alluded to by Charles Dickens, is stationed there as if to keep off all but "respectable" people. And yet, when we come to think of it, what place have those "non-respectable people"—the poor—got to pray in, if their church is closed against them? Their miscalled homes are often not fit places to live in, much less to concentrate the mind on prayer. There can be little doubt that the more frequent practice of this private devotion in church among the Roman Catholics is one reason (among other obvious ones) of the greater hold that communion, and those who in our communion imitate its regimen, have over the poor. They feel that the church is their home; the region of their best emotions; the place where their prayer is wont to be made. There is no more imposing sight than the poor peasant in a continental church utterly absorbed in prayer when no service is going on, and deaf to the sounds of the busy world outside the sacred house.

By way of realizing anew something of this idea, I accepted the invitation one sees every Tuesday morning in the *Times* to attend the Merchants' Lecture at the Weigh House Chapel in Fish Street Hill, close to the Monument, at noon of that day. The lecture was, I perceived, to be preached by the Rev. W. W. Aveling, of Kingsland. All seats were free, the advertisement went on to assure me, and there would be "no collection."

Being safely landed at the Mansion House, after a more than usually protracted journey by the Metropolitan Railway, I sped towards the Monument, when it wanted only some two minutes to the meridian hour. Of course under such circumstances one is button-holed by an acquaintance who has something important to communicate, and equally, as a matter of course, one has to shake him off almost rudely. This occurred to me just as I was getting into a fit state of mind to note the contrast between the quietude of the Weigh House Chapel and the din of Fish Street Hill. In my state of absorption I recollect suggesting to my acquaintance that he should accompany me to a pew, and that he fled precipitately at the bare idea.

I had never been in this chapel before, among all my devious wanderings, and was struck with the handsome arrangements of the interior. At the end farthest from the door was a fine pulpit of carved stone, an alto-relievo representing the Last Supper. Behind this, occupying the apse, was an organ with richly-gilt pipes, and beneath it the usual table, at which Mr. Aveling was, at the time of my arrival, standing and reading from the Bible. What with the Metropolitan delays and my button-holing acquaintance I had got quite late; however, there were many later. In fact people kept dropping in and out during the whole service and sermon, which I interpreted as a sign that they were really of the class for whom the lecture was intended—business people able to snatch only a few minutes from the midst of their occupations. There was a considerable majority of men too, which—without being ungallant—I also recognised as a good sign. One seems to be always able to get a congregation of ladies. There was a very fair contingent at this chapel; and I know not why, but there was a pervading characteristic about them which I should find it quite impossible to put into words, but which made me feel that I had met them before at every dissenting chapel I had ever attended. Probably their numbers would have been larger but for the simultaneous meeting for the Week of Prayer, and also for the Noontide Prayer in Moorgate Street, which I have described in these pages.

Mr. Aveling then, standing at the table underneath the pulpit, was reading a psalm appropriate to the occasion (for it was the first lecture in the New Year), in a clear distinct voice, and with marked, but by no means exaggerated, emphasis. He was arrayed in simple clerical dress without any gown. To the reading of this psalm succeeded a rather long

—but not too long—extempore prayer. It struck me as curious that when Mr. Aveling prayed that we might be blessed in our domestic relations he specified "husbands," but not "wives." Considering the service was meant for merchants, I understood this at once to be a *lapsus linguæ*, and thought it argued that Mr. Aveling must be as much accustomed as myself to a preponderance of the female element in week-day services. But the prayer was exceedingly eloquent, and the modulation of the voice perfect, especially when, at its close, he besought, in well-chosen periods, that when our time came, the sun might set for us, not in a blaze of splendour, but calmly and quietly, so that those who loved us should feel that, though we were absent from the body, we were present with the Lord.

The single hymn, too, which was sung was appropriate, and the congregation bore their parts in it as though its chords were familiar. I am always struck by the singing power manifested in these chapels. A woman behind me sang in a rich clear voice, so as to be heard all over the large building, the words—

> "Time is earnest, passing by:
> Death is earnest, drawing nigh.
> Sinner, wilt thou happy be?
> Time and Death appeal to thee."

There was more of the "destructive" element in the composition than I liked; but I did not forget that I had wandered beyond my own limits, and was not there to criticise, but to listen and describe.

As the text of this lecture, Mr. Aveling took the words occurring in Ecclesiastes ix. 10—"Whatsoever thy hand findeth to do, do it with thy might; for there is no work, nor device, nor knowledge, nor wisdom in the grave, whither thou goest."

There was an old adage, he said, that whatever was worth doing was worth doing well. There was a place assigned for everybody, and a definite end for each one's existence. Our wisdom was to find out what that place and what that end was, and then to obey in reference to it the injunction of the text. Standing at the opening of the year we should remember that thought and action projected their consequences into the future, and touched chords that would vibrate throughout eternity.

Dividing duties into Relative or Social on the one hand, and Individual or Personal on the other, he proceeded to pass in review the former. As he did so, I found it necessary to move somewhat nearer the pulpit, and then perceived that, opposite to the gaily-decorated organ, at the other or street-end of the chapel, was a bright-coloured window, being a copy of Raffaelle's cartoon of St. Paul preaching on Areopagus.

Personal duties, however, said the lecturer, were more appropriate to the occasion. It might seem a work of supererogation to tell a man he should take care of himself; but "many don't," he observed. They cared for the visible, the present, the material. The body was so clamorous that it would be attended to. The mind was cultivated, too, but though the spirit's necessities were really as clamorous as those of the body, we were often deaf to them. We might go on ignorant of the existence of the spirit within us, if God did not find methods to reach our consciences. To neglect the spirit was to commit suicide.

What, then, must we do? Without answering that question exhaustively, he would say—Apply to every duty the injunction of the text. Bring to bear on spiritual matters the same energy as was given to worldly concerns. "Will you pardon my saying," he continued, "that many of you would have been in the *Gazette* long ago, if temporal interests had not weighed with you more than spiritual?" He had not one word to say against attention to temporal interests—his text enjoined it. "But I don't believe," he said, "in doing anything in a half-hearted way.

I am going to speak strongly—but if I made up my mind to do a wicked thing I would do it with all my might."

We Londoners, he went on to say, were not usually considered deficient in energy. If you crossed London Bridge of a morning, you saw earnestness on every face. The very mode in which men moved along showed that their whole soul was in what they were about. If that were only carried into religion all would be well.

He traced this principle through such duties as attendance on the means of grace, and especially dwelt on the importance of hearty singing. So in Bible-reading. He traced back to its original the word rendered "Search the Scriptures." It was a word of great energy—the word that would be used of searching a mine. If they so sought, they would find gems flashing round them. Looking for brass, they would get gold; seeking for iron, they would find silver. Prayer, self-examination, self "crucifixion" were also subjected to the same searching analysis.

Finally, he would speak one word as to the reason given in the text for this earnestness, "There is no work," &c. That was a solemn thought; work could only be done on this side of eternity. It reminded him of Matthew Henry's quaint saying, "If the work of life be not done when our time is done, we are *un*done for ever."

"If I read the Bible 'aright," continued Mr. Aveling, "probation is confined to earthly life. There is nothing to encourage hope for another opportunity. It is *not in the Book*. Even if there be hope of a chance in another world (and I know it is a favourite theory with some people), it ought not to regulate our actions, because God's express condition is that work shall be done here and now. We don't dream of evading death—at least, any of us except that 'poor mother among the Shakers.' See, then, that the end of life be realized before death comes."

The lecture became a little too theological towards its close, and then, of course, it exceeded its limits, but only by a few minutes. On the whole, it was very practical and appropriate, and concluded with heartily wishing us a happy new year.

A brief prayer and the apostolic benediction sent us forth into the whirl of the Great City again; and the contrast came sharply back when a boy clamorously demanded of me to buy "Jon Duan" for ninepence.

BRAMOISM IN LONDON.

PROBABLY since the era of the homöousian and the homoiousian so great a difference has not turned on a single syllable as that between Brahminism and Bramoism. The former is, as is well known, a religious system abstruse in matters of faith and ornate in practice as Romanism itself; the latter, rendered familiar to us by the presence in our midst some years ago of Baboo Keshub Chunder Sen, head of the Bramo Somaj, is very much of the same kind of revulsion against Brahminism which Protestantism is against Roman Catholicism; only Brahminism has run, as in some cases Protestantism seems not disinclined to do, into the antithesis of a pure Theism.

Being informed, then, that the coadjutor of Chunder Sen, and present representative of the Bramo Somaj in London, was to preach at Mr. Conway's chapel in Finsbury, I adjourned thither for the purpose of learning from personal observation something of the principles of that vast confraternity which I had heard was spreading in India. He had already preached for Mr. Voysey, and at St. George's Hall, and at the Unitarian Chapel in Stamford Street, Blackfriars; so that one could gather by the nature of his sympathies and associations something of the preacher's principles. It was no doubt a similar proclivity that led him to Finsbury, to the shrine once known as "Fox's Chapel," the presiding genius of which is now Mr. Moncure D. Conway.

It is a significant evidence as to the spread of the very broadest theological—or anti-theological— opinions, that it was with some difficulty even I, as a favoured individual, could find a seat in Mr. Conway's chapel. The bustling pew-opener was all politeness, and, moreover, knew my purpose in attending; but for a long time she could only offer me the alternative of a draughty seat at the back, which would have involved rheumatism, or one in front which might have endangered dislocation of my neck, had I endeavoured to catch a glimpse of the preacher. However, she presently disposed of me in a populous pew, and I had leisure to look round and notice how the well-filled chapel was dotted over here and there with brighteyed Asiatics, who had come to witness the once rare phenomenon of their countryman delivering himself in an English pulpit. It may be worth while to repeat a brief outline of the service at this, which is very much the most advanced place of worship in London; in fact one where any form of worship at all strikes one almost in the light of an incongruity. Proceedings began with the singing of a hymn from a collection recently made for use in this chapel, and which is really a manual of very eclectic poetry indeed. It was performed with unusual musical ability, and I regret I have not the hymn-book by to quote the words. Then Mr. Conway read from his own book, the Sacred Anthology, first of all the manifestation of God to Elijah as the Still Small Voice; secondly, a Puranic myth of King Vena; and thirdly, a Meditation from the Vedas, commencing, "May that soul of mine which mounts aloft in my waking and my sleeping hours, an ethereal spark from the Light of Lights, be united by devout meditation with the Spirit supremely blest and supremely intelligent;" each of the six portions of which the Meditation was composed concluding with the same aspiration which ran through it like a burden or refrain. A second hymn followed, sung to the tune, "Alla Trinita Beata," and then succeeded a quasi-prayer, or rather meditation, wherein we were exhorted to attain by an effort to a proper exaltation of mind. I could not help noticing the different attitudes assumed by the congregation during this religious exercise. Some bent as if in prayer, and others sat listlessly, according, as I suppose, to their different temperaments. The preacher, who was a dark, negro-like man, sat by while Mr. Conway conducted the service. He was clad in the conventional Hindoo coat, long as a Ritualist's soutane, but toned down with a gold Albert watch-chain. An anthem was sung while we sat; and the brief "devotions" were over.

The preacher then took Mr. Conway's place at the desk, and gave out as his text, in a strange musical voice, some Sanscrit words, which he said contained a deep well of meaning and truth, and which he afterwards translated thus:—"In the golden recess of man's soul dwelleth the immaculate Spirit of the Supreme God." It saddened him, he said, to think how the greatest privileges were often abused. This was exemplified in the word Revelation. It was a blessed word, the noblest man could utter, the making-known of the supreme unseen Spirit to the aching heart of humanity. It had been painfully abused, and its subject misunderstood, until it was made to apply to matters little calculated to inspire religious ideas. He had for instance, he said, great reverence for sacred books; a sincere reverence for that book outspread before him, the Christian Bible. So had he for the "Scriptures of his Fatherland," which had been a fount of truth over all the world, and his veneration for them was, as it should be, great and sincere. But, he added, my book or your book is a book only. In my country it is usual to divide revelation into two classes—(1) That revelation of which we hear, of which we are reminded as a matter of memory, and (2) that revelation which is spoken to us, and which we hear directly. There could not, he held, be a deeper or truer division. It would not "do" to say that the Bible revealed nothing, that the Hindoo Scriptures suggested nothing; and he did regard the Scriptures of the Hindoos, of the Mahometans, and of the Christians as revelations, but in the secondary, subordinate, and indirect sense. He would be the last to discourage Scriptural studies, because he knew from experience that the Bible, the Vedas, and the Koran had taught him many things, and developed in him principles which he never had before. Our men of the Bramo Somaj, he said, do read from books the revelations of great thinkers. We have a little book of our own containing such utterances, which we read from week to week, and treasure, honour, and reverence; but we are always alive to the dangers attending such regard for a book. In the north of India, in that classical spot the Punjaub, the country of the Five Waters, there was a race physically and morally strong amongst whom there grew up a simple soul that gradually put aside the deities of Hindoo Orthodoxy and the fanaticism of Mahometanism. Such a one sat down beneath the shade of the trees and by the banks of the lordly rivers, and composed hymns and anthems. That man died; the Sikhs degenerated in spiritual matters; they became political and orthodox; and they now worshipped the book containing those simple utterances. Such, he said, is the fate of all books. We of the Bramo Somaj remember this, and fear lest it might attach to the little book we have compiled.

When we raise our eyes to the figures described by the stars on the map of God's Heavens; when, from the material universe, there stand out before you the wisdom and love of God, then all books are lost. Before any books—Koran, Bible, or Vedas—existed, that was where men got their inspiration. The spirit of worship was older than the oldest book. Star, bird, flower, sun, told men of God; and man said, "These are Thy glorious works, Parent of Good!" The universe supplied the elements out of which books were subsequently compiled. To us in the Bramo Somaj the universe is such a book. My country is a beautiful country. My heart swells when I think of the cloudless skies of my fatherland, its majestic rivers, its mountain chains. It swells, too, when I remember the sublime traditions of my Aryan forefathers. And thus also it was with every land. But, as was the case with books, so, too, the material universe was a secondary source of revelation. There was a world which the eye saw not, the ear heard not, yet the light from which came pouring into the soul. It was well to study the external universe around us, but better still the universe of the spirit within us— that unseen world into which we should go when we shuffled off this mortal coil. Let us, he urged, learn the sweet Gospel of Truth and Peace in the world of the heart.

The soul of the true teacher was the best source of revelation. Because we had left some errors should we, therefore, he asked, defy the authority of religion? Should we disregard great men? If he could not advise his hearers to disregard books or the material universe, how could he advise them to disregard these teachers of the Gospel of Peace? He referred to no one man or country. Truth was incarnated in great souls who came into the world to tell of life here and hereafter. So did he reverence the name of Jesus (blessed be His soul!) Often did he think how he would like to sit at the feet of those great Teachers, and like a child learn the truths they knew. No matter whether they were men or women; whoever spoke so to him was to him a revelation, and he would confide his sorrows to such a one. He would ask such ones how he might approach his God, and profit by their joys and sorrow, and aspire to be crowned with that crown of success God had put on their brow in the tranquillity which God's servants always enjoy. No, we must not disregard the stream of revelation which comes from the hearts of *men*, and which was far more real than the cut-and-dried dogmas of which the volumes of the world were full. Of these he was weary and sick at heart. He had read book after book, he had seen dogma opposed to dogma. Let all be silent. Let the Word of God speak. By His words I receive strength. Such revelation is from the world of spirits.

But—Vanity of Vanities!—what avail books or men, if there be in me no corresponding chord of sympathy? We live in different worlds. The wicked man lives in the world of self, and the influence of the good man is lost. Jesus is persecuted and crucified, as others have been like Him, because there was no chord of sympathy between Him and those who heard Him. Then where, he asked, was the final appeal of simple humanity? Only one direct source of might existed for all—and again he almost chanted the musical words of his Sanscrit text. There, he said, I take my final stand. There is medicine for the sick; there food for the strong. The true revelation is here (and he laid his hand on his heart). It is silent. There is no noise when it comes; but the feelings stand transfigured. Doctrines come flashing, and flowing; motives of life no book can teach. God speaks: let the whole world be silent. What mattered it to Saul of Tarsus that he had persecuted Christians? What matters it to me that I have lived in idolatry? You perhaps have been great sinners; but the voice of the Lord came, and Saul was made a new man, and the heathen was sanctified before the throne of the Great God of Love. The Kingdom of Heaven is brought into the world! The spirit is always ready to speak. Do you tell me of seers and prophets of old, and say that inspiration is dead now? I decline to accept your dogma. Prophets and seers did and *do* live wherever God is worshipped in spirit and in truth. Has creation ceased? Are not men born now as of old? Then why should the stream of truth have ceased? Why is it only the soul that has stagnated? It cannot be. The stream of revelation is still flowing; not perhaps to you or me; but there are some souls that still look up to heaven just as seers of old did for guidance.

We do not, he concluded, hold the material universe as identical with the Spirit of God. We have discarded Pantheism; but still we hold the world as the throne of God. The star-spangled heaven is His canopy. The sun and moon are the lights of His cathedral. The flower-decked earth is the floor of His temple. When the soul opens to Him, the Sun of Righteousness streams in as the light at yonder windows. It is the law of the Universe. It streams into palace and hovel alike. We have the real source of revelation open when we open our hearts to God. This is the true Atonement. There is one pulse between divinity and humanity, and men stand sanctified and glorified, children of one Father with whom they shall dwell in time and eternity.

He followed up his sermon with a brief but eloquent prayer, standing picturesquely with upturned face, as if consciously enjoying the revelation of which he had spoken.

A MOZOOMDAR'S SERMON.

SINCE the visit of Baboo Keshub Chunder Sen to this country, several years ago, the subject of Bramoism has been kept pretty steadily before the British public. The Bramo Somaj in India is a body which, in its recoil from Brahminism, has lighted pretty nearly on pure Theism with a sort of proclivity towards Christianity. As such it claims kinship with Unitarianism in England; and it was in the chapel of Mr. James Martineau, then of Little Portland Street, that Baboo Keshub Chunder Sen made his *début*. Seeing that his cousin, the President of the Bramo Somaj, was to deliver a Sunday sermon at the same place, I made up my mind to be present, and went in good time, anticipating a crowd, for it used to be difficult to get a seat at Little Portland Street. But since I was last there, Mr. Martineau had left; and so—it might almost be said—had the congregation. I had no difficulty in getting a front seat that Sunday. This was once the focus and centre of London Unitarianism; but the glory had departed, or rather had ramified from the centre to the circumference. The new church in the Mall, Kensington, seems to have absorbed a good many of those who formerly worshipped at Little Portland Street. Mr. Martineau, too, was a man of mark, whose place will not be easily supplied: a fact significantly attested by the circumstance that, since his resignation, the post of preacher at that chapel had not been filled up.

Mr. Martineau's influence still lingers in Little Portland Street in the shape of the Prayer-Book and hymns which he compiled for the use of its congregation. By the former, with its ten services, is secured a fixed ritual; two of those services being almost abridgments of the Church of England Morning and Evening Prayer. On the occasion of my visit the third service was used, which is not quite so much like that of the Established Church, but still such as to secure congregational worship, and to warrant a brief description here.

The officiating minister, habited in a black Geneva gown, took his seat under the pulpit, and the preacher —on this occasion the Indian gentleman above-mentioned—took his place in a pew. He was a fine stalwart man, quite dark, and arrayed simply in the long cassock-like coat of every-day life. The service commenced with a sentence or two from Scripture, and a brief exhortation. There was neither confession nor absolution, and the Jubilate was sung by an excellent choir in the gallery, in place of the "Psalms for the Day." Then was read the 1st Lesson (Proverbs viii.), followed by Isaiah xliii. (headed "*Ecce Servus meus*") as a Canticle. A second Lesson (St. John i.) came next, and then the Psalm "*Benedic, anima mea.*" There was, of course, no recitation of a Creed. Prayers and a Proper Collect followed, the Sundays being reckoned after Christmas and after Whit-Sunday respectively. This was the Sixteenth Sunday after Whit-Sunday. It struck me that the service was cold, though the musical arrangements were perfect, and that the congregation were rather present to have something done for them by a reader and choir than to do it for themselves in the way of social devotion; an instance, surely, of the way in which extremes meet—the severe theological cultus of Unitarianism approaching in this respect the *opus operatum* of the Catholic Church, except in so far that the service was directed purely to the ear instead of the eye of the congregation. A remarkable feature was a Commemoration of the Departed, which occurs, I believe, in every service.

Three hymns were sung during the morning prayer: but I could not follow them, as the young lady next me in the pew did not offer me a sight of her book. There was an absence of the *petits soins* strangers usually experience in an alien place of worship; but by-and-by a gentleman saw my desolate condition, and brought me a hymnal from the other end of the chapel. The service ended with the Jewish Benediction.

The preacher then passed to the pulpit, and gave out, first in Sanscrit, and then in English, a text, the source of which he did not mention, consisting of the words, " Infinitely true and infinitely wise is the Lord of Lords." Ages ago in India, he said, they recognised the power of God. Ages ago the Universe was a wild waste, over which brooded the Spirit of God, and all that has been subsequently evolved was involved in Him then. The cause is always before the effect; and He is the cause of causes—the great uncaused cause. In Him reason means harmony, goodness, love, reconciliation between truth and truth, and between all things good and true.

Reason alone does not represent the mind of God; but the whole heart does. I am not prepared to define reason as one faculty. It is the entire essence of humanity which makes the greatness of man's soul. One essential attribute is that it reveals itself. Accordingly God's reason revealed itself in the beginning in external nature. Its first characters were written on the glorious firmament, the sun, moon, and mystic stars, and the vast volume of the world.

In the material world reason coincides with revelation. There is no conflict. All laws are harmonious. Reason is reflected on the revelation of the material universe. What are the special applications of this harmony? All our wants are satisfied, our instincts called forth by the world in which we live. Here is perfect adaptation. But still there are certain wants which the world cannot satisfy. Man's nature demands greater revelations than those of the material world, something higher, deeper, and more beautiful. Our spirit is still unsatisfied. I am pleased, he added, to find that some of the greatest thinkers of your country do admit those deeper wants of the soul. Sceptical as the age is we cannot ignore those deeper wants. That higher revelation *is* furnished by history. Do not be startled; to me history is not dead. It does not merely relate the past. To me it is a progressive dispensation. To me history means a record of God's dispensations to the world. God is not dead or inactive, nor is history. It is a grand unfolding of that light which man's soul demands. In the progressive services of great men I find that deeper revelation which the world cannot give.

But then here lies the problem of problems. How are we to reconcile reason with the revelations of history? This is the question we must answer or remain for ever unsatisfied. I solve the question of the revelation of the external world by the faculties with which I am furnished. Then shall my soul hunger and thirst in vain? If my physical nature is satisfied, so will my spiritual nature be. I shall interpret God's revelations through my own instincts.

But no. Men stand up and try to interpret them for men according to their prejudices. They could manufacture artificial wants, dogmatize, philosophize. Let theologians write as they will; but O, let the simple man alone who wants to know his God through nature and history! Let me stand face to face with God!

Do not accuse God because men try to intercept the light of his revelation. No; let all human theology be put aside, and let us stand directly before God, as His nature is expressed in the great events of the world.

Very simple are the instincts which interpret God's

events. 1. The world is moving on, and we must seek and accept the new truths. Let the great discoveries of the physical world come; and by them let us interpret God's other revelations. If we do not so discover them, we must be content to live in darkness. Not only do I not fear, but I hail the light that science is emitting. By it I interpret God's mind. Light can never be against light, or truth against truth. The first test, then, is the test of the *enlightened intellect*. That which does not bear the test shall fall. Best that it should do so. 2. But *love* is a test beyond the enlightened intellect. This instinct of love interprets God's love. So too (3) there is the element of *righteousness and purity*. I dare not charge God of that of which I should be ashamed. Do not charge God with the impurities encrusted upon human action. Let the three instincts of the intellect, the emotions, and the conscience judge of the revelations of God in history. The sense of necessities quickens these instincts. Man wants to know God as the old Indian anchorites did. They sought and found Him; and I trace in their utterances evidence of the fact. After these sages came others who tried to discover God's attributes. In India they did discover much of this, but not the relation of man's soul to God. Centuries after there came another. Jesus came and revealed that relation. In India they merged themselves in the depths of deity until they lost self-consciousness. "Humble Jesus" found God speaking to the depths of the human heart. He stood and found He was one with His God.

The true saintliness of Jesus consisted in discovering these relations, which would conquer all that was gross and little in man's nature, and make him like God. All cannot retire from the world; but all can discover God's light in their own conscience. Jesus recognised this light in all, even in the publicans and sinners; dormant, perhaps, but there still. This is the one common bond among all our differences. This bond Jesus sought to bring out. So must we try to find this light in ourselves and others. I cannot understand religious bitterness. Once recognise this light, and every sect and religion, past and present, is illumined by it. The ultimate light we need will not be found in books, but by direct communion with the Spirit of God. Thus, and thus only, will the difficulties of individual souls and of communities be ultimately removed.

The preacher concluded with an eloquent extempore prayer to the Great Spirit for this reconciliation; and the service ended with the hymn—

"Restore, O Father, to our time restore,
The peace that filled Thy infant Church of yore."

MR. DE MORGAN ON CHRISTIANITY.

I HAD fondly hoped that the *National Reformer*, with its exuberant "Guide to the Lecture Rooms," gave me the clue to the whole of unorthodox London. I had no idea that heterodoxy contained within itself anything in the shape of an "Index Expurgatorius" equivalent to that in which naughty volumes are chronicled at the Vatican, or, more nearly still perhaps, the "Episcopal Black Book," in which erratic curates are judiciously inscribed by the bishop of the diocese. But Heresy, it appears, is as highly organized as Orthodoxy itself; and the name of Mr. John de Morgan is, for some reason or other, not permitted to appear in the pages of that journal which I had adopted as my guide, philosopher, and friend. "Acting," however, "on information I had received," I journeyed, like an ecclesiastical detective, to Castle Street, Oxford Market, on Sunday evening, in order to sit at the feet of Mr. de

Morgan, the apparently heretical gentleman whose erroneous views had exiled him even from the columns of the "leading unorthodox journal." The announcement, in fact, which drew my pilgrim steps towards this particular shrine was substantially as follows— for there is no need to be mysterious even on so abstruse a subject as the ramifications of metropolitan heterodoxy:—

"CHRIST THE GREAT REFORMER.

MR. JOHN DE MORGAN

Has arranged to deliver a Course of Lectures on the

LIFE AND TEACHINGS OF CHRIST,

IN THE CASTLE STREET HALL,

25, Castle Street East, Oxford Market, as follows :—

Sunday, April 19th :—' Christ ! Man or God ?' Sunday, April 26th :— ' Did Christ teach the Immortality of the Soul ?' Sunday, May 3rd :— ' What is Christianity as taught by Christ and the Early Church ?'

Each lecture to commence at 7.30 punctually. Admission 2*d.*; front seats, 4*d.* Discussion invited.

The whole argument and proof will be drawn from the Bible, and it is hoped that disputants will adhere to that Book."

Although I had long ceased to be beguiled by any pretentious names attached to the temples of unorthodoxy, I was still led into an error on this occasion. I jumped to the conclusion that Castle Street "Hall" was the Co-operative Hall in that street, which really deserves its name, and where I knew Sunday evening lectures were wont to be delivered. Thither, accordingly, I turned my steps, and, finding the door open, mounted the stairs. I climbed until it seemed I must be at an elevation equal to the upper storeys of the Tower of Babel; and when I had got up to the very attics, I heard the sound of a harmonium, and a male voice. I thought, perhaps, Mr. de Morgan was regaling himself with a preliminary hymn; but when I listened, I found the particular composition was of so exceedingly orthodox a nature that I would not scandalize him by supposing it could have issued from his lips. I descended the stairs again, and went out into the street, leaving the minstrel still tootle-tooing his pious strain to an accompaniment of one finger on a nasal harmonium.

Opposite, on an exceedingly mild dwelling-house, I perceived the sign of which I was in search. The mansion was certainly not, as Horace says, *invidendis postibus aula*; and, moreover, it was closely shut, though it was now after half-past seven o'clock. A respectable woman stood at the door, evidently bent, like myself, on hearing Mr. de Morgan. I joined her, and found she was the landlady of a certain public-house whereat Mr. Odger is accustomed to air his oratory, and where I hope to pay a visit shortly, if the excellent hostess will excuse my making thus free with her name. She gave me much valuable information, for which I here publicly tender her my thanks; but was inclined to take a desponding view of free-thought prospects in general, and especially lamented the dissension between two of its most shining lights—Mr. Bradlaugh and Mr. de Morgan. Let me do her justice; she was no partisan, and simply dwelt with sorrow on the recognised fact that, in these movements, to divide is not always, or often, to rule.

When the hall was at length opened, and I paid my twopence (which was all the young lady at the door asked me for), I thought I had never seen such a pill-box of a place. A good many intelligent-looking artisans were already there, and had commenced a warmish discussion in their seats on the subject of intuitions. One voluble man had, incautiously, I fancy, used the word, and a fierce black-bearded opponent in a front bench, who had been deep in his Bible, flew at him, and told him he was talking nonsense. There was no such thing as an intuition; it was all experience. Had a child any intuitive ideas? Yes, said the former speaker. Pope wrote poetry at eight years of age. Could that have been experience? The aggressor retaliated, illogically enough, by saying Cowper did not begin to write until he was fifty. However, the argumentation served to beguile the time until Mr. de Morgan, a very juvenile and rather good-looking man, took his seat alone on the little platform, and became engrossed in a ponderous family Bible which was on the table. This gave me time to take stock of him; and I am afraid I began to despise his youth. He looked a full ten years younger than the youngest of his auditors; had a fluffy head of hair parted devoutly down the middle, an incipient moustache, and wore a gay flower in his button-hole. One always expects to see these heretical gentlemen thick-bearded, and with a savage scorn of the proprieties. Mr. de Morgan was quite the reverse.

When he began to speak I found his voice was as pleasant as his appearance. He was the very model for a "duck" of a curate, and I am sure his eyes and voice would have been irresistible with the young ladies. He touched first of all briefly on one or two events of the week. First, he said, the *Flag of Ireland* newspaper had received a warning from Government. Next, the authorities of Grafton Hall, where Hibernian patriots gather, had been informed that, if their treasonable talk was continued, the Hall would be closed. He very much wished they would give *him* a similar warning. It really was most incongruous to hear this sweet-voiced preacher enunciate such startling sentiments. One would just as soon have expected them from the ideal curate at a petticoat party!

In a passing reference to the Budget, he satirically remarked that it was proposed to pay off, in twenty years, half a million from the National Debt, while the "poor Republicans" in America had accomplished a similar feat in one month. He then passed definitely to the subject of his lecture; and, as an instance of the absurdities, "nay, blasphemies," which were current as religion, read a handbill which had been given him as he passed St. George's Hall that evening, when it was announced that a Mr. Herbert Taylor would preach "the Salvation of God." Was it possible that God needed salvation, or was it only bad grammar? Mr. de Morgan meant this for a *coup;* but his audience evidently considered it clap-trap, and failed to applaud.

Nothing daunted, however—and I should think Mr. de Morgan was not easily daunted—he went on to explain that the question of the evening was, not whether there was a soul, and that soul was immortal, but whether Christ taught it. He claimed that they, namely, Mr. de Morgan and his followers, represented the real teaching of Christianity—that old familiar tale I had heard so many Sunday nights in such a variety of places—and that Christ's doctrines referred solely to this world and man's temporal interests. Take the word Damnation, he said. Scott and Henry, Kitto, and other commentators, agreed that it referred to judicial punishment in this world. It was a judgment which could be pronounced at any time. There was, indeed, as Mr. de Morgan strongly put it, "no date for damnation." So, too, of the word Hell. In the Old Testament it often meant the grave. When it did not, it referred to the valleys of Hinnom and Tophet, where the fires were kept burning for purposes of scavengery outside the walls of Jerusalem. There was a heavy punishment if those "eternal fires" were allowed to go out; and the consigning a man to Gehenna was simply saying he was unfit for the Christian Commune, and deserved to be cast out of it, as offal was cast into Hinnom and Tophet. "Everlasting" simply meant enduring, and was applied to these fires, which had burnt for a thousand years. Christ had, he said, warned those whom He taught that He spoke all these things to them "in parables." He had definitely sanctioned the teachings of the old Hebrew Scriptures, and in Eccl. iii. 18, it was said that what happened to the spirit of a beast happened to the spirit of a man; as one died, so died the other. Each went to the same place.

Then with regard to the expression "The kingdom of God." Josephus continually used the expression with reference to the succession of high priests, that such and such a priest introduced a "kingdom." In such a transferred sense the Americans used the word "platform" to distinguish a certain set of political principles. So Christ used the word kingdom to symbolize the principles of the Christian Commune. He touched at length the case of the rich young man who went away sorrowful when he was told to sell all he had before he could enter into life. That meant enter into the Commune of Christ, which was a Commune of hard work and perfect equality. Light, he said, might have been thrown on these and similar passages if the new Revision Committee had been a company of scholars, instead of a company of dogmatists; but the fact of Dr. Vance Smith being objected to as a member, showed that the ecclesiastical authorities did not want to get at the truth, but only to have their prejudices confirmed. The parable of the grain of mustard seed was a case in point too. "Heaven doesn't grow," he said, "but the Christian idea does, and Christ, in His enthusiasm, thought He had only to promulgate His principles for them to take the world by storm. I thought so once," continued the lecturer, talking as if he were a very Nestor. "Years ago, I thought if I could only tell people how great a man Christ was, they would listen and follow. I found them sunk in Conservatism. Christ thought the same, and met with the same disappointment." The kingdom of God was, in short, Communism. It was within men. It consisted of the benevolent ideas of Universal Brotherhood. "This is, in fact, the position we take. We are a community. We have nothing to do with the men at St. Stephen's or with the woman (*sic*) who sits on the Throne!"

Really one would not have expected this from a jaunty little curate-like young man, with the sweetest of voices, hair parted down the middle, and a flower in his button-hole! Her Majesty might have looked for more respect from so sweet a young creature!

His object, he concluded, was purely eclectic, and he only wanted his hearers to think over the passages on which he had dwelt. The general judgment, he submitted, was a physical impossibility. "Years ago," again repeated the juvenile Methuselah, while he was preaching to his people on the text, "Every eye shall see Him," his own words shook his faith, for the idea crossed his mind, *Where will they all stand?* His final broadside was against Sunday Schools, which he quoted the Bishop of Manchester for setting down as hotbeds of immorality. I very much hope that Prelate never did commit himself to such a statement. I certainly never heard of it, and beg to say I only set down the words *auctoritate* Mr. de Morgan. Out of 724 criminals somewhere or other—again I am not responsible for the statistics—no less than 644 had been seven years in Sunday Schools. And with this tremendous fact Mr. de Morgan sat down.

The fierce-looking gentleman who disbelieved in intuitions was then appointed chairman, and the discussion, if so it could be called, commenced. The intuitional artisan began by saying he believed every man had a soul and was immortal, but then he shot off at a tangent and girded at the upper classes, which I found to my regret was this particular gentleman's one subject. I say regret, for he cheated me out of my discussion, and went off into high-falutin, until the chairman could bear it no longer, and made him sit down abruptly by calling "Time." Poor man! I was really sorry they shut him up; for he began much to the point. There was a rough pathos in his words when he said it was a poor prospect for the working man if the soul were not immortal. No one would ever do anything for him if Christ did not. How, he asked, would they ever "resurrect" such great men as Robespierre, if the soul were not immortal? It was, I think, a casual reference to the House of Commons which roused this gentleman's ire, and so caused his collapse. In "a rhapsody of words" he said Christ pointed him to the bright blue sky, but how was he to soar up there, when the House of Commons told him to look down to them, and treated him as a marketable commodity? The House of Commons was ruled irrelevant, time was up, and the excited artisan was heard no more.

The next speaker, a good-looking elderly man, was, if possible, more inconsequential still. He began by quoting the clause from the Lord's Prayer, "Thy kingdom come;" and then said the sun, moon, and stars were not private property, simply because they could not be got at. He hit out fiercely at "a hireling priesthood and a rotten press;" but Mr. de Morgan and the chairman knew their man, and occupied themselves in reading, simply reminding him when "time was up."

The Chairman, having sought in vain to get other speakers on their legs, declared that he had long since given up the subject as incomprehensible, and so harked back to the National Debt, about which he said nothing in particular, but a good deal in general. When he was a young man that text about the camel going through the eye of a needle made him afraid of getting rich, but he lived on in the hope that science would one day make "a thundering" big needle, and the camel would go through.

A full-flavoured Hibernian gentleman at the back of the room apologetically ventured on Biblical criticism, by suggesting whether " camel" in the passage might not be a wrong rendering for " cable ;" but the version did not find favour, and he sat down discomfited.

Then everybody cut in, and the discussion was waxing irregular, when Mr. de Morgan rose to reply. After disposing of the Christian miracles as magnetic, he protested against scoffing at Christianity, but claimed the right to criticise. I wondered whether I discovered the cause of his exclusion from the *National Reformer* when he instanced as what he meant by scoffing Mr. Bradlaugh's description of Christ as "an impostor riding on a donkey!"

Robespierre, he said, in conclusion, proved the resurrection of ideas, not of the individual. Nature was always reproducing herself; and the Parisian Communists in their deaths represented a risen Christ! Christ was a law-breaker, and—said this suave young man—"I glory in being a law-breaker, too!" Montesquieu had said, and he repeated, the best way of getting rid of a bad law was to keep on breaking it.

If one could have seen our little assembly break up and file out of that exceedingly modest domicile near Oxford Market, he would hardly have guessed the strangely tall talk in which we had been engaged that Sabbath eve. I suppose it serves some purpose as a safety valve. I am sure the two irrelevant artisans felt better when they let off their fiery speeches against the House of Commons, the hireling priests, and the rotten press. In fact, from Mr. de Morgan down to the Irishman and his cable, it might be said that the statements of their opinions amused them and could not hurt anybody much.

THE JUBILEE SINGERS.

My eye happening to light upon an announcement that a "Service of Song" would be given by the American Jubilee Singers at the great Metropolitan Tabernacle on a Wednesday evening, I determined to be present.

Seeing that the doors opened at seven, and proceedings commenced at half-past, and being provided with a press ticket of admission, I thought I would still get there by a quarter past, for I reckon punctuality among the cardinal virtues. I know the capacities of Mr. Spurgeon's great building, and was not a little surprised to find it crammed to the doors to hear these nine emancipated slaves sing their "Songs of Zion;" no longer, thank God, hanging their harps on the willows, and chanting those strains sadly "in the strange land," but singing them half jubilantly, half plaintively, in the way of recollection; for it is so, in half sadness the reminiscence of a past joy or sorrow ever comes back to us with something of sadness still.

My magic pass took me to the foot of the pulpit, where I could hear splendidly, but only just see the heads of the singers, who had entered Mr. Spurgeon's rostrum before I got quite settled—three rows of faces, all of pure African type, and several of real African tint, though some were nearly as white as the Teuton. Mr. Spurgeon said a few characteristic words by way of opening, and informed us that nearly all these ladies and gentlemen had been slaves themselves, while all were closely connected with those who had been in bondage. For his life, he said, he could not imagine anybody "owning" them, except it might be some gentleman possessing one of the ladies as his wife—at which the ladies smiled complacently, and I daresay blushed, only I could see none except the "dark" ones, and blushes were invisible in their case. They would sing, he said, the songs they used to sing in old slave times, and when the Northern army was coming South to their deliverance. They seemed to him to "preach in music." There was a force in their singing which went to the heart. His own sluices of tears did not lie very near the surface. It was not easy for books to make him weep, but the sluices were drawn when he heard the Jubilee Singers.

Some of their words, he went on to say, were grotesque, and seemed nonsense (in truth, they looked almost profane to me when I read them on the programme). When such appeared to be the case we must take it for granted that we lacked intelligence to understand them—a canon of criticism which I thought would be very convenient to many an aspiring poetaster. There was a real mystic deep philosophy which we could not understand without having been in the position of these people, in the cotton plantation with a "tingling back." To an audience who had been in slavery their effect would be electric. So might it be to us who sympathized with them. They had then got, he added, 8000*l*. They wanted 14,000*l*. for the buildings at Fisk University. They ought soon to get the other 6000*l*., be off quickly with it, and soon come back for 6000*l*. more. Mr. Spurgeon talks of his thousands as lightly as the Shah of Persia!

Then there burst on our ears, soft, low, and weird, the first strains of the song, "Steal away to Jesus," which, I confess, was one of those whose diction sounded strange, until I learnt that it was what they sang at night when they were precluded from coming to religious service, and literally "stole away" to it in disobedience of orders. Then the words took a new significance; and I was even able to follow Mr. Spurgeon's application of them to the dying Christian—

"Steal away to Jesus,
Steal away home,
I ain't got long to stay here."

These words were sung by way of burden after every verse, the last being—

"Tombstones are bursting,
Poor sinners are trembling,
The trumpet sounds in my soul,
I ain't got long to stay here."

Then, with a burst of exultation, in full chorus—

"Steal away to Jesus!"

The song itself was very plaintive and touching, but came to a really majestic climax, ending as it did in the Lord's Prayer, exquisitely harmonized, and recited softly, as if by stealth, until it came to the words, "For Thine is the kingdom," when it swelled into a noble crescendo, diminishing again to almost breathless pianissimo at the final "Amen." I could understand the thrilling effect of the Jubilee Singers then, and how the pathos of their wild harmonies made bearded men weep.

Next came a Jubilant Song of Liberation, bearing the quaint title, "Go down, Moses." Pharaoh, or "Ole Pharaoh," as he is disrespectfully termed, is, naturally enough, the *bête noire* of the coloured people. The defiant way in which the chorus yelled out after every line "Let my people go," was something that must be heard to be appreciated. When one of the gentlemen had to represent Pharaoh in solo, he made him a very distressing person indeed, as though the reiterated "Let my people go," had really been too much for him. This strain was encored vociferously; for its dramatic effect was most striking; and the minstrels, whose répertoire, especially on the subject of "Ole Pharaoh," is an extensive one, replaced it with another—

"Did not ole Pharaoh get lost
In the Red Sea?"

Commenting on what had been sung, just to give the singers some rest, Mr. Spurgeon said, "I'm uncommonly glad old Pharaoh did get lost. Slavery was our old Pharaoh; and wherever slavery of blacks or whites exists, may it be like old Pharaoh, and get lost in the Red Sea."

"Many Thousand Gone" was the next song. These words were again the burden, and followed each of the lines—

"No more peck o' corn for me,
   Many thousand, &c.
No more driver's lash for me, &c.
No more pint o' salt for me, &c.
No more mistress' call for me," &c.

And after this, at special request of Mr. Spurgeon, though it was not in the programme, was sung the well-known "Glory, Hallelujah" chorus of "John Brown," with a wonderful climax at the Hallelujah.

Parenthetically, Mr. Spurgeon said he was glad there was no more possibility of "fugitives"—some of whom he feared "took us in mightily." He referred to one in particular for whom they had subscribed, in order to enable him to buy back his father. He didn't believe he ever had a father. He believed he was like Topsy, and "growed;" at all events he "growed" rich by their contributions.

"Mary and Martha's just gone 'long,
To ring those charming bells,"

was the title of the next piece, the burden being—

"Free grace, and dying love."

Some of the verses provoked audible mirth in the audience, especially one which alluded to the two great theological schools coming under Negro observation, and which bore a special significance as sung there in the very focus and head-quarters of the English Baptists—

> "The Methodist and Baptists just gone 'long,
> To ring those charming bells.
> *Cho.* Crying, Free Grace and Dying Love,
> O, 'way over Jordan, Lord,
> To ring those charming bells."

"I am trying to find out what the title of the next song means," said Mr. Spurgeon. "O Brother, you ought to be here, to hear the Jordan roll!" "I think," he added, "it means you ought to be a Baptist. Read it thus, my Wesleyan and Congregationalist friends; and may it be blest to some of you 'unwashed brethren.'"

> "Roll, Jordan, roll!
> I hope to go to Heaven when I die,
> And hear the Jordan roll."

I could not get the idea of pious "Ethiopian serenaders" out of my mind, as they sang thus in a weird unison, with just a harmony at the final cadence, and a real roll, like a deep full river, on the last word.

Then came a solo by the very darkest lady. Again a wild touching song, taking us back, as we were told, to the times when there was little prospect of the "hallowed grave" for the Negro bondsman—

> "You may bury me in the east,
> You may bury me in the west,
> But I'll hear the trumpet sound
>   In the morning!"

This was repeated, at vociferous request, and fresh verses added from the apparently inexhaustible store.

The last strain to which I stayed to listen—for the service promised to be lengthy, and prolixity in such matters always appears to me a mistake—was one the words of which had struck me as singularly irreverent when I saw them on the programme—

> "Gwine to write to Massa Jesus
> To send some valiant soldiers,
> To turn back Pharaoh's army,
>   Hallelujah! Hallelujah!"

This last interjectional word "Hallelujah"—like the traditional "Mesopotamia"—seemed really to do these singers good as they enunciated it. The song itself bore reference to the time of the Liberation, when, as Mr. Spurgeon pertinently observed, there was a "good deal of that kind of writing done down South." They were waiting for the Northern army to come and free them; and these were the words that expressed their terrible tension—

> "You say you are a soldier, fighting for your Saviour,
>   To turn back Pharaoh's army. Hallelujah!
>   To turn back, &c.
> When the children were in bondage they cried to the Lord,
>   He turned back Pharaoh's army. Hallelujah! &c.
> When Moses smote the water, the children all passed over,
>   And turned back Pharaoh's army. Hallelujah! &c.
> When Pharaoh crossed the water, the waters came together,
>   And drowned ole Pharaoh's army. Hallelujah!" &c.

So ended my experiences with the Jubilee Singers. I seemed the only one out of those congregated thousands who came away when the "ladies and gentlemen" went to refresh. When I passed into busy Newington, I was haunted with those wild weird strains, as one who hears the bagpipe pictures the Highlands. While I sped along the Metropolitan Rail, on my homeward way, I smiled as I read "The Gospel Train" in their strange libretto, and mused how many ways there are of doing God "acceptable service"—

> "The gospel train is coming,
>   I hear it just at hand,
> I hear the car-wheels moving,
>   And rumbling through the land.
>   *Cho.* Get on board, children,
>   Get on board, children,
>   Get on board, children,
>   For there's room for many a more.
>
> " I hear the bell and whistle,
>   The coming round the curve;
> She's playing all her steam and power,
>   And straining every nerve,
>   *Cho.* Get on board, &c.
>
> " No signal for another train
>   To follow on the line,
> O sinner, you're for ever lost,
>   If once you're left behind.
>   *Cho.* Get on board, &c.

"This is the Christian banner,
　The motto's new and old,
Salvation and Repentance
　Are burnished there in gold.
　　Cho. Get on board, &c.

"She's nearing now the station,
　O sinner, don't be vain,
But come and get your ticket,
　And be ready for the train.
　　Cho. Get on board, &c.

"The fare is cheap and all can go,
　The rich and poor are there,
No second class on board the train,
　No difference in the fare.
　　Cho. Get on board, &c.

"There's Moses, Noah, and Abraham,
　And all the prophets, too,
Our friends in Christ are all on board,
　O, what a heavenly crew.
　　Cho. Get on board, &c.

"We soon shall reach the station,
　O, how we then shall sing,
With all the heavenly army,
　We'll make the welkin ring.
　　Cho. Get on board, &c.

"We'll shout o'er all our sorrows,
　And sing for evermore,
With Christ and all His army,
　On that celestial shore.
　　Cho. Get on board, &c."

A CAMPANOLOGICAL CONCERT.

THERE is a distinct advantage gained by adopting for a treatise or an entertainment a nice long unpronounceable name that shall be, as the Article says, "not understanded of the people." I remember one of the earliest criticisms on my own sermons when, ages ago, I was a country curate in the wilds of West Somersetshire, was to the effect that the critic, an old peasant woman, "liked 'em so much because they were chock full o' hard words as nobody couldn't understand." I fancy if the canons of criticism were always stated with such outspoken candour as this, that remark would be found to apply to a good many more pretentious works than my incipient discourses!

Even, however, when the epithet "campanological" is translated into the vernacular, and it is made evident to the uninitiated that a Campanological Concert simply means a handbell ringing entertainment, there is still a nice weird sound about the very name of bells which fits them for the subject of an article when Christmas is drawing near, and everybody is preparing to quote Tennyson's "Ring out, wild bells, in the wild sky." One would be puzzled to account for this epithet "wild," except by presupposing poetic licence, which covers as many incongruities as the digamma itself. Edgar Allan Poe's romantic jingle of "The Bells" also occurs to the mind, and might seem to some of us to justify the epithet "wild," were it not that Poe is already undergoing the process of whitewashing, or semi-canonization, which Mr. Froude has applied to Henry VIII., Mr. Jesse to Richard III., and somebody else to Nero. Fresher still in the recollection of all of us is the perpetual ding-dong of the sleigh-bells in the ears of Matthias at the Lyceum; so that, on the whole, when two mild-looking tickets came inviting me to a "Campanological Concert," I decided, yes I would go, just as I was on the point of consigning them to my capacious waste-basket. I would go and hear what a Campanological Concert was like. The last I had heard was in the old cathedral town where I was born, and where the ringers, every Christmas, used to come round in the dead of night, and, after a very wild campanological exercitation indeed, extemporize a benediction on the inmates of the house whom they had aroused, and feel injured if they did not receive a substantial fee for their delicate, but somewhat dissipated, attentions.

It was, strangely enough, to a Baptist Tabernacle the tickets invited me; and when I entered I found the space below the pulpit occupied with a long table on which were placed multitudinous bells of all sizes, up from the muffin-bell of domestic life to the size of a small pail. I was accompanied by a young lady of the mature age of twelve, who, of course, insisted upon selecting a front seat, exactly under the twelve biggest bells; and was only induced to shift her quarters on the expostulation of the worthy pastor of the chapel, who I fancy had fears of my cerebral safety if we retained our original position.

Our Campanologists were the Royal Poland Street Temperance Handbell Ringers, who are proud of being able to boast that they have four times been commanded to perform before Royalty. Their conductor, Mr. Miller, on entering with his four confrères, immediately proceeded to request the expulsion of all babies, and then the five indulged in a sort of burlesque opening in verse, about which I will only say I think it might be judiciously omitted.

All sorts of entertainments are suggested, just as in the opening of a pantomime; and, of course, everybody knows that campanology will eventually carry off the palm. It does, and the five gentlemen commence a pretty waltz-like air called " The Snowdrop," and taken pianissimo. I had seldom heard anything sweeter; and it was some time before I could analyse my campanologists sufficiently to see how they produced their effects. Mr. Miller and another performer, who seemed to have their hands full of bells, I found were responsible for the air, or soprano part, and made up an octave between them, having two bells in each hand, and rapidly snatching up from the table those which represented accidentals, or which were above or below the octave. A young gentleman, apparently of a nervous turn of mind, who was answerable for the alto, kept scrambling about among his bells as though he were catching a mouse or searching for something in a hurry. The tenor was calmer, but liable to spasmodic attacks, due, perhaps, to sympathy with the adjacent alto. The bass was cool as a cucumber, and swung about his huge pail-like bells with the ease of an Atlas: but so gently did he do his spiriting that I might—as my young companion reminded me—have sat *inside* one of his miniature Big Bens without being seriously discomposed.

Mr. Miller was a gentleman running over with fun, and his appearance really justifies one's anxiety as to whether the continued strain on his brain and biceps may not be too much for him. He is so thin as positively to make one's eye ache to look at him; but how thoroughly I appreciated his fun when he introduced "The Keel Row" as "The Newcastle, or Tyneside Anthem." It brought to my mind an exercise in which I myself once engaged whilst a guest in a Durham house. A "Geordie," or pitman, wagered that he would dance to the tune of "Weel may the keel row" longer than I would play it on the fiddle. He had unlimited confidence in his legs, I in my fingers. We played and danced until everybody else was tired, though we were not; and the result was a drawn battle.

After this piece, the excitable young alto descended to a harmonium, and we all sang, campanologists and audience, a ditty printed in their programme—

"SCATTER SEEDS OF KINDNESS.

"Let us gather up the sunbeams
  Lying all around our path;
Let us keep the wheat and roses,
  Casting out the thorns and chaff;
Let us find our sweetest comfort
  In the blessings of to-day,
With a patient hand removing
  All the briars from the way.

CHORUS.

> Then scatter seeds of kindness,
> Then scatter seeds of kindness,
> Then scatter seeds of kindness,
>   For our reaping by-and-by."

I fancy we thought we did the chorus rather well; but the irrepressible Mr. Miller said he was glad he found himself in face of a conscientious audience, for he found we had given ourselves no applause for that performance, and that was—exactly what we deserved.

Handel's "Harmonious Blacksmith" followed, and I confess I did not know, until Mr. Miller told us, that the particular blacksmith in question lived at Little Stanmore, "just up the Edgware Road." The variations on this air were a perfect marvel of manipulation. The first soprano looked and acted like a distracted muffin-man, and the excitable alto fairly threw one of the bells over his head, to the great danger of Mr. Miller, who was performing his part with a grim air of determination on his face, as though he would do it or die in the attempt. Then we had the sweet old chimes of boyhood rung out, but with a considerable "difference"—as Ophelia says; and several familiar tunes interspersed, such as "Hark, the vesper hymn is stealing," "Home, sweet home," &c. Then Mr. Miller gave us a sermon on tract distribution, which was a mistake, and a recitation on "People *will* talk"—good, but out of place. The sweet air "Mandolinata" followed on the bells; and then Mr. Miller meandered into a dissertation on change-ringing, winding up by telling us the number of changes that could be rung on twelve bells, and how long it would take to do—viz., 479,001,600 in seventy-six years and three days, at twelve per minute.

The *chef-d'œuvre*, if one may judge by difficulty, was Sir Michael Costa's March in "Eli," in which no fewer than sixty-six bells were manipulated by the five executants. The bass is elaborate in the extreme; but our placid performer went through it without turning a hair. More singing followed; then the "Men of Harlech" and the "Westminster Chimes Polka," by Mr. Miller; the composer giving us a brief history of big bells in general, from the Giant of Moscow down to Big Ben. Then came what I thought—and what, it appeared, Her Majesty considers—their masterpiece, "The Blue Bells of Scotland." The variations on this air were brilliant in the extreme; but the *ppp* of the original melody was to me far more overpowering, and unapproachably pathetic. Why should this weird effect attach to bells more than any other instruments to tickle the senses?

By way of doing justice to all the component parts of the British Empire, Mr. Miller would add an Irish air—one of those soft, soothing Irish melodies; and straightway the band broke, at presto, into—" Rory O'More!"

The whole entertainment concluded with—" God save the Queen," and when it was done, I really felt I could sympathize with the sentiment of the worthy pastor of the chapel, however much I might join issue with the expression. He said he should like to "*lay* in bed all day and dream of the music he had been hearing that evening."

LADIES ON LIBERTY.

THERE was once a popular prejudice that the best guardians of English liberties were Englishmen; and even now in certain quarters the idea obtains that, journalistically speaking, the Englishman is the British Palladium; but, on the whole, it is beginning to be true of this, as of a good many other exploded theories, *nous avons changé tout cela*. Since the development of the strong-minded element in what was once—wrongly again!—deemed the weaker sex, woman and not man holds the shield of our liberties. Did not Jove himself concede the ægis to that strong-minded lady Minerva? Which thing, no doubt, was an allegory.

Though it was not a Sunday to tempt one forth or make folks forego the post-prandial nap—the custom of most of us on that particular *après-midi*—yet the announcement that Miss Fenwick Miller, " of the Ladies' Medical College," was going to devote an hour at St. George's Hall to an apotheosis of that Apostle of Liberty, John Stuart Mill, murdered sleep for me at least, and made me dare even the Sloughs of Despond left by the Fulham District Board of Works —alas, the misnomer!—in Western London so as to present myself in due season at the shrine of St. George—fitting locality for our young Pallas to brandish her ægis!

Very softly be it spoken, the fact that it was a youthful Athenë, and not one of the cod-eyed spectacled Minervas, who was to assume that mythologic shield, lent alacrity to my steps. I entertained pleasant recollections of Miss Fenwick Miller's bonny face and musical voice from certain experiences at the Dialectical Society, where I had heard her handle the most tremendous topics in presence of those Socratic gentlemen—topics from which a middle-aged Pallas Athenë would have shrunk in spinsterly horror, and whereat all the genus Grundy lifted up their hands, eyes, and noses in blank dismay. As for me, I am afraid I rather liked it. It seemed as if it were the first instalment of that "liberty, equality, and fraternity" which are to prevail when Astræa Redux brings back the golden age of Paradisiacal innocence. I would go and get a second instalment in the shape of that young lady's lecture on "John Stuart Mill and his Critics."

A very manful—no, I mean a very womanly—apologia was that with which Miss Miller favoured the large audience who deprived themselves of their Sunday snooze to listen to her musical cadences. I could not help thinking how much the success of an orator —or oratress, if there be such a word—depends on the intonation of the voice. Miss Miller's is suave as the voice of Spurgeon or the proverbial sucking dove.

It is not my present purpose, however, to follow Miss Miller in her elaborate defence of Mr. Mill. In fact, it only occurred to me to bracket Miss Miller along with another lady whose utterances on the subject of Liberty I proceed to narrate. The coincidence of two smooth-spoken ladies taking up their prophecy on the same subject in the course of one short week seemed too curious to pass unnoticed, and might not unreasonably be read as a sign of the times.

In the second instance where the ægis of liberty was, during the same week, wielded by female hands, Pallas Athenë was not a spinster but a married lady, whom for that reason I forbear to mention by name. Pallas Athenë proper has only herself to think of; and, when she announces her name publicly, I feel I may do the same. But where a possible Mr. Pallas comes in as a factor in the problem with the additional contingency of Misses and Master Pallas, I am not sure that I have the right to print names, and content myself, therefore, with speaking of the lady who lectured on the Tuesday evening at South Place Chapel on Civil and Religious Liberty as Praxagora—a term I have used before in the same connexion. Praxagora, the classical scholar will recollect, is the heroine in Aristophanes' comedy of the "Ecclesiazusæ," who assumes the marital costume in order to obtain admission to the Athenian House of Commons. The name struck me as typical of those advanced ladies who purpose scaling the walls of St. Stephen's by the ladder on which Woman's Suffrage is only the first round.

The weather during the week had certainly been most adverse to the female champions of our liberties. It rained piteously again when I betook me to South Place Chapel on the Tuesday evening: but the large building was well filled with an audience of more than average intelligence, who had paid 1*s.* or 6*d.* each to hear Praxagora state, as we knew she would, some of those defects of liberty, civil and religious, which existed, and to hear her remedy for the same.

When I entered, a little late, I found proceedings had commenced. The lady, supported by Mr. Conway alone, was in the midst of a glorification of the French Revolution. No contrast could be greater than between the quiet, ladylike appearance of the lecturess, her gentle bearing and silvery voice, and the tremendous doctrines to which she gave utterance. After eloquently defending the French Revolution, Praxagora went on to say that though things were not exactly the same in England as they were in France on the eve of the outbreak, still there were existent among us many of those remains of feudalism which were swept away by the French Revolution. We had not free thought in religion, or free action in politics.

Among the minor evils thus surviving in our midst she specified those appertaining to the tenure and transmission of land, the law of primogeniture, a standing army with promotion on account of birth, &c. These, she said, "must be swept away." This was an ever-recurrent phrase with Praxagora. Everything that did not quite coincide with her notions was to undergo the sweeping process forthwith. These legal infringements on liberty we could "sweep away," if we would.

In France, before the Revolution, and in England

now, the king, nobles, and clergy, thought all was going on very well and comfortably, while the Republican clubs were growing up in their midst. She passed on to draw a vivid picture of the "homes" deemed good enough for the poor, and especially instanced the huts appropriated to married soldiers at Woolwich, in which she said Her Majesty would not allow her cattle to be stowed at Windsor. And yet there was no rebellion. Only the talk in the Republican clubs before mentioned was not exactly loyal; in fact, it might be said that treason was talked there. The Government thought they could crush this out; but the leaders of popular opinion knew the forces they could reckon upon. The Queen and the Prince of Wales thought they made us supremely happy by occasionally driving through our streets. Now Praxagora would be the last to disparage loyalty, but it must be the golden loyalty due to some great man or great principles, not the "pinchbeck loyalty" which attached itself to the Duke of Edinburgh, or any member of the Royal household. Praxagora inveighed bitterly against taxation of the necessaries of life, and claimed that all taxation should be direct, and those who paid the taxes should have a voice in imposing them; whereas a large proportion of the working classes, and (which was evidently where the shoe pinched) "all women" were unrepresented. Why was there no Hampden to teach us how to resist this unjust taxation? Had we not courage enough to say, "These things shall not be so?" Reading from a tabular statement by Mr. Watts in the *National Reformer*, Praxagora stated that while the upper classes were taxed only to the extent of 10d. in the pound, the lower classes, by means of indirect taxation, were mulcted to the extent of four shillings and fourpence. On the fertile subject of the Game Laws, Praxagora went deeply into the item of Deer Forests, to which one-tenth of the area of Scotland was now devoted; so that you might walk from Aberdeen to the Atlantic entirely through forest. "Clear out the people!" was the principle avowedly acted upon in laying down the land in these forests. But the land, like the air, argued Praxagora, was nobody's property.

Speaking of a standing army as a standing menace, which must be got rid of—"swept away"— Praxagora sarcastically supposed the Duke of Cambridge attained to the dignity of Commander-in-Chief by personal bravery, as did the Duke of Edinburgh to his naval captaincy. Praxagora's powers of—shall I say it?—"chaff" are unlimited, and the extreme quietness of her demeanour made her sarcasms even more telling. The proposal to "sweep away" the standing army was applauded to the echo. Look what the standing army had just done in Spain, and was likely soon to do in France. What good was it here except to corrupt the society in garrison towns, and put men to saunter up and down outside Royal palaces, taking care of those who had no need to be taken care of?

As to Electoral Reform, that would not be perfect until every adult person was represented. To strike at the House of Lords was to strike at a dying institution. But persons and institutions took a long time dying. The House of Lords was a disgrace to a free country, and stood in the way of every reform until menaced. Therefore it, too, must be "swept away." Puppet kings and queens would be less injurious when this "toy-house" was gone, and then might come the times of the glorious Republic.

So ended this rather fierce tirade on the political side, not bawled out with the lungs of a female Cleon, but lisped as some pretty flirting girl might simper love sentences at a ball. Then Praxagora diverged to Religious Liberty.

She spoke not as a Freethinker or Secularist, "though Freethinker and Secularist I am," she added, amidst vociferous plaudits, but as a citizen of a community pretending to be free. She pleaded for the Roman Catholic as for the Atheist, that conscience should be held sacred.

The Church of England as by law established was an egregious monopoly. It had been an anachronism ever since the Church had ceased to be co-extensive with the nation. It was a mere creature of the State. Of the truth or falsity of its tenets Praxagora said nothing. She protested against the establishment of any religion or irreligion, and, as she had before asked for a Hampden, she now called for a Cromwell, and this time not in vain. A voice suggested Sir Charles Dilke as the Coming C.

The law affecting infidels and against blasphemy were passed under review, and Mr. Woolrych's decision on the previous day, not to accept the testimony of a witness who avowed his disbelief in a God, came in for very severe comment at Praxagora's hands.

She demanded that a fair fight should take place on platforms without aid from the strong arm of law; and having impeached one and all of these violations of civil and religious liberty at the bar of public opinion, Praxagora wound up with a beautiful peroration full of day-stars and figures clad in white, cloudless skies, and all the rest, and sat down overwhelmed with applause.

When I saw Praxagora afterwards jogging along by the Metropolitan, I thought anybody who sat opposite that comely matron would be puzzled to guess that ten minutes ago she had been demolishing Queen, Constitution, and Church with her scathing oratory from the tribune at Fox's Chapel.

AT THE CITY TEMPLE.

AMONG the noteworthy institutions of religious London the Thursday morning sermon at the City Temple occupies a prominent place. It is a favourite fallacy to represent the London clergy as gentlemen who merely drone away existence in a *laisser-aller* kind of way; who have booked a comfortable sinecure, and only ask to be let run quietly along in the old ruts. Will anybody who feels inclined to bring this indictment against the clergy simply calculate the amount of labour involved in getting up two sermons for Sunday, and one for an intermediate week day—not sermons of the class which are advertised as sold at 2s. 6d. a dozen lithographed by the sermon-mongers—veritable sermons in stones—but such as will bring an educated congregation of men to church or chapel at inconvenient hours or working days. The labour of the leader-writer or magazine contributor is child's play in comparison.

Working men—by which I mean not only artisans, but workers with brain and muscle alike—do throng the commodious aisles of the City Temple at midday on a Thursday—though the day and hour are not exactly the most commodious for either the brain or body-workers. I proved this on a recent Thursday, when I paid a long-proposed visit to this place, rendered famous by the episode of Mr. Fremantle's frustrated *début*. I could see at once there was going to be a congregation; for it was a few minutes after the stroke of noon when I alighted at the Farringdon Street Station, and quite a little stream of people was busy scrambling up the steps to the Holborn Viaduct. By some kind of freemasonry which I cannot explain, I knew they were bound, like myself, for the City Temple, though we were not any of us of that sex generally supposed to be the exclusive attendants at noontide services on week-days. No sooner did we present ourselves breathlessly in the spacious aisles of the handsome building than we were ushered by courteous male attendants into the best seats empty. There was a large congregation present, nearly two-thirds of the pews being full when I arrived.

Mounted in a goodly pulpit, the gift of the Corporation of London, Dr. Parker was reading in a singularly impressive voice the conclusion of the Sermon on the Mount as I entered. So strangely does one's eye catch trivial details, that I believe one of the first objects I noticed was a large bouquet lying by his side, and seeming to illustrate graphically enough the words he was reading. He was attired in Geneva gown and bands, and his delivery at once gave the idea of a consciousness of power. I was not at all surprised at the largeness of the congregation that had assembled, though a bitter north-east wind was blowing outside, and the second of Messrs. Moody and Sankey's services was on at Exeter Hall, and might have drawn the curious thither. I should fancy Dr. Parker's was a steady congregation. They all looked as though they were *at home;* at least, the large majority did. When the Scripture reading was over, Dr. Parker offered an extempore prayer embodying the ideas of the passage. It was somewhat florid—perhaps on such a theme it could scarcely be otherwise—but very fervid, eloquent, and, above all, brief.

Then a hymn, still bearing on the topic of God's Providence, was sung without accompaniment, the melody being led by a bearded gentleman sitting in an official chair under the pulpit. It was a good old standard tune which everybody could sing; and I believe everybody did sing it. There were certainly more men than women in the congregation, and I always think a strong unison of male voices very fine. This was the whole of the simple service—Bible-reading, Prayer, and Praise; then came the sermon.

Having first read through Psalm cxxxviii. in the same emphatic manner as he had the passage from the Great Sermon, Dr. Parker fixed on the concluding words as his text: "Forsake not the works of Thine own hands." He proposed to examine the natural claims we had on God. We did not ask to be here in this world, but here we are, and therefore we had a right by *nature*, by the state of things in which we found ourselves, to say that, under such circumstances, we ought not to be forsaken. It was not enough to bring us here. If we had asked to be brought, then we might have divided the responsibility.

You yourselves, he said, allow the efficacy of such an appeal. A child, it may be, left you ten years ago, and though that child could not plead virtue, it could groan forth the heart-breaking word, "Bad as I am, I am your own flesh and blood. I have done wrong, but don't let me rot. This flesh is your flesh. May I not come home on that natural claim?" So we could say to God: "Thou didst not make us thoughtlessly. That would have been unworthy of a work which comprised within it the stars and the angels. *Don't forsake us.*"

Some said, the preacher continued, that, as vessels of wrath, God had the right to dash us to pieces just as the potter had the work of his hands. No; God might dispose thus of masses of men, but he dealt differently with individuals. The text was a lawful, a pathetic, and an universal appeal.

Now what was God's answer to this pathetic cry of forsaken man? The whole constitution of nature, he again submitted, was God's answer by anticipation. It would have no meaning else. For every desire of man there was a provision: for his hunger a table, for his thirst fountains of living water—springs perennial and inexhaustible. The answer came before the cry. Nature would be one huge waste if this were not so. We might prove it by common things patent to all.

Suppose, for one moment, though it might tax imagination to do so, nature without man. Let an angel come down to look over and note it. Let him be a Recording Angel with pen and tablet. Here he would see food in abundance—the teeming orchard, the golden field—see flowers and fruits on all sides. When he had made his inventory, he would ask,

Why these things? He would listen for a footfall, and hearing none would say, "There is something wanting. Here is a feast spread, but no guests—a Banqueting Hall deserted!" Then let the human race be introduced; and the angelic heart is satisfied. "Ye are the guests," the Doctor exclaimed in a fine apostrophe, "ye who are created in the image of God!" Now might the angel say, "I can enter the last line, and go back to Heaven with a full report."

Take another picture, nearer home now — a miniature. Here is a dwelling—and still we know nothing of the human race. We look on with wonder. For whom is all this arrangement? There is a dog sleeping yonder. But is it all for the dog? No. There are books on the shelves. These can't be for the dog. There is a little bright bird. Ah, that's it. It's all for you. But no; there are pictures, which the bird can't appreciate. There is a sleek "long-backed" cat; but there is an instrument of music, which cannot be for the cat. All is a solemn irony so far; when lo, a bright-eyed child comes in, and all is explained. The inferior creatures are there on sufferance; but this life absorbs, or will one day absorb, all these surroundings. So with nature. The lion and the leopard, the behemoth and the fowl do not explain it. Man's nature is the key that opens the lock. It is he who makes the great house a *home*.

So when we are asked, Will God forsake the works of His hands? we may take the whole scheme of nature for our answer. The whole constitution of things—mountains, streams, forests, fowl, and fish— are a pledge that God will *not* forsake man. He makes His rain to fall and His sun to shine on all— on the man who prays and on the man who blasphemes.

You ask what is man's natural claim on God. This is the infinite reply.

No bird ever sang the pathetic refrain of the text. The young lion finds his mouthful of food. It is man only that realizes the idea of being forsaken. The greater the life the greater the need; just as it had been curiously said, the more glorious the intellect the nearer to insanity. It is man who cries, "Why standest Thou so far off, O God?" Millions of human voices were gathered up in that cry from the Cross, "My God, my God, why hast Thou forsaken Me?" We see man's greatness in his distress. As man suffers more than beast or bird, so he can enjoy, and know, and realize more. Are ye not much better than they?

It is we who have forsaken God. The forsakenness is not on man's side. His children have gone from Him to be guests at the devil's table. All we, like sheep, have gone astray.

Does God forsake the righteous? Don't let us give an opinion to-day. Let an old man speak—a bright old man, with silver locks on his shoulder, and an eye like a star. He has a harp in his hand; and thus the old minstrel sings: "I have been young and now am old, yet saw I never the righteous forsaken nor his seed begging their bread." David never saw the child of God dead on his Father's doorstep. If you are forsaken, ask yourselves whether you have been righteous. Paul and David—the great reasoner and the greater singer—answer, "Cast down—but *not* forsaken!"

> "Make you His service your delight,
> He'll make your wants His care."

The above is only a condensation of a long and eloquent discourse. Some of the "bits" were worthy of Charles Dickens. For instance, picturing the abode of a poor widow, Dr. Parker spoke of "a place out of which even a sheriff's officer could not take more than the shadow, and would not take that *because he could not sell it.*" "I have been as nearly forsaken as any man in the world. I looked around on all sides, but could see no way out—no lateral way, only a *vertical one!*"

It was, one could not help thinking, just the sermon many a man with care upon his forehead might want to carry back with him to his counting-house or his shop that Thursday morning, and the listening to which might be the greatest possible relaxation and relief for him. There was nothing showy or sensational in the sermon, though it was full of sustained eloquence, and glittered with bits of quiet humour. But you knew it was a sermon that came from the heart, even had the preacher never uttered the pathetic words, "I have been as nearly forsaken as any man in the world!"

A PRESIDENTIAL SERMON.

In my examination of the different outlying bodies beyond the pale of the Church of England, I am free to confess that I have done scant justice to the Wesleyans, a religious community which, whether by its numbers or nearness to my own form of faith, ought, I am aware, to have a very early claim on me. I resolved to repair my error by going to head-quarters and hearing Dr. Morley Punshon, the President of Conference for the current year, and simultaneously to examine as much as I could in detail the different sections into which the main body has, since its foundation, broken up.

Dr. Punshon's chapel stands in Warwick Gardens, Kensington, and is such a handsome Gothic building that the Bishop of Lincoln himself might mistake it for a church. I knew it of old, however; and, having taken care to assure myself that Dr. Punshon was going to preach, presented myself at the portal somewhat late, so that the congregation might get seated before I intruded. I looked in on the basement, where a female of grim aspect, after scanning my outer man, suggested sharply I had better go upstairs. I ought to mention that I had arrayed myself in a kind of subdued Evangelical clerical costume, so that I might at a pinch pass muster for a Nonconformist; but the female Cerberus evidently sniffed the Establishment, and told me, in the accents of a tartar, I had better go upstairs. I always get on better with male than female pew-openers, and was quite relieved to find one of my own sex in charge of the gallery, whereto I retired discomfited. He at once beckoned me to a seat, and volunteered to supply me with a hymn-book. He put me in the back row, and behind a pillar; but I did not expect a chief seat in the synagogue. Before I started that morning, some one suggested I should want a prayer-book, which I, in my ignorance, declared would be unnecessary. I was soon corrected, however. When I got settled in my gallery, I found a youthful curate was reading a lesson from one of the Prophets in a large pulpit inside the communion rails. This young man wore no gown, but a very clerical costume—much more like the Establishment than my own. His tie was of the very nattiest;

and a budding beard and moustache formed no incongruous additions in these hirsute days. While he read the lesson with admirable emphasis and clear articulation, I had time to take stock of my surroundings. There was generally a shiny look about the chapel, as though everything, including the congregation, had been newly varnished. The seats were low, the galleries retiring, and everything in the most correct ecclesiastical taste. The position of the pulpit was strange to me; and the addition of a table covered with red baize surmounted by a small white marble font with a chamber towel ready for use, did not diminish the peculiarity. There seemed to me a sort of struggle between order and chaos discernible, ending in a drawn battle between the conflicting elements. The pulpit had succeeded in attaining the "Eastward position," but the table at its base did very well for a quasi-altar, and was flanked, north and south, by two semi-ecclesiastical hall chairs of oak. The font was locomotive, and might be supposed to occupy its abnormal position under protest. After the lesson was finished, I was surprised to hear the Te Deum commenced by an excellent choir of men and boys who occupied the front of an organ gallery over the pulpit; and still more surprised to find the congregation using the Church of England

Book of Common Prayer. The very lessons themselves were those I should have heard if I had gone to my own church. The Jubilate followed the Second Lesson, during which the curate ran down the pulpit steps quite in a frisky manner, and Dr. Punshon took his place and resumed the service with the Apostles' Creed. The suffrages and collects followed, and the service ended just as our own, the General Thanksgiving being taken by the whole congregation with the minister.

Then there succeeded a baptism of a female infant—which explained the chamber towel. Again the service was an abridgment of the Church of England form, even the portentous word "regeneration" occupying its accustomed place. Dr. Punshon took the child from the father and handed it, after sprinkling it thrice, back to the mother, saying, "I return you your child," and adding a brief but very telling extempore address. In its course he defended infant baptism, and pictured the "proud and blushing mothers of Salem" bringing their little ones to Christ. He attributed no magical virtue to the water, he said; yet still, if the ceremony wrought its proper effect, that water might be to the child as a "holy chrism."

Then followed the sermon, delivered in a clear

voice, and—as far as I could see by twisting my neck round the iron pillar—with just enough gesticulation to mark the emphasis, without ever for one moment degenerating into the faintest semblance of "rant." The text was the beautiful one from Col. i. 12, and the subject of the discourse "The inheritance of the Saints in light." Truly did St. Paul say, observed the preacher, that if in this life only we Christians had hope, we should be of all men the most miserable. Sad, indeed, were it if all our hopes ended in the sepulchre; and the Gospel flashed a new revelation on God's purposes in this respect. It told us that the grave was not the goal. The great thought of the text was that preparedness was necessary for this future life. In that word "meet" lay the pith of the whole. The ignoring the claims of this world gave a handle to the Infidel who—one class of infidels at least—looked upon the present life simply as a parenthesis between two eternities, and having no affinity with either. Even many so-called Christians deemed that we had no personal connexion with the world to come. But we should remember that the present was not only a condition of probation, but of discipline. We were always scattering seeds, and the trifles which made up the sum of life constituted our characters for ever. So it was the Apostle pressed on triflers that assurance, "Be not deceived; God is not mocked; for whatsoever a man soweth that shall he also reap." The character now being formed should endure for ever.

Owing to the taint of original sin, a change must supervene, so as to fit us for heaven. Even analogy pointed out this fact. This world was adapted as a dwelling-place for the creatures placed upon it, and the creatures were in turn adapted for it. There was a theology which depreciated this world, and prescribed austerity as the rule of life. It ignored all the Bible except its lessons of self-denial. It enjoined a perpetual cloud on the brow and a sequestration from all enjoyment. Professors of such a system so exalted the blessedness of death as almost to justify suicide; but all analogies were against this "savage, sour theology."

No; this world, he said, was not a dungeon where the spirit should chafe for freedom. It was a very Alhambra of delight and beauty apart from sin: and sin was in the man, not in the world. It was not in woodland, stream, or mountain, not in the songsters of the grove. All nature was "loyal to God!" These false friends, however, led the Infidel to argue that he must exalt the present life; and so it was that old-fashioned errors were dressed up under the name of Secularism; but let us not, he urged, yield to this "impudent unbelief." Godliness, said the Scripture, was profitable to all things, having the promise of the life that now is as well as of that which is to come. Christianity was so large that it must have two worlds as its theatre. It claimed and needed both worlds, the present to toil in, the future for rest. So regarded, it was a sunny and beautiful thing to live, even while the cloud might be weeping sweet tears. Yes; those words were true, "This world is very lovely!"

If, then, we saw in this world such adaptation, let us extend the analogy to the next. That was the leading idea of the text. If the same tastes remained with the man then he might be happy if heaven were but a repetition of earth. But the circumstances of Heaven were different, and demanded certain conditions of mind which the natural man had not. Therefore the man must be prepared for the place as well as the place for the man. Were man to enter Heaven as he now is, it would be unparadised for him at once.

Had this change, he asked his hearers, come to them? It was not enough that in time of sorrow or of reverie they should picture Heaven as embracing all earth's beauty without earth's changes—

even as the daring painter had represented the Plains of Heaven—and that so they should cry out for the wings of the dove that they might flee away and be at rest. They might do all this, yet be making no preparation for the Heaven of the Bible—might be only sighing for a Paradise of Poetry. In fact, it was not a "real honest heaven" for which by such anticipations men were made meet.

Let us ponder it well, then. If we educated our children with a definite view towards their future life, " why, in God's name," did we not educate ourselves after the same fashion? We were but infants yet to come of age. When the Books were opened it might be that among those books should be the very primers and school-books out of which we had educated our children, and that the Judge should say to us, " You admitted the principle in your children's case, but you neglected it in yourselves!"

It was a consummate sermon, spreading, in one unbroken flow of eloquence, over more than forty minutes. Dr. Punshon speaks in a rapid manner though with perfect articulation, but so as to render it difficult to transfer to paper the richness and copiousness of his illustrations. The above, it need scarcely be said, are only a few headings of one of the finest sermons to which it has ever been my good fortune to listen, and which nothing but the absence of gown or surplice would have informed me was other than the utterance of an exceptionally eloquent preacher in my own Church; just as, under the same reservation, I might have followed the service without being conscious of anything save one or two very judicious abridgments, or dreaming that I had wandered past the frontier of orthodoxy into the confines of the larger Church of England.

"WAKING" THE PARIS COMMUNE.

THERE are some historical events so eminently and *per se* eligible that in commemorating them one is apt to let imagination outstrip reality as to the period of their recurrence, and, by an eager prolepsis, we forestall the actual day or epoch of their celebration. Jubilees, for instance, have been made to succeed one another at intervals of less than fifty years; and in like manner the fourth anniversary of the Paris Commune was so obvious a reason for congratulation that the working men of London anticipated the actual birthday by twenty-four hours, and celebrated that event on the 17th instead of the 18th of March, 1875. Perhaps some national fitness of things was discovered in thus making the apotheosis of the Commune synchronize with the festival of Ireland's patron saint; indeed, so strongly was I impregnated with this idea that the ceremony to which I was bidden at Franklin

Hall, Castle Street East, gradually assumed less and less of the character of a birthday, and approached nearly to that of an Irish wake. There was considerable truth as well as beauty in the idea; for the Commune died young; and, moreover, the death-day of the Martyrs in old ecclesiastical language was touchingly spoken of as their birthday. Presumably, then, as an "earnest worker for the emancipation of the proletariat" I formed one of a gathering which was neither numerous nor select at the loftily-titled Hall of Franklin. This was evidently a small Dissenting Chapel that had missed its vocation, and degenerated into a meeting-place for earthly instead of heavenly citizens. Every one on the occasion was a *citoyen*—or a *citoyenne*, for there was a sprinkling of the fair sex —and I felt bound to array myself as much in the garb of a "citizen" as possible; that is, I wore a loose coat that had seen better days, a sombrero hat, and voluminous black tie with turn-down collar. So successful was my *tenue* that, though Britannic in build, I had the inexpressible felicity of being addressed in French by an Englishman. He sat in front of me, and my arm was resting on the back of his bench. He suddenly sat back, and we "collided," when he said, "I beg your pardon," but, looking round at the same time, altered his phraseology and said "Pardon, M'sieur." I was not going to betray myself by the dialect of Stratford-atte-Bow, so simply raised my hat in silence; and I feel certain he set me down as a morose "citizen" brooding over my individual losses in the days of July '71. A few of the small assembly were evidently exiles, refugees from the Commune; some of them fine, handsome men, with evidently a history of their own; but most of the attendants, and nearly all the speakers, were clearly what they purported to be, British working men. Their speech "bewrayed" them, even had their appearance not done so. With one or two exceptions, it was halting as that of Moses himself. However, this is hypercritical. It was not the men's eloquence, but their grievance, I had come to hear. I only allude to the last-mentioned fact as an evidence that the speakers really belonged to the class they claimed to do. They were London artisans, not pseudo-patriots from elsewhere assuming the character. Citizen Maltman Barry took the chair, and certainly made up in the substance of his speech anything that was lacking in the manner of its delivery. Citizen Barry had a knack of enunciating the most tremendous doctrines in a calm matter-of-fact way, just as though he had been saying a proposition of Euclid. One-half expected to hear him wind up with a Q. E. D., but he did not; he read a Public Declaration of English working men on the Paris Commune of 1871, of which the following are the exordium and peroration :—

"Fellow working men, the event which we commemorate to-night was one of the grandest in human history. Four years ago to-day France had sounded all the depths but one of national humiliation and disgrace; three months later she had sounded the last and deepest. Four years ago to-day the naked throat of France was under the iron heel of the most pious and brutal of modern conquerors; three months later her professional betrayers were drunk with the life-blood of her best and bravest sons. The Revolution of the 18th of March was essentially a social one. The aim of the working men of Paris, in taking hold of the political machinery of the national government, was not so much to secure their own political ascendancy as to establish by its means a just and true social system, in which the lords of the land and the lords of money would no longer be permitted to *exploit* the working class. . . ."

Then—but at the end of four octavo printed pages read in Citizen Maltman Barry's most deliberate and incisive tones—came the conclusion :—

"The memory of that ruthless massacre will never die. The precious blood of the martyrs of the Commune has not been poured on stony ground, but upon the fertile soil of sympathetic human hearts, where it will some day bring forth fruit even of an hundredfold!"

Citizen Maltman Barry's ambition was to lead the heroes in this new crusade, and to pave the way for the return of the refugees. He would be one of the first to draw the sword in the cause of the workmen of Paris. I suppose I am very unimaginative, but I could not for the life of me picture Citizen Barry with a sword. It seemed as incongruous as Dr. Johnson's idea of helplessness—a man with a fiddle which he couldn't play!

The following resolutions were then proposed, seconded, and carried with scarcely a dissentient:—

" Resolved—

" 1. That this meeting of English working men endorses the principles and approves the actions of the Paris Commune of 1871.

" 2. That this meeting considers the suppression of the Paris Commune to be one of the foulest deeds in the history of the world, and denounces not only the professional assassins of Versailles, but also their bloodthirsty and infamous instigators in this and other countries.

" 3. That this meeting, being of opinion that the

time is come for the consolidation of the militant forces of the working class, with a view to the speedy achievement of its own economical emancipation, recommends to the English working class the fellowship of the International Working Men's Association."

The flowers of oratory in which these resolutions were recommended I can only recall from memory. My note-book, in which I began to enter them, was regarded as so decidedly obnoxious that I had to put it away, lest I should earn the imputation of being a *mouchard*. The ideal hero of Citizen Barry, who proposed the first, was Robespierre; but the seconder reserved his admiration for the Sepoys in the Indian Mutiny, though there was considerable difference of opinion on this subject in the assembly. The one object of execration was the Press, and it was agreed on all hands that the true history of the Paris Commune had yet to be written. The making away with the Archbishop and the hostages was a disagreeable necessity. (Here a voice suggested that all Archbishops should be crucified!) But the working man was always merciful, while the propertied classes were always cruel. The citizen who advanced this proposition hoped to God he might not be mixed up in any revolution; but the one who followed—quite an elderly and anything but Herculean citizen—was all for physical force.

Citizen Johnson, a fine fluently-speaking man, was troubled at comparing the small numbers present with the thousands at that time sitting at the feet of Messrs. Moody and Sankey, and he also waxed wroth at the misrepresentations of the "specials" in the Franco-Prussian War. He himself hoped one day to be the historian of the Commune; and he ran over in rough outline, but with unquestioned eloquence, and amid loud applause, the chief names on the muster-roll of its martyrs, whose example he would make it the sole object of his life to follow.

Finally, Citizen Lessner, speaking to the third resolution, said that a simultaneous demonstration in England would, four years ago, have made the Commune a success. Trades Unionism, he suggested, was not enough; work, as well as capital, must be international. The International was not dead, though it might be dormant, nor was the Commune. All that was wanted for the resuscitation of both was organization.

A collection was made in the course of the evening, and most of those present contributed their coppers to the cause of the Communists. Copies of the Declaration, too, were sold at a penny each, and I managed to possess myself of one of those documents. There was a good deal of discussion during the collection, people talking in little groups of two and three, but the refugees and myself only looked on and listened. It was emphatically a British Communistic meeting. The chief topics of debate were the relevancy of the Indian Mutiny to the subject and the character of Marshal MacMahon, one very enthusiastic man contenting himself with replying to everything that was said to him by anybody, or on any subject, "MacMahon was a brave soldier." He was as persistent in the enunciation of this formula as Wordsworth's little girl, or Citizen Barry in the delivery of his Euclid-like opening address.

When we emerged from the Franklin Hall the little boys greeted us with derisive cheers, "Hooray for the Commoo-noon!" and the bigger boys said to the young ladies by whom they were accompanied, "There goes a lot of sanguinary Frenchmen;" only the young gentlemen used a stronger and more Saxon equivalent for "sanguinary."

THE MUSIC OF THE SPHERES.

A CERTAIN popular comic song contains the following couplet—

> "Much it amazes, to view all the phases
> Of this very versatile, go-ahead age."

And of all the varied subjects in which this same versatility crops up, none is more remarkable than Modern Spiritualism. Some of us once fell into the mistake of considering this rather a static, if not actually a retrogressive, element in society; though the very name of that which is its centre and focus—the "Progressive" Institution and Library—should have told us differently. But facts are more stubborn things still; and a fact it is that we continually find Spiritualism breaking out in new departments and among fresh strata of society.

Table-turning, tilting, and rapping were among the earliest developments. The normal condition of ghosts would appear to be moving furniture and "working the telegraph"—as I believe it is now customary to call it. Then they took to talking and making faces. Fiddling and tambourine-playing have always been favourite accompaniments of the light porterage: and eventually vocal music formed a frequent item in every spiritualistic programme.

I own then I expected some "manifestations" of this last-mentioned character when I received, one day, a circular headed "Marylebone Association of Inquirers into Spiritualism," and saw that it was simply a programme of the "Third Annual Concert," to be held in the Quebec Hall, Seymour Street, Portman Square, on a Monday evening, in the bitter spring of 1875. Failing to see any other connexion between "Inquiring into Spiritualism" and an evening concert, I jumped at once to the conclusion that the spirits were going to sing and play. I looked down the programme more carefully. Yes; there was a spiritual element in it, though at first all had looked secular and materialistic. Two ladies were to open with the overture to "Semiramide." No doubt the ghost of Ninus would put in an appearance at the appropriate passage in the music. "The Chough and Crow to roost are gone" was there—that was weird and ghostly too. "Come where my love lies dreaming" savoured of Messrs. Moore and Burgess, true, but was still capable of a nice mesmeric meaning. "Hush thee, my babie!" might apply to Mrs. Guppy's infant, who was a writing medium at five months. Yes; there could no longer be any doubt about it. A spice of *diablerie* itself was to be introduced, for the last item but one was a "Fra Diavolo" duet. I must go. Whatever other engagements stood in the way, I would sacrifice them all as sternly as Mr. Disraeli when bidden to the Speaker's dinner.

Forth I went then, that bitter Monday night, in quest of the Music of the Spheres; and found the Hall in Seymour Street pretty well filled with what looked very like an ordinary concert audience. There was one well-known female medium in the front seats, it is true; and I located myself as near her as I decently could, feeling sure that the "influences" would centre there as a nucleus. Ladies and gentlemen, too, kept appearing and disappearing through a sort of secret door that opened beneath the platform, and there was considerable delay in commencing, which I thought looked favourable—like "getting up the conditions."

One fact came home vividly to my consciousness during this period of enforced delay, and that was that the feminine portion of the Marylebone Inquirers into Spiritualism (who, I could see, were going to be the exécutantes) differed entirely from the ordinary run of medium, being neither antiquated, portly, nor frumpish; but exceedingly juvenile and comely withal. An erratic sort of notion crossed my mind that, if I "inquired" anywhere, I should like the "sphere" to be Marylebone.

Whilst I was thinking thus a violent rapping suddenly took place, and then I knew that I was not to be disappointed. The rapping spread all over the building. It was commenced on the ground-floor, and soon spread into the gallery. It was exactly like the stamping of human feet on the floor varied with the perpendicular "prods" of umbrellas. In fact, the raps so thoroughly resembled the effects which would be thus produced that I discovered these were actually the efficient causes. The audience were getting impatient, and used their feet and umbrellas in the ordinary manner to signify that fact.

Then two of the comely young ladies played the overture to "Semiramide" on an asthmatic cottage piano, from which it required an act of thaumaturgy to extract the ghost of a sound. No other ghost came. I looked in vain for the apparition of "Ninny's Tomb." Two well-known male mediums entered during the performance; and the circumstance cheered me, as I hoped the powers might be increased. The

Chough and Crow did not go to roost as announced; but, in place of that ornithological retirement, Barnby's beautiful four-part song, "Sweet and Low," was as beautifully rendered by two other of the comely and *spirituelles* young Inquirers, aided by two capable male Investigators. It struck me that the spirits must be deaf indeed to calls from the vasty deep, if they could hear that delicious quartette warbled round a Marylebone table, and still keep away from the N.W. postal district. As a rule, the singing at séances is enough to scare any sensible or sensitive spirit, far more effectually than the crow of chanticleer. I felt still more than I had done previously that Marylebone is the place to inquire in. Peter—I mean Miss Showers's Peter—was by no means equal in vocal power to the Investigator who followed, requesting Maud to join him in the garden, or another who gave himself out, in a basso profondo, as a "Friar of Orders Grey." I was just beginning to feel that, whether the music came directly or indirectly from the "spheres" or not, certainly the invisibles must have "impressed" those who compiled the programme; when, lo, the weird duet from Trovatore was over, the irrepressible tenor's love had lain dreaming, despite the efforts of four other masculine Inquirers to awaken her, and the First Part was at its close, when an incongruous Inquirer marched to the piano and tumbled down all my beautiful Castles in the Air—that is, in the spheres—by playing a selection from "La Fille de Madame Angot." I never in my life realized so forcibly the truth of the adage that from the sublime to the ridiculous is but a single step. I should have left abruptly, only I wanted to hear a pianoforte solo played by a lady whose fame had already reached me as volunteer organist at the Sunday spiritualistic services.

Between the parts occurred another "hiatus valdè deflendus." The audience seemed to like it; for all the Inquirers knew one another, and talked and told spirit-stories to their hearts' content. They were all very friendly and sociable with me, too; and one gentleman, seeing my loneliness, came right across the room to give me the latest thing in ghosts. I should have liked to commence inquiries forthwith; but I fancy the Marylebone maidens had seen me making notes, and perhaps fancied I was "taking them off." Personally or artistically, certainly there was no temptation to do that, except in a literal sense, which would occur to no well-regulated mind. I realized the position; I had been present at an exceptionally good evening concert, and the music only came from the spheres in the same sense as all good music is confessedly a matter of inspiration.

When the interval was over, the fair young organist appeared in due course, but sang, "She wore a wreath of roses," instead of playing her solo, and I left when the excellent quartette I had before listened to with so much pleasure had sung "Hush thee, my babie." There was no baby—certainly not Mrs. Guppy's—only a sweet little frizzle-wigged, golden-haired girl in the stall before me. I wondered whether she were a Marylebone Inquirer. I adore little curly-headed girls of three, and should have liked to have an "Inquiry" with this one. She sat prim, as though she had been thirteen or thirty, instead of three, and I knew it was no use waiting for Fra Diavolo. I had as little chance of anything from that sphere as from the others.

One thing I had gained by my visit, above and beyond the enjoyment of an evening's music, and that was I had got out of the silly notion that spiritualists were only spiritualists, and that Marylebone Inquirers must of necessity be always inquiring. It was a social aspect of the subject; a friendly gathering of those who were joined together by common interests in one engrossing subject, but who wisely refrained from bringing that subject always to the front. When I remembered my hasty conclusion that I should get some music from the spheres, it put me in mind of the story I once heard about a "lion-hunting" lady who was vulgar enough to trot out any celebrities for her own glorification as showing that clever people came to her house. She had secured a well-known singer as her guest; and no sooner had the unlucky tenor set foot within her drawing-room than, with vulgar and offensive impetuosity, the hostess said, "O, dear Mr. ——, I am so glad to see you. Will you give us one of your charming *morceaux?*" In reply the justly offended vocalist said, "With pleasure, madam, in one moment. But I see Captain ——, of the Artillery, just entering the room. Ask him to *fire off a big gun,* and when he has done that I will sing you a song!" What right had I to expect the Marylebone Inquirers to be always inquiring, or the Marylebone spirits to be perpetually laying on for my edification the Music of the Spheres?

A SPIRITUALISTIC TEA.

It ought to be a great consolation to those who mourn over the spread of materialism in England to learn that the London Spiritualists observed the twenty-seventh anniversary of the Rochester Knockings on the evening of—one hesitates to say it—All Fools' Day. Without dwelling unduly on the suitability of that particular day for such an epoch, it may safely be averred that the unquestioned spread of Spiritualism in England is the best guarantee possible against the advance of Materialism, as that term is generally understood, for it is quite certain that if the doctrines of the Spiritualists are right, science must to a great extent be wrong. If, for instance, a single case of levitation of the human body were adequately proved, it would be quite opposed to the idea of gravitation being that universally diffused force which we have fondly believed it to be since the days of Sir

Isaac Newton. But we were thinking of no such ponderous subjects as this when we adjourned to the Co-operative Hall on All Fools' Day. What had gravitation to do with us or we with gravitation when five-and-twenty pretty lady mediums—bearing such idyllic names as Lottie Fowler, Annie Eva Fay, and the more mundane one of Mrs. Guppy—were going to " preside at the urns?" It sounded like a warning of impending fate, but it was not the urn of destiny, but the urn of domestic tea at which these *spirituelles* ladies were to preside. There certainly was no absence of regard for the "material" comforts of this sphere observable on the part of those hungry and thirsty souls who came early so as to have a long evening before them, and seemed determined to have their eighteen-pennyworth for their eighteenpence. By the way, very few of the lady mediums put in an appearance, and those who did had a hard time of it. An hour and three-quarters having been allowed for tea, the tables were put back as though we were going to "co-operate" like ordinary mortals for a dance. But it was the soirée that was coming on now. "Swarry" was to be, as Sam Weller says, not "on the table," but on the platform at eight o'clock. The chair having been taken by a Mr. Everitt, and the various speakers ranged duly round the president, a most imposing cordon of spiritual ladies encircled them as with a garland of many colours, and filled up every inch of the platform, which, being fitted into an apse at the extreme end of the hall, had a most unsatisfactory effect on the eloquence of the speakers. The Chairman read (instead of speaking) the opening address, wherein he mentioned that one purpose of the evening's gathering was to present to a "veteran medium," Mr. Wallace, a purse of money which had been collected for him. The origin of this Wallace fund was curious and characteristic. Mr. Wallace had been working as a medium for more than twenty years, but his professional associations did not seem to have been commercially successful, and Mr. Wallace being involved in difficulties, another medium saw a vision of an empty bag resting on the veteran medium's shoulders surmounted by a legend which bade him "go and fill it." He took the hint, and the result was the presentation on All Fools' Day of the very satisfactory sum of 112*l*. to the veteran medium, together with a handsome vellum testimonial beautifully emblazoned by a writer "under spirit control." Speeches of ten minutes' length were made by several orators, and among them Mr. Jencken, a barrister, who had recently married Miss Kate Fox, the recipient of the original Rochester Knockings, their union being blest by a medium baby, who wrote automatically at five months old. Then Mrs. Tappan delivered an inspirational address and improvised a poem. Next came the presentation, and Mr. Wallace bore away the well-filled bag in triumph (one would venture to hope not without "remembering" his mediumistic friend whose vision occurred so opportunely). The ladies warbled; and one clever gentleman imitated a fiddle and a flute, and the sharpening of a saw, and the buzzing of a blue-bottle fly. Another, almost as clever in his way, recited the "Death of Montrose," until it was close upon eleven o'clock, and all the virtuous people sheered off. If they got anything like through the programme they must have stopped until the small hours. The Co-operative Hall is a large one, and it was quite full, and this gathering, we must recollect, only represents one moiety of the London Spiritualists, for there is what less transcendental people would call a "split" in their ranks, one-half following the lead of Mr. Burns at the Progressive Institution, the others having seceded and established an organized body, bearing the portentous title of the British National Association of Spiritualists. Mr. Everitt beautifully embodied the ideal of perfect fairness which should appertain to a chairman by presiding at this meeting, which was set on foot through Mr. Burns, though he himself is a prominent member on the Council of the British National Association. The association, by the way, has just established itself in head-quarters at 38, Great Russell Street, near the British Museum, so that London now possesses two great "national" institutions in the same street, and almost within a stone's throw of each other.

A FREE CHRISTIAN CHURCH.

There is something at first sight as fascinating in the idea of a Free Christian Church as in Mr. Bright's notion of a Free Breakfast Table—a sort of Rule-Britannia, Britons-never-never-shall-be-slaves ring lurks in the very title; and the more judicious Unitarians who are anxious to keep *au courant* with the times are wise in their generation to merge the more distinctive in the general title, which has the transcendent merit of not saying more than is necessary, and leaving imagination to expatiate to any extent as to the immunity from all restraint of those who assume the title.

And if a Free Christian Church seems so attractive in its point of contrast to our tolerably liberal Establishment, with its easy discipline and liberties only prevented from degenerating into licence by the prospective action of the Public Worship Bill, what must such a cultus be to a man who passes to its influences from the very midst of Roman bondage? I had heard of such an one on the outskirts of London—for West Croydon is but a London suburb now—the Rev. Robert Rodolph Suffield, at whose chapel Mr. Voysey made his *début* when he left the Established Church some years ago; and it struck me I should like to see in what direction the mind of an ex-priest would run when it shook off the fetters of Roman responsibility, and became free to act for itself. Mr. Suffield left the Church of Rome simply, I had heard, because the dogma of Papal Infallibility was fulminated from the Vatican, and had no further quarrel with the Holy See. He was not, I was given to understand, a vulgar convert who went about crying "Unclean, unclean!" as to all the institutions he had left behind him; and yet here he had shot off from Rome to a very advanced stage of Rationalism. Clearly the Père Suffield was a man to be interviewed, and I interviewed him accordingly.

Mr. Suffield's little iron church stands close to the West Croydon Station, and the congregation was already assembling when I arrived. It is the very tiniest of its race; and was fairly full some time before service commenced. A large harmonium stood about the centre, and an excellent choir performed the musical portion of the worship, which consisted of hymns taken from the Rev. J. Martineau's collection. The prayers were extemporaneous, or read from MS., I could not discover which. They were very eloquent and impressive, and had the rare merit of not erring on the side of prolixity. There was, of course, a distinct theistic tone traceable throughout. I had come, however, to hear the sermon.

Taking for his text the words from St. Paul's Epistle to the Thessalonians (i. 5, 21), "Prove all things, hold fast that which is good," Mr. Suffield—who, by the way, wore no surplice or gown throughout the service—stated that Revivalism and Ritualism were the two popular religions. Were they true? Were they beneficial? If not, should they be supplanted by some other creed, or by a principle, a method of action? He thought we had had enough of creeds, new and old. The answer, of course, was by an appeal to common sense—in other words, by Rationalism.

"Rationalism, as I understand the term," he said, "does not by any means exclude mystery or disparage poetry, romance, and the ideal. It says they are beautiful and glorious, but they are handmaids, not masters. Rationalism does not deny the mysterious in the universe. In the very depths of our reason we recognise the mysterious. Rationalism does not deny the hidden influences of God, but Rationalism says even such must be judged by our common sense and conscience, by the laws of right reason, which God has given to man, whereby he can be saved from becoming the slave of absurd and dangerous illusions. Two of those illusions I now proceed to glance at, namely, Revivalism and Ritualism. I use these words in the way they are understood in England by the common sense of people who have no object to be attained by playing at words. I address honest, straightforward persons, and not those induced by Dr. John Henry Newman or Mr. Maurice to use words in a non-natural sense, whereby language, creeds, and formularies can be made to mean anything but what straightforward persons know full well was originally meant.

"Thus persons wishing to darken counsel with words, might enter on sophistical arguments to prove that we are all Revivalists and all Ritualists. It is very easy to prove that a Quaker is a Ritualist, and that a Rationalist is a Revivalist; and as there is no one in the world but what deems reason to have an office, it would be easy to prove that a Romanist is a Rationalist. I would commend such amusing but deceptive subtleties to the ladies and young people who belong to the mystical æsthetic section of a well-known Church party, and to all other people who, like Dr. Newman, are rather ashamed of their religion, and therefore defend it with the most pertinacious, subtle, and indignant skill. Juvenile dreamers must dream their dreams, and fanciful persons must weave their fancies, and clever ecclesiastics must explain away encyclicals, trusting to Providence and to the confusion of tongues that the Pope may never hear the explanation. I speak to those who, when they say a thing, mean it, and not its opposite; who, when they read poetry, mean poetry; when they recite a creed, mean dogma —to those who consider that accuracy of language, that simple straightforward veracity of word and act is an essential in religion as in business.

"Thus, by Revivalism I understand the Evangelical Religion in prominent action. The Evangelical Religion, though of small numerical consideration in the world generally, is in England numerically strong, embracing as it does about half the Established Church, and all the less intellectual members of the Congregationalist, Presbyterian, Baptist, and Wesleyan sects. Dr. Arnold defines the Evangelical to be 'a good Christian, with a narrow understanding, a bad education, and little knowledge of the world;' but as some of the disciples of Ritualism might equally lay claim to be comprehended in that definition, we must particularize. The Evangelical, like the Ritualist, believes in the depravity of all mankind, the eternity of future punishment, and the redemption procured for a few by the satisfaction rendered to God by the death of His Son, who is also the eternal and coequal God. So far the Ritualist and Evangelical agree; now comes the difference. The Evangelical says that the saving effect of that blood of the God-Son is obtained through an act of the mind, through a strong feeling generally called forth by an external mode. The Ritualist says it is obtained through Sacraments, that is, through certain rites administered by men divinely appointed for that office. Thus, Anglican Ritualists and Romanists entirely agree in principle; the only difference is, that each considers the other damned in consequence of a mistake about the persons commissioned to administer these rites. The Anglican Ritualist regrets that the Romanist is in the deadly sin of schism, he being separate from Archbishop Tait, while claiming that he himself is the true sacerdotal successor of the Apostles. The Romanist at once anathematizes and ridicules the Anglican Ritualist as entangled in the double devilry of schism and heresy. The Evangelical applies the blood of Christ to his soul by the vivid effort of his imagination. The Ritualist applies it to his soul by the more elaborate process of a mechanical act performed in the spirit and way prescribed to him by his priestly superior. The Evangelical gets his minister, or evangelist, or deacon, to decide for him whether the vivid act of his imagination has been of the right degree and sort.

"The act of the imagination whereby an Evangelical persuades himself that he has got the blood of Christ applied to his good is called conversion. When such conversions are wrought on a large scale, it is called a Revival. Thus an absurd and lowering superstition is all at once brought to light and propagated in England. Most chapel-going people, and a very large number of church-going people, hold the Evangelical Religion; thus a well-advertised Revival ought to attract great numbers, almost as many as would be attracted by a popular idol in Northern India, by a miraculous Madonna in France, by a prophetical utterance in the Holy City of the Mormons, or by a Kenealy gathering in Hyde Park. The Revivalist seeks Mr. Moody in the inquiry-room. The Ritualist seeks Mr. Mackonochie in the vestry. These superstitions are melancholy, but as they exist it is best that they should be made manifest. Amidst these superstitions Rationalism is advancing with firm and onward steps.

"Rationalism would triumph much more widely if Rationalists were not so compromising, so timid, and so diffident. Many Rationalists say there have always been superstitions, the world is full of superstitions now. Consistent Rationalists only form the smaller groups of the independent and the thoughtful, therefore we have not courage to proclaim our Rationalism. Many Rationalists are inconsistent, and conceal themselves under forms they disbelieve, or content themselves with an indolent freedom—rearing their children as serfs. As Rationalism, according to my definition, implies the supremacy of conscience as well as of common sense, I do not acknowledge under that religious and honourable name those indolent people who have not the courage to avow their convictions.

"The Evangelical Religion, never strong in the intelligence and learning of its votaries, has been losing more and more amongst the thoughtful members of churches and chapels. Ministers of Orthodox chapels are compelled to keep in the background the real basis of their sect, and to retain the presence of their more educated hearers by adopting the rationalistic methods, and softening down those dogmas which chiefly shock the natural consciences, and are chiefly opposed to science and common sense; but the rank and file still cling to the mediæval theology.

"The hopeful sign of the recent revivalist movement has been its rationalistic basis in external management; it has traded upon the principles of common experience. Miracles in the way of sudden deaths have come in afterwards to magnify the Divine mercy; but all the groundwork has been laid for months. The two Evangelists formerly visited England, and took their measure of us, and then laid their plans with a prudence deserving of success. A special newspaper was started; all the Evangelical agencies had been put in motion for months; all rational means adopted with consummate care; the system of large outlays and large returns; all the Evangelical ministers and clergy united to co-operate and to speak; all the Orthodox chapel and church-going population appealed to for the whole of the existing Evangelical element; the very music and hymns practised for months; advertising on an enormous scale; telling anecdotes invented, and discourses carefully prepared and repeated over and over again. When the *Christian World* commenced reporting the Evangelical utterances, the editor received a solicitor's letter warning him that the Evangelists would prosecute him for breach of copyright if he continued the publication. Indeed, the publication of their discourses and anecdotes had already led to serious inconveniences. So the preparations of this movement were eminently business-like, and therefore deserving both praise and success. In its progress the rationalistic element has never been quite absent, and therefore the mischief done has not been so great as might have been. Thus the medical statements testify that this movement has not produced so many cases of insanity and immorality as frequently arise in America.

"The reckless statements as to miraculous interventions made by the Evangelists, I regard as amongst the proofs of their convictions and inaccuracy. For what conceivable reason their sincerity and personal goodness should be doubted, passes my apprehension. We have daily experience as to the positiveness of credulity, and the power of personal conviction as to foolish and mischievous superstitions, and all superstitions have elements of truth, goodness, and common sense. No good man will impute insincerity and bad intentions to another unless compelled to do so by irrefragable evidence. I attach as little credence to Mr. Moody's anecdotes as to his superstition and his sudden deaths; but when a man has persuaded himself that he is a divine agent, arguments easily arise.

"'The Apostles were ignorant and foolish men; I

am an ignorant and foolish man, therefore I am an Apostle.' 'Clever people laughed at the Apostles; clever people laugh at me, therefore I am an Apostle.' 'The Apostles worked miracles; I am an Apostle, therefore I work miracles.' 'Saul was suddenly converted on his way to Damascus and became a Christian, therefore no one can be a Christian unless he be suddenly converted.' 'The Evangelists spoke about Jesus Christ; and I speak about Jesus Christ, therefore I am an Evangelist.' 'Those who opposed the Apostles, thereby blasphemed Jesus Christ, and unless converted went to hell; those who oppose me, blaspheme Jesus Christ, and die and go to hell;' and Mr. Thomas Walker blasphemed Jesus Christ, in Mr. Moody his Evangelist; he was struck dead in his hotel, and would have gone to hell, but a newspaper reporter, in spite of the prayers against a critical spirit, thought he should like to hear what the coroner said about the sudden death. It appeared that Mr. Thomas Walker, though deserving death, had not actually died, but had made a hearty breakfast and driven off with a companion in a fly the morning after his very sensible jokes at good Mr. Moody's absurdities.

"No wonder that Evangelists object to reporters as much as they denounce argument, proof, and criticism. Dr. Rowland Williams, Vicar of Croydon, and a

Canon A.D. 1497, preaching at St. Paul's, said:—
'We must root out printing, or printing will root out us.'

"However, they cannot escape all the inconveniences of publicity.

"All this is very sad. It is the same absence of mental ballast which leads others to seek the like superstitious support from a priest, a cope, chasuble, and confessional.

> "Leave your dry unfruitful dogmas,
> Faith unreasoning, credence blind;
> All the little narrow circles,
> Where you wander self-confined,
> Splashing in the mire and puddle
> Of your small sectarian pond,
> Heedless of the mighty ocean,
> And the boundless Heavens beyond.
>
> "Is there nothing more to preach of
> Than the letter of your law?
> Nothing left to feed the people
> But the barren husk and straw?
> Nothing for the unbelievers
> In a creed their souls disclaim,
> But eternity of torment,
> And the unconsuming flame?
>
> "Nobler themes than these invite you,
> If you'd throb as throbs the time;
> And would speak to hearts o'erburdened
> Words more human, more sublime!
>
> "God—our God—whose works surround us,
> Preaches in the summer wind,
> In the tempest of the ocean,
> In the silence of the mind;

In the sparkles of the planets,
In the splendour of the sun,
In the voice of all Creation—
'God is love, and God is one!'

" God is love—and love eternal;
All things change, but nothing dies;
Find this Gospel, and expound it
In the Bible of the skies.

" O'er the starry vault of midnight,
See the countless worlds outspread—
Homes perchance of nobler creatures
Than our planet ever bred;
Larger than the earth and fairer,
And then limit, if you can,
God's great love to one poor corner,
And one little creature—man!"

The sermon, which I have thus abridged, was full of humour, and often soared into eloquence; but I am quite sure either a Revivalist or Ritualist would have joined issue with its logic; while of course those who heard it had come with the foregone conclusion that Rationalism was the only panacea for all the ills that religious flesh is heir to.

In the afternoon Mr. Suffield lectured at St. George's Hall on Monasticism; and I followed him as devoutly as though I had been a promising convert myself. He sketched most amusingly the monastic institutions of the Middle Ages, and insisted on it that the ascetic portion was only one exceptional adjunct of their system. Monasteries were the centres of intellectual culture and artistic taste, and agricultural skill; while the fathers excelled even in such pursuits as horse-racing and steeple-chasing. They acted plays in their sacristies and refectories which were so broad as to shock even the barons of the period. Therefore, argued Mr. Suffield, the best way to reproduce them was not by copying literally their ascetic institutions and customs, but to keep *au courant* with the times in all these different departments of social progress. A very pleasant and possibly not an untrue view to take of those same Monks of old.

It was the doctrine of the Papal Infallibility which drove Mr. Suffield from the Roman Catholic Church out into the far countries, as it seems likely to drive many more; but the way in which he speaks of the old system shows what a hold it takes and keeps upon its votaries. I quote from a pamphlet of his entitled "Five Letters on a Conversion to Roman Catholicism":—

For twenty years I was Apostolic missionary, and discharged duties not unimportant in many parts of England, Ireland, Scotland, and France. I published a work ("The Crown of Jesus"), which obtained the widest circulation, was publicly commended by all the archbishops, and received the Papal blessing. I left the Roman Catholic Church on the day on which the Papal Infallibility was proclaimed. I never incurred, even in the smallest matter, the censure of any ecclesiastical superior. I never even had a quarrel with any Roman Catholic, lay or ecclesiastic. Therefore I have none of the bitterness which sometimes is found as the result of conflict. I have the most perfect and intimate acquaintance with all the minutest workings of the system in all departments of the Roman Church. All who have known me in public or in private during the last three years, can testify to the affectionate kindness of my feelings and speech as to all the Roman Catholics whom I have known at any period of my life.

* * * *

For myself, under the circumstances I felt bound to speak, but it has been with pain. When Anglican converts have left the English Church—in which they had passed so many happy and holy years, they speedily published against it diatribes, in which they seemed to delight, for they dipped their pen in gall. I cannot say that it is with any approach to such feelings I write of Roman Catholics; I know that, theoretically, they cannot reciprocate my affection and esteem; but it has been always a delight to me when I have been able to clear them from unjust aspersions; it is with sadness that I warn against that fearful despotism, under which they must, as time advances, be prostrated more and more. May some of these, dear to me by a thousand memories, obtain courage to investigate, and then, conscientiously shaking off the incubus, arise as the freed children of the Universal Father.

A SCOTCH SYNOD IN LONDON.

THERE is something almost pathetic in the position of a faith, strongly bound up with one country, located in another, however tolerant. It always savours of singing the Lord's song in a strange land; and though Presbyterianism may be said to be thoroughly domesticated in England, yet I can never hear the broad accents of a Scotch minister south of the Tweed without feeling as if I were listening to those same Jewish captives "by the waters of Babylon." I was attracted to Edward Irving's old church in Regent Square, one Monday evening in May, by an announcement that the Scottish Synod for England would commence its annual sitting there, when the Rev. Donald Fraser would preach; and on bending my steps thither found a large congregation assembled, or rather assembling, for they dropped in by detachments during the entire evening, the service commencing at the unusually early hour of six.

I was handed to a seat by a tall verger in a dress-coat, with the most unmistakably Caledonian visage, who smiled blandly as familiar members of Dr. Dykes's congregation took the seats he assigned them, many of the front pews being separated by a red cord from the rest of the church to accommodate the impending Synod. Precisely at six o'clock Dr. Fraser ascended the pulpit, habited in gown and bands, his snow-white hair looking from the distance almost like a forensic wig, and giving him the appearance of a barrister. A curious oak canopy surmounts the pulpit, probably by way of sounding-board, but it looks very much as though it would topple over and precipitate the preacher from its dizzy height into the pew below.

The service, which was striking from its utter simplicity, began with the singing of a metrical psalm to one of the quaint old Scottish tunes. This was followed by an Old Testament reading from Ezekiel, in which Dr. Fraser's well-known powers of elocution were admirably displayed. An extempore prayer bearing on ministerial duties came next, and then one of the hymns following the psalms in the collection used at the Church, and specially adapted "for ministers." The singing was of course unaccompanied, and led by a precentor with powerful voice, who occupied a position below the pulpit. Then Dr. Fraser read 1 Peter v., and immediately proceeded to the exposition, which was to form his sermon for the evening. The chapter commences, it will be remembered, with the words—" The elders"—that is, the presbyters—" which are among you I exhort, who am also an elder"—or presbyter; but in nearly every instance Dr. Fraser used the term bishop as equivalent in its sense of overseer to that of presbyter. The Episcopate was needful now as then, he said. It was necessary that each congregation should have its group of bishop-presbyters, and that these should meet in Presbyteries and Synods. Peter had an overwhelming claim to personal authority, but it was, said the preacher, only little men who stood on official importance. Real heroes like Peter and Paul put themselves on a level with their fellow-men. Feed the flock—" episcopize" the flock—was the command. (It is perhaps impossible for those out of the Anglican Church to understand how strangely these "episcopal" terms sounded coming from such a source.) This shepherding of the sheep was the crucial question of the day. It was no use to say that all presbyters are bishops, unless the Christian episcopate could be recognised in the presbyters above the chaos of system, anti-system, over-system, and under-system. Then, again, they were not to lord it over God's heritage. They were not "lord bishops." So, when the chief-shepherd, the archbishop (and there was no archbishop but Christ), should appear they should receive a crown of glory at the great day of coronation!

Another hymn called "Pressing on" followed, and then Dr. Fraser descended from the pulpit, and, occupying the Moderator's chair, "constituted the Synod by prayer." Names were called over, and Dr. Fraser proposed as his successor in the office of Moderator for the ensuing year one who had been thirty years in the ministry, and nine years in his present charge, the Rev. John Mathieson, minister of Hampstead. The name was received with much applause; and Mr. Mathieson, being fetched from the vestry by the smiling man in the dress-coat, passed to the Moderator's chair, and read from MS. his inaugural address.

In broad Scottish accent quite different from Dr. Fraser's diction, which had not the suspicion of a "brogue," Mr. Mathieson eloquently dwelt on the present aspects of Presbyterianism in England. He congratulated his co-religionists on their unity, while they were, he said, "broad" enough to embrace different opinions on minor matters. He threw in a word of commendation on the American evangelists, "who have moved the myriad-peopled city," he said, "as it has never been moved before." It might have been that their own ministers had relied too much on intellect, and that God was teaching them a lesson in these men, whose lips had been touched by a live coal from the altar. In the last ten years the English congregations had increased from 106 to 160, and that not chiefly in the North, where such increase might have been expected, but in the South, where they were more scattered. Perhaps the state of the Church of England might lead people to look at Presbyterianism as the safeguard against Romanism under the form of Ritualism. He concluded a most interesting excursus by dwelling on the prospects of Church extension, of union with the United Presbyterians, and eventually of a complete unanimity which might once more make people say, "Behold, how these Christians love one another!"

COMMUNION SUNDAY.

It is only under some reservation that the following ecclesiastical experience can be said to bear reference to Unorthodox London, or indeed to the metropolis in any sense, since its locale is the Highlands of Scotland. But of the Cockney traveller, even more than of the Parisian, it may be said that he carries his nationality with him; and in the land where the Presbyterian is the established form of faith, I felt myself very literally indeed "Unorthodox London." My subject and myself seemed for the moment to change places.

With that charming inconsistency observable in some perverse natures, I found myself one year waiting until summer and autumn had quite departed, excursion trains were at an end, and tourist tickets all expired, when I set out on an unseasonable journey to the capital of the Highlands. From thence I wrote, with a bright November sun shining down on the Ness which flowed under my windows, as if that luminary were disposed to fool me to the top of my bent, and make believe that it was only rather late summer; while the salmon were leaping as though they enjoyed the joke too.

I invented something I called "business," which was sufficient to satisfy myself, if nobody else, as to the sanity of the step I took in suddenly rushing off from London to Inverness, and by the way I stopped at Perth to pay a visit to the home of the "Fair Maid" (which I found remarkably like other third-rate tenements, rather out of repair, down a back street), and also to have a look at the round tower which forms a curious appendage to the Cathedral at Brechin, the meaning whereof is just as obscure as it was before I left the flags of Fleet Street. Having attended to these preliminary details, I pushed on to Inverness.

It is very refreshing "to one who hath been long in city pent" to notice the first symptoms of having got across the Scottish border. It came to me in the shape of an exceedingly intoxicated Caledonian drover who got into my carriage in mistake for his own, somewhere north of Carlisle, after alighting in an infructuous search for more "whusky." He had been selling cattle at Manchester, and told me twenty times over of a certain little "Hieland bull" which he had bought for "eight pun" and sold for "twenty-fower pun." He boasted that he "niver tell't a lee to a mon; but, egh, I have tell't lees to t' weemmen," he added, and the old goat told me lots of unsavoury stories of his youth, illustrating his faculty for "tellin' lees to t' weemmen."

When I landed in the High Street of Inverness with a small boy carrying my bag, it seemed as though I had entered a city of the dead, and I asked the lad whether the shops were usually shut by 6.25; but the youthful aborigine was thinking of his impending "saxpence," and did not care to enter on the matter. At the lodging I had engaged I found the landlady had gone out. It was "Fast Day," the servant girl informed me; and it seemed likely to prove literally so in my case. I went back to the station, and I found nothing but sandwiches, which I rejected, as I had been living on them for the last two days. At the Station Hotel the waiter was much too genteel to realize the idea of a chop, and proposed a heavy dinner, which I declined, much to his disgust, and was going home resolved to fast like the rest of the good folks at Inverness—though I had no idea what they or I had done to be reduced to such a measure—when lo! I saw the hospitable door of the Queen's Hotel standing open, and on representing my bonâ fide travelling condition to the landlady was soon supplied with all I wanted, and tended by the prettiest waitress it has ever been my lot to see on either side of the border.

If it was easier to find a god than a man in ancient Athens, it is certainly easier to find a church than a house in Inverness; and I had arrived on the day of preparation for the six-monthly celebration of the Communion. During the whole of Thursday the shops were shut, and thus it was I found the Highland metropolis so silent. I no longer regretted—especially after its pleasant sequel—my little difficulty as to a meal, since I should be in a position to see some of the observances of a Scotch Communion Sunday.

On "Sabbath" morn, however, a sort of *esprit de corps* led me to attend first of all the celebration of the Communion according to the Scottish office at the Episcopal Cathedral. I went thither on Friday to morning service, when I formed the only adult male element in the congregation, the rest consisting of three ladies and a boy. There was a goodly gathering on the Sunday morning, however, and the Cathedral is a splendid building only just consecrated. As I went along Ness Walk, and by the fairy-like islands, I saw every imaginable sort of conveyance bringing the country folk in to Communion Sunday. Indeed, throughout the two days previously, the city resembled some Catholic place on the Continent; the good wives, in their clean white caps, coming and going incessantly, with their Prayer-books in their hands. No possible devotion to the Mass could exceed that of the Scotch folk in prospect of Communion Sunday. No doubt the infrequency of the celebration has something to do with the solemnity of its observance.

The morning service and sermon at the Cathedral were both taken by the Provost, who was quite unassisted, and had a hard morning's work. The choir was good, the boys' voices being especially clear, putting one in mind of the fresh crisp Highland air the children breathed; while the faint Scotch accent, discernible in their articulation, rather added to the piquancy of their singing. The chants were Anglican, and everything was exceedingly hearty, without a symptom of anything that could be called *excess*. In fact the cultus of Inverness Cathedral would hardly be deemed "High" in London, but it was exceedingly imposing.

The sermon was a special one on the subject of the death of a member of the congregation, and the

Provost took a double text—"The heart knoweth its own bitterness, and a stranger doth not intermeddle with its joy;" and "Rejoice with them that do rejoice, and weep with them that weep." He traced the growth of Christian life here as consisting to a large extent in the development of sympathy and elimination of selfishness. When we took a larger view and looked beyond we saw that, except in so far as individuality was retained, there would be no bounds to sympathy, none of those limitations which here made up personality. The address was short but exceedingly eloquent and much to the purpose; so that the previous disappointment which I felt at not hearing the Bishop himself was quite removed.

The Scottish Communion office bears considerable resemblance to the English, but has its points of difference as well. It opens with the Lord's Prayer and Collect for Purity, but the use of the Ten Commandments is optional, their place being supplied alternatively (and it was so on this occasion) by Christ's Summary of the Decalogue. After this the final Kyrie was sung; and then came a prayer for grace and strength, or a collect for the Queen. Provost Powell, like a loyal subject, chose the latter. The Collect, Epistle, and Gospel for the day succeeded, and the general congregation left after the Offertory.

The special Communion Service then commenced with the Sursum Corda and Sanctus. Immediately came the Prayer of Consecration, which is longer than in the English office, comprising, besides our prayer, a special Oblation of the Elements (as in the Greek Eucharistic office), an Invocation, and certain portions of our Church Militant Prayer. Then came the "Prayer for the whole State of Christ's Church," which, again, is longer than ours, and comprises the following beautiful sentences—which were specially appropriate under existing circumstances :—

"We bless Thy holy name for all Thy servants who, having finished their course in faith, do now rest from their labours.

"And we yield unto Thee most high praise and hearty thanks for the wonderful grace and virtue declared in all Thy saints, who have been the choice vessels of Thy grace, and the lights of the world in their several generations, most humbly beseeching Thee to give us grace to follow the example of their steadfastness in Thy Faith and obedience to Thy holy commandments, that, at the day of the general resurrection, we and all they who are of the Mystical Body of Thy Son, may be set on His Right Hand, and hear that, His most joyful voice, 'Come ye Blessed of my Father, inherit the kingdom prepared for you from the foundation of this world.'" Then followed the Lord's Prayer repeated, the Confession, Absolution, and Comfortable Words, as in our office. The sentences of administration were simply 'The Body of our Lord Jesus Christ which was given for thee;' and 'The Blood of our Lord Jesus Christ which was shed for thee preserve thy body and soul unto everlasting life,' the communicant responding 'Amen.' I noticed that the celebrant maintained the Eastward Position throughout. The office concluded with a Thanksgiving and the Gloria in Excelsis.

After leaving the Cathedral I went to the Free High Kirk, where I believe there was just one place vacant, into which I was put; and I fear this one place was obtained by undue compression of the polite pew-opener. I was rather dismayed to find that I was among the faithful, the non-communicants being in the gallery. The desks in the pews were covered with white linen, and the deacons were already bearing round huge plates of bread and immense chalices of wine. The bread was cut into long slices, and I passed it on when it came to me; but the civil pew-opener would not hear of this, and I had to break a piece off and eat like the rest. The wine seemed to be unfermented, and had to be continually replenished from flagons which the deacons carried round with them and placed on the ground when not in use. A more complete contrast to the office I had just heard in the Cathedral could not be imagined. The minister (Dr. Black), a young man clad in academic gown and Geneva bands, sat beneath the pulpit, and during the administration kept reading passages of Scripture and reciting verses of hymns from memory. In the interim between these the silence was profound. This minister had a most pleasing voice, without a *soupçon* of Scotch accent, and was peculiarly happy in his quotations, recitations, and expositions. The ceremony concluded with an address from another minister, who spoke in a broad Scotch dialect, and based his remarks on a strange mystical passage in the Song of Solomon. The address, however, was extremely apposite; but I could not help thinking how little the worthy gentleman would have liked the resemblance which still struck me between a continental Sunday and this Scottish Communion Sabbath. He was bitter against the Papists, exhorting them to carry the influence of this Communion in their hearts, not to wear it in the shape of a crucifix round their necks. He scarcely wondered that a Roman Catholic never knew any real peace (a fact of which I had not been aware), because they only worshipped a dead Christ. It seemed to me just another instance of how much better we are than our creeds, and how of all Christian virtues the " greatest is Charity."

When I narrated my morning's experience to certain friends I had formed in Inverness—the most sociable and hospitable of places!—they at first shook their heads in incredulity, but eventually laughed heartily over their toddy at the idea of " Unorthodox London" having been put into a pew and allowed to communicate, nay, invited to do so, by mistake. "We couldn't have done it," they assured me.

Perhaps the good folks were in a proselyting mood, and thought they would convert me.

BREAKFAST WITH EARLY CHRISTIANS.

I THINK I never realized so intensely the fact of my being a working man as I did when I accepted the invitation of the Young Men's Christian Association to breakfast at their rooms in Aldersgate Street, London, at six A.M., and afterwards attend their annual meeting. I sped through the clear air of a genial spring morning and caught the first workmen's train to the City, and found by the time we had got two or three stations down the line we had only nine workmen standing in our compartment in addition to the ten who were seated. The accommodation on the Metropolitan is utterly inadequate, and all distinctions of class quite disregarded. If any one wants to see the "working men in their thousands," he had much better take one of these early trains than attend a Hyde Park demonstration; only he will be considerably more "scrowged"—to adopt the artisan's phraseology. When I reached the institution in Aldersgate Street I found the whole place laid down to a heavy breakfast, and it may be supposed our appetites were sharpened by our early rising. I fancy the Christians young and old did considerable justice to the viands. I know I did.

As soon as breakfast was over—and I must not omit to mention that the Early Christians were female as well as male—we adjourned to the large lecture-hall, where Mr. Alderman M'Arthur took the chair, and after a hymn had been sung from the special collection of the Association, commencing with the words "Early my God," &c., and prayer by the Rev. J. Webster, we proceeded to business. We were informed by the chairman that the Young Men's Christian Associations of Melbourne and Chicago were represented by two gentlemen who would address us, and Mr. M'Arthur then gave us some interesting details of his early experiences of the Young Men's Christian Association when he came as a young man to London. He often used to take his cup of coffee there, and was pleased to find that the old waiter "James" was still alive. He owed further obligations to that Association, for when he was in business and wanted an assistant he got one from them, who proved a treasure to him, and rose rapidly to be a partner, but was removed by an early death. The Association was in fact a young men's club. He concluded by reading amid great applause a portion of Lord Chief Justice Cockburn's speech at the opening of the Manchester Athenæum, on the value of intellectual pursuits.

The Rev. J. J. Halley, from Melbourne, then made a most telling and humorous speech, saying he was commissioned to convey the love of the Christian young men in Australia to the Christian young men of London; and he was quite sure that had the former known that ladies would have been present they would have sent their love to them too. He gave a graphic account of life in the colonies, where he said there was a fine opening for good men but none for fools.

Dr. Barnardo, of Stepney, preached a sermon—though he disavowed any intention of doing so—on the subject of earnestness in Christian work; and on sitting down was violently attacked by the next speaker, the Rev. R. C. Billing, who said early rising had made him pugnacious, and he had a quarrel with both the preceding speakers—with Dr. Barnardo for contrasting his own excellent speech with ministerial utterances, and with Mr. Halley for wanting to decoy all the best young men over to Melbourne. The

Rev. M. C. Osborn, who was introduced by the chairman as his own pastor, said it was difficult to say when men ceased to be young; some in that assembly had grey hair or bald heads. In manner as well as matter this gentleman was most successful, displaying genuine enthusiasm without a tinge of what the most fastidious could call fanaticism. I could not help noticing, that although he belonged to the Methodist Connexion, his dress was intensely clerical, with orthodox coat, and something remarkably like Roman bands. This was the case with most of the Nonconformist ministers present. Then came the gentleman from Chicago. The Hon. Mr. Farwell—such was his name—had a most telling American accent, and claimed for his people on his side of the river the characteristic of being wide-awake. He had just come over, and had already conveyed the greetings of the Young Men's Christian Association in Chicago to the Convention at the Opera House and to the Presbyterian Synod. He had come four thousand miles just to look in on Brother Moody's meetings, and told some most interesting stories of his own work in the inquiry-room. On the very first day he had gained a great "large-looking" Scotchman and his wife, which he thought a very wide-awake thing to have done. Several other speakers followed, and then, as it was near nine o'clock and many had to go to business, the Doxology was sung; but we who remained had the privilege of hearing Mr. Hunter, the Baptist Missionary in the Highlands, sing a most characteristic hymn. In responding to the vote of thanks, the chairman remarked that Charles Lamb said he did not like getting up until the world was comfortably warm, but he thought that if he could have been at that meeting he would have found plenty of warmth of heart. It was indeed a most hearty gathering, and gave one a vivid notion of the work being done all over the world by Young Men's Christian Associations.

The Association was formed in 1844, in order to the improvement of the character and social condition of young men engaged in commercial pursuits. Its objects are both missionary and educational. It seeks to bring men under the influence of Christian principles, and to lead them to exhibit the appropriate results in all the duties and engagements of life. It has, during the twenty-eight years of its existence, enlisted the voluntary missionary efforts of 4365 young men, who, as members of the Association, have sought (as many hundreds of them are still seeking) to lead their companions in the paths of virtue, to protect the young from temptation, and to reclaim those who have fallen into evil habits. Its useful labours have secured the support of some of the largest commercial houses in London, while the fruits of those labours, in addition to the membership of the Christian Church, and in the supply of efficient agents in every department of religious and benevolent service, have been acknowledged by the representatives of the Church in all its sections. The public lectures at Exeter Hall, inaugurated by the society, and sustained for more than twenty years, have been circulated in a total of 100,000 volumes, while of the single lectures the sale in one year reached 111,500, and was in every year considerable. The work is at present sustained in the City of London as follows:—By the activities of 750 members in the spheres of their daily calling; by Bible classes, held every Sunday afternoon, attended by a weekly average of 200 young men, probably by a yearly aggregate of not less than 3500; by devotional meetings thrice in each week; by frequent addresses by ministers of the Gospel; by the annual distribution of tracts and invitations to the extent of 50,000 copies; and by its library and reading-rooms, which are frequented by an average of 1000 young men per annum, and in connexion with which classes are formed to afford to young men opportunity of acquiring a knowledge of the French, German, Spanish, and Latin languages, Mathematics, English composition, and vocal music. There are nine branches of the Association in the metropolis. In Great Britain and Ireland 200 similar associations have been formed through its example, many of them by its direct operation. The movement has spread itself, from this centre, over France, Holland, Belgium, Switzerland, and Germany; is represented in Spain, Italy, Greece, and Egypt, in India, China, and the Australian Colonies; and exercises in British North America, and in the United States, an influence even larger than in the mother country. The total number of Associations exceeds fifteen hundred.

The attention of the Baptist Home Missionary Society for Scotland, to which reference has been made, is chiefly directed to the Highlands and Islands of Scotland, containing a population of about 400,000—one-fourth of whom inhabit the Islands. Some of the parishes are about sixty miles long, and from sixteen to forty miles broad; and a single parish extends, in some cases, over six, in others over eight, and even ten islands. A great portion of the people are thus precluded from attending their parish churches, while their poverty, for the most part, prevents them from supporting preachers. To these, therefore, the Gospel can generally be made known only by itinerant labourers. The Society employs from eighteen to twenty-five approved and tried missionaries.

POLITICAL LADIES.

It is perhaps prejudging a great social question to include the proceedings of the Women's Suffrage Association in a volume bearing the title of "Unorthodox London;" but I use the expression only in the most conventional way, and without for a moment expressing any opinion or feeling on the matter. If I did express an opinion, it would certainly be in favour of giving ladies the franchise; while the tone I adopt in the following notes, made at one of the Association meetings, will, I think, show that I could even contemplate the presence of ladies at St. Stephen's without, at all events, feeling that we should lose anything in the way of eloquence in the debates.

The Women's Suffrage Association had a grand field-day on a Saturday, winding up with an evening meeting at St. George's Hall, London, over which that fortunate man Mr. George Dixon, M.P., presided. When I got to the hall, which was even then getting crammed, I found that happy individual sitting, like "Jack-among-the-maidens," on the platform, surrounded by the prospective orators—one cannot say oratresses—of the evening. The object of the meeting was, as on previous occasions, that the ladies might discuss the speeches of those who had opposed the second reading of the Women's Suffrage Bill. Each lady, to a great extent, devoted herself to one speaker, and scarified him after her own fashion.

Mr. Dixon gallantly made his opening speech of length sufficient to cover the inevitable noise caused by the assembling of the audience, and one irrepressible old gentleman made frantic efforts to speak. He had come from a long distance for the express purpose of talking against the ladies, and could not be persuaded to rest at any price until he had been promised a hearing after all the ladies had spoken. With this he professed himself satisfied, and sat down with a sardonic smile, occupying himself by making notes of each oration in a gigantic note-book. I don't know why, but I could not rid myself of the notion that this old gentleman was dreadfully henpecked, and had come to vent his wrongs on the Association.

Somebody told me he was a Mormon, but I do not believe that.

Miss Becker was the first speaker, and devoted herself principally to the vivisection of Mr. Chaplin, whose historical research she called in question. He had said there was no historical precedent for giving political power to women. Where, she asked, had Mr. Chaplin learnt history? It put her in mind of the way they acted plays at Stonyhurst, cutting out all the female characters, and acting "Macbeth" without a Lady Macbeth in it.

Mrs. Fawcett followed, and with that simple, attractive eloquence which seems to run in her gifted family, undertook the anatomization of Mr. Smollett, who was, of course, the bugbear of the evening. She dwelt strongly upon the indelicacy of his speech, and suggested that modesty might not be out of place even in the House of Commons. As to the indifference about politics, which he affirmed to be the characteristic of women, she protested against taking the tittle-tattle of "butterfly ladies" as representing the feelings of the women of England. They were quite as anxious about their political status as the agricultural labourer, in illustration of whose ignorance she told the story of a poor man who mistook his rating-paper for a vote, and offered to give it to her. "I've just apaid two and eightpence vor un," he said, "but he baint no good to me!"

Mrs. M'Laren, an elderly lady, introduced by Mr. Dixon as the sister of John Bright, and who announced herself as the wife of Duncan M'Laren, of Edinburgh, took Mr. Leatham to task, as a member of the Society of Friends. She read her speech from MS., and went on so long that time was called by the impatient audience; in fact, several ladies displayed a diffuseness in dealing with their subject which unkindly critics would perhaps say was characteristic of their sex. She contrasted Mr. Leatham disadvantageously with George Fox, and appealed to the Revivalists to teach him that the duties of women were not bound up within the four walls of a Quaker meeting-house; in fact he was, she added, but a "shabby specimen of a Quaker."

Then Miss Rhoda Garrett followed with a charming ironical speech, perfect in matter as well as manner of delivery. Sir Wilfrid Lawson, she said, dreaded two enemies of England—the Pope and the Colorado beetle; but there was a third, and this foe was literally of our own household; in fact, it was the female householder. The Pope might crush the Church, the Colorado beetle destroy the crops, but the women would reverse the decrees of Nature, Providence, and—the House of Commons. "When I sat in the Women's Gallery, and listened to the debate of April 7th," she said, " I felt bewildered, and that, like Artemus Ward, I would give five dollars to anybody that would tell who I was, and whar I was goin'!" She spoke solemnly—a statement which provoked great laughter—because she felt solemnly. She felt that those 187 senators who voted against the Bill were like the Jews who had the custody of the Ark, the covenant of national safety. What would become of them if these custodians should be defeated at the next general election? Changing her tone, she elicited cheers by mentioning the name of Florence Nightingale, and reminding us how she was decried for going to the Crimea (said the irrepressible old gentleman, "Never!") and finally reverted to her original strain, arguing that a woman might vote for an M.P. without losing her head or heart; might, in fact, drop her ballot-paper in the box, and return to cook the family dinner. Sir Henry James came in for a considerable share of Miss Rhoda Garrett's badinage; but the insults of Messrs. Leatham and Smollett, she said, would tell in favour of the movement.

Miss Tod, of Belfast, came next—a lady with a

beautiful brogue and lots of Irish humour. In fact, "chaff," if one may use so vulgar an expression, was the distinguishing characteristic of the speeches. She congratulated herself that no Irish member had spoken against the Bill, and therefore she had no native orator to vivisect. She therefore turned her attention to Mr. Smollett, and went over the same ground as her predecessors, though in her own fashion. She did not regard the vote as a panacea, but thought it would remove much righteous discontent. She especially combated the idea that giving the franchise to widows and spinsters was a slur on married women.

Miss Wilkinson said a few words as the representative of the working-classes; and then Miss Sturge took as her text the words quoted by Sir Henry James—

"Oh, the good man little knew
What the wily sex can do."

We'll show him, she said; and then treated us to a speech as ironical as Miss Garrett's own, only it came too late in the evening, and was too long. One enthusiastic gentleman liked it so much that he called out "Encore" at the end.

It was very late by the time the irrepressible gentleman got on his legs, and he displayed considerable aversion to mount the platform, or to give his name, but eventually did both, announcing himself as Captain Jones, of London. His words were utterly incoherent, and he was by-and-by laughed down, but not until he had warned the audience (whom he denounced as packed by the society) that they were preparing a stick for their own backs, and he hoped they would get well punished. Decidedly the Women's Suffrage Association meeting is getting to be an annual treat, and one of the liveliest events in the London season. I should strongly advise senators, before they deliver themselves of any sentiments hostile to women's franchise, to picture themselves as being "sat upon" at St. George's Hall, with no one to say a word in their defence except some adventurous Captain Jones, about whom they would be ready to exclaim—"Save me from my friends!"

THE JEWISH NEW YEAR AND DAY OF ATONEMENT.

THERE is no more curious link binding the present with the past than the persistent traditions and ceremonies of modern Judaism, surviving as they do in the very busiest centres of modern life, and amongst a people exceptionally qualified to play their part in the active business of the world. To pass along the London streets on a Friday evening or Saturday morning, and see the shops of the Hebrew tradesmen closed when commercial life is elsewhere at its zenith, shows that the old faith is still alive in the hearts of this singular people just as it was " in the brave days of old" in Palestine. Whether that which is now called Judaism adequately represents the Mosaic faith and practice (a question which is debated to some degree within the pale of modern Judaism itself) we will not discuss. The Jew finds in his religion what the Christian poet Keble has so well expressed under the words—

> "The trivial round, the common task,
> Will furnish all we need to ask—
> Room to deny ourselves, a road
> To bring us daily nearer God."

The occurrence of two of the great annual festivals furnished material for illustration—first, in the Reading of the Law on the Day of Atonement; secondly, in Waiting for the Shofar (or "Cornet") at the New Year.

The Day of Atonement—or rather, as it is called in the Hebrew, the Day of Atonements (Yom Kippurim)—is called by the Rabbinical name of Yoma, that is, the Day *par excellence*. It was celebrated on the tenth day of the seventh month, called in the Old Testament Ethanim, but by the Jews in later times Tisri. According to the uniform voice of tradition (says the "Speaker's Commentary") it was the first day of the civil year, in use before the Exodus, and was observed as the festival of the New Year.

To us this would imply a season of joy, but not so to the Jew. It was said in the Rabbinical writings that "as the merits and the sins of a man are weighed at the hour of his death, so likewise every year, on the festival of New Year's Day, the sins of every one that cometh into the world are weighed against his merits. Every one who is found wicked is sealed to death; but the judgment of the intermediate class is suspended until the Day of Atonement. If they repent they are sealed to life, but if not they are sealed to death" (Hilchoth T'schuvah, c. iii. 3, quoted in McCaul's "Old Paths").

With this great annual fast of expiation was connected, in ancient times, the significant ceremony of the scapegoat, still retained among some of the orthodox Jews to the extent of sacrificing a cock on the eve of the Day of Atonement. The Order of Atonements, published at Breslau in 1830, gives minute directions for this sacrifice. Having taken the fowl into his hand, the sacrificer repeats certain verses of Scripture, and then, "moving the atonement round his head," he adds, "This is my substitute—this is my commutation. This cock goeth to death; but may I be gathered, and enter into a long and happy life, and into peace." "As soon as one has performed the order of the atonement, he should lay his hands on it, as the hands used to be laid on sacrifices, and immediately give it to be slaughtered." "This custom," says Dr. McCaul, "extensively prevalent among the Jews, proves abundantly the internal dissatisfaction of the Jewish mind with their own doctrines, and the deeply-rooted conviction of their hearts that without shedding of blood there is no remission of sin" ("Old Paths," p. 302).

The ordinary sacrifices and atonements of the year did not suffice to complete the reconciliation between the congregation of Israel—which was to be called a holy nation, but in its very nature was still altogether involved in sin and uncleanness—and Jehovah, the Holy One—that is to say, to restore the reconciliation and true vital fellowship of the nation with its God, in accordance with the idea and object of the old covenant—because, even with the most scrupulous observance of these directions, many sins and defilements would still remain unacknowledged, and therefore without expiation, and would necessarily produce in the congregation a feeling of separation from its God, so that it would be unable to attain to the true joyousness of access to the Throne of Grace, and to the place of reconciliation with God. This was met by the appointment of a yearly, general, and perfect expiation of all the sins and uncleanness which had remained unatoned for and uncleansed in the course of the year.*

The Feast of Trumpets (*Dies Clangoris et Tubarum*) came in on the first of Tisri, and was one of the days of Holy Convocation and commencement of the New

---

* Kiel and Delitzch on the Pentateuch.

Year. It was to be a Shabbath Shabbathon, or Sabbath of Rest, and on it were blown both kinds of trumpets, the straight horn and the cornet. Thus was the Shofar, described by Professor Marks as "a loud sounding instrument, made of the horn of a ram, or a chamois, sometimes of an ox, and used by the ancient Hebrews for signals, and, among other purposes, for proclaiming the New Year." Rabbinical traditions represented this epoch at the anniversary of the Creation of the World; and besides its significance as the opening of the year, it was, so to say, the introduction to the immediately succeeding Day of Atonement. The "Sounding of the Cornet" no doubt bore reference to the words of the prophet Joel, "Sound the trumpet (cornet) in Zion, sanctify the fast, proclaim the solemn assembly." This custom is still retained; and Professor Marks adds, "The sounds emitted from the cornet in modern times are exceedingly harsh, although they produce a solemn effect."

The following prayer is said by the person who sounds the cornet before he begins:—"May it be acceptable in Thy presence, O Lord, my God, and the God of my Fathers, the God of Heaven and the God of the Earth; the God of Abraham, the God of Isaac, and the God of Jacob; the great God, mighty and tremendous, to send me the holy and pure angels who are faithful ministers, and faithful in their message, and who are desirous and willing to justify Israel; and also the great angel Patzpatziah, who is appointed to present the merits of Israel, when they sound the cornets this day; and likewise the great angel Tas-h-bash, who is appointed to declare the merits of Israel, and confound Satan with their sound of the cornet; and the great princes who are appointed over the cornet, Enkatham and Pastam; and the great angels Hadarniel and Sandalphon, who are appointed over our sounding, who introduce our sounding before the throne of Thy glory; and also the angel Shamshiel, who is appointed over the joyful sound, and the angel Prasta, who is appointed to superintend קש"דק, that they may all be expeditious in their errand; to introduce our soundings before the veil, and before the throne of Thy glory; and mayest Thou be filled with mercy over Thy people Israel; and lead us within the temperate line of strict justice; and conduct Thyself towards Thy children with the attribute of mercy, and suffer our soundings to ascend before the throne of Thy glory."—*Prayer for the New Year*, p. 81.

Among the ceremonies connected by some of the orthodox Jews with the Day of Atonement, the following are mentioned by Dr. Kitto in his "Cyclopædia of Biblical Literature:—"Towards evening of the 9th of Tisri, and before they take their last meal for twenty-four hours, they repair to the synagogue, and each inflicts on his neighbour thirty-nine blows with a piece of leather. This infliction is called סלנרת, in expiation of those sins which are punished by the law of Moses with flogging. Most of the Jews on that day (of atonement) wear a white gown—the same shrouds in which they are buried; while *all* of them are obliged to stand the whole day without shoes or even slippers."

APPENDIX.

By way of making this work useful as a book of reference, it has been thought desirable to append brief statistical notices of some of the more important religious bodies. The figures have been generally taken from documents issued by the respective communities during the current year, and have been in many cases checked by some member of the community.

ROMAN CATHOLICS.

According to the Catholic Directory for 1875, the following are the statistics of the two metropolitan dioceses for the year 1875 :—

Ecclesiastical Statistics of the Diocese of Westminster.

Priests
- Secular (including Oratorians 18 ; Oblates of St. Charles 20 ; unattached, invalided, or retired, 14) 201
- Augustinians 3, Carmelites 6, Charity (Fathers of) 3, Dominicans 10, Franciscans 5, Jesuits 17, Marists 9, Missions (Pious Society of the) 4, Oblates of Mary Immaculate 9, Passionists 10, Servites 6 . . 82

Total: 283

Public Churches, Chapels, and Stations 101

Attendance of Children at the Poor Schools of the Diocese.

Year.	Present at inspection.	Average attendance.
1857–58	8,333	8,648
1858–59	9,470	9,820
1859–60	9,414	10,008
1860–61	9,981	10,521
1861–62	10,536	10,734
1862–63	10,827	11,318
1863–64	11,642	11,640
1864–65	11,342	11,132
1865–66	11,145	11,112
1866–67	11,870	12,056
1867–68	13,146	12,665
1868–69	14,027	13,260
1869–70	14,839	13,751
1870–71	14,886	14,058
1871–72	16,353	14,913
1872–73	16,699	15,220
1873–74	17,585	15,624

Ecclesiastical Statistics of the Diocese of Southwark.

Priests { Secular	143	
Priests { Regular	74	227
Priests { Unattached, or on sick leave	10	
Public Churches, Chapels, and Stations		134
Other Chapels, of Communities, &c.		48
Registered for Marriages		76

Statistics of Clergy, &c., in Great Britain.

	Clergy.	Public Churches, Chapels, and Stations.
ENGLAND AND WALES:		
Archbishops and Bishops	18	
Priests:		
Westminster	283	101
Beverley	137	109
Birmingham	172	103
Clifton	71	38
Hexham and Newcastle	127	91
Liverpool	233	122
Newport and Menevia	55	56
Northampton	37	40
Nottingham	71	58
Plymouth	44	36
Salford	155	83
Shrewsbury	98	70
Southwark	227	134
Total in England and Wales . . .	1728	1041
SCOTLAND:		
Archbishop and Bishops	3	
Priests:		
Eastern District	70	78
Western District	133	109
Northern District	32	40
Total in Scotland	238	227
TOTAL IN GREAT BRITAIN	1966	1268

THE CATHOLIC HIERARCHY.

The governing Hierarchy of the Catholic Church consists: of his Holiness the Sovereign Pontiff, who is assisted by the Sacred College of Cardinals, and by several Sacred Congregations, or permanent ecclesiastical committees, of which the Cardinals are the chief members; and of the Patriarchs, Primates, Archbishops and Bishops, the Apostolic Delegates, Vicars, and Prefects, and certain Abbots and Prelates.

I. GENERAL SUMMARY.

HIS HOLINESS THE POPE,
BISHOP OF ROME AND VICAR OF JESUS CHRIST,
SUCCESSOR OF ST. PETER PRINCE OF THE APOSTLES,
SUPREME PONTIFF OF THE UNIVERSAL CHURCH,
PATRIARCH OF THE WEST, PRIMATE OF ITALY,
ARCHBISHOP AND METROPOLITAN OF THE ROMAN PROVINCE,
SOVEREIGN OF THE TEMPORAL DOMINIONS OF THE
HOLY ROMAN CHURCH.

SACRED COLLEGE OF CARDINALS,

Consisting, when the number is complete, of six Cardinal Bishops, fifty Cardinal Priests, and fourteen Cardinal Deacons.

PATRIARCHS.

Of the Latin Rite, seven; and five of Oriental Rite, with Patriarchal jurisdiction.

ARCHIEPISCOPAL AND EPISCOPAL SEES.

ARCHIEPISCOPAL SEES.

Latin Rite.
- Immediately subject to the Holy Seee . 12
- With Ecclesiastical Provinces . . . 126

Oriental Rite.
- With Ecclesiastical Provinces:
  - Armenian 1
  - Greco-Roumaic 1
  - Greco-Ruthenian 1
- Subject to the Patriarchates:
  - Armenian 5
  - Greco-Melchite 4
  - Syriac 4
  - Syro-Chaldaic 5
  - Syro-Maronite 5

⎬ 164

EPISCOPAL SEES.

Latin Rite.
- Suburban Sees 6
- Immediately subject to the Holy See . 84
- Suffragan, in Ecclesiastical Provinces . 567

Oriental Rite.
- Immediately subject to the Holy See:
  - Greco-Bulgarian 1
  - Greco-Ruthenian 3
- Suffragan Sees in Ecclesiastical Provinces:
  - Armenian 1
  - Greco-Roumaic 3
  - Greco-Ruthenian 4
- Subject to the Patriarchates:
  - Armenian 11
  - Greco-Melchite 9
  - Syriac 8
  - Syro-Chaldaic 7
  - Syro-Maronite 3

⎬ 707

The foregoing summary of what may be called the Residential Sees (*Sedi Residenziali*) of Archbishops and Bishops, amounting, with the Patriarchal Sees, to 883, is taken from the list published in Rome, Feb. 25, 1874.

The total number of Patriarchs, Primates, Archbishops, and Bishops, at the above date (including those who were *retired* and those who had the title of sees *in partibus infidelium*), was 1081.*

Cardinal Manning addressed a Pastoral Letter to the clergy and laity of his diocese, in the various churches of which it was read on Trinity Sunday, 1875, in which he states:—" 1. That the aggregate church room, giving the succession of masses, does not at this time nearly suffice for the Catholic population of London. 2. That the intervals between church and church are in many places so great as to render attendance at the offices of Divine worship impossible to many. This is especially true in some of the outskirts of London, where the poorest of our people are often congregated in great numbers. 3. That the multiplication of smaller churches is the only certain way of ensuring the attendance of our poor. They are often reluctant to frequent our larger churches, which are also already so filled by others as to leave comparatively little free space. 4. That in the course of last year two churches were opened among the poorest of our people—namely, in the neighbourhood of Drury-lane and Covent-garden, and in the Isle of Dogs. 5. That the first stone of a church in the mission of Barking-

---

* The titles of sees *in partibus infidelium* (in infidel regions) are, for the most part, conferred on Archbishops and Bishops who are appointed to Apostolic Delegations, Vicariates, or Prefectures; or to the office of Administrator, Coadjutor, or Auxiliary, in a Diocese.

road, in the midst of a population of 2000 poor, was laid on the 8th of this month; and a church, to replace the Church of St. Boniface, for the use of the German population in London, is already begun. It will be remembered that the Church of St. Boniface fell to the ground in the year 1873. The priest had hardly time to remove the most holy sacrament when the whole fabric came down. 6. That two other churches are urgently needed—namely, at Wapping and at Homerton. If we possessed the means they would be at once commenced. 7. That in other parts of the diocese the existing buildings, now used for divine service, ought to be replaced by fitting churches. Nothing but the prior and overwhelming claims of London have delayed our making this effort. 8. Finally, the diocese possesses no means whatsoever for the building of churches, except the proceeds of this annual collection."

THE RIGHT REV. MONSIGNOR CAPEL.

Recent controversy has brought into even more than usual prominence the names of Monsignor Capel and Canon Liddon, perhaps the most representative preachers, at the present moment, in the Roman and Anglican branches of the Church respectively. An accusation was brought by Monsignor Capel against the Ritualists of disseminating Roman doctrine in the Church of England; and Canon Liddon, narrowing his remarks specially to the doctrine of the Real Presence, which he claimed as pre-Roman and Catholic in the larger sense of the word, stood forth as the champion rather of those views which are known as High Church than of Ritualism technically so termed. The unecclesiastical mind, it is true, fails to distinguish accurately the difference between these two schools of thought, which is indeed rather one of degree than of kind;

and the columns of the *Times* had for some while been made the vehicle of controversial letters and articles which, to lay readers, had grown not a little wearisome. Monsignor Capel is, however, not so much the controversialist or the preacher—though under these aspects we most commonly regard him—as he is the educator. It is mostly to education the greater portion of his life has been devoted. This he claims to be the essential feature of his work. Preaching and propagandism are but accidents in comparison. This zealous Roman ecclesiastic is only in the thirty-ninth year of his age, and is not, as many persons fancy, a convert from Anglicanism. The style of his preaching, and even the pronunciation of his words, lead one to suppose that he has been brought up under English academical influences. Such, however, is not the case, or rather, the influences of our Universities have only been, so to say, indirectly brought to bear upon him. His earliest work, whilst he was yet only in minor orders, was at the training-school of St. Mary, on Brook Green. This institution he was partly instrumental in founding, under the superintendence of Father Glennie, a convert from Anglicanism and a veteran in the work of education. To his early association with this gentleman Monsignor Capel attributes not only the academical bias of his thoughts and form of speech, but also that intimate acquaintance with High Church doctrines and practices which stood him so well in stead during the recent controversy with Canon Liddon. At St. Mary's he led for years the life of a recluse, cut off to a large extent from the outside world, and living only in his lecture-room and study. This kind of existence he continued too long, for it told upon his health, and he was obliged to go for a season to Pau. The retirement to the Pyrenees Monsignor Capel calls the end of Chapter I. in his life. He returned too soon, again broke down, and commenced Chapter II. by taking up his residence at Pau, where he lived seven years and a half; though when he came thither his health was so shattered that, according to all human probability, he had only come to die. He had now been admitted to the priesthood, and besides engaging in his favourite work of private tuition, he ministered among the Catholic residents of that motley community who were health-seekers like himself at Pau. In association with these representatives of different nationalities he outgrew those habits of the anchorite which he had imbibed at Brook Green, and studied the manifold phases of his own religion as represented in the devotees of Spain and Italy, the colder German, and withal in his own fellow-countrymen; whilst such outlying bodies as the Greek and Lutheran Churches were also forced upon his notice. Here, too—to use his own expression—he first "crossed swords with a Puseyite," his antagonist being the Rev. Richard Temple West, now Incumbent of St. Mary Magdalene's, Paddington, who came to Pau to preach at a "High" Church recently established there, and adopted the somewhat questionable course of inviting Father Capel and his co-religionists to "assist." This the young priest denounced as inconsistent with the principles of Anglican Sacerdotalism—viz., inviting in a Catholic country Catholic priests to take part in what was an act of schism. During his residence at Pau Bishop Colenso's book appeared, and Father Capel preached a series of sermons against it. Cardinal Wiseman offered to print and publish the volume; but the young preacher declined. In fact, Monsignor Capel does not seem to share the penchant of most controversialists for printing. His celebrated lectures on Tractarianism, like those on Dr. Colenso's works, still exist only in manuscript. When these seven years and a half were over, Father Capel returned to England, with his health established and the ideas of the bookworm broadened by association with people of all ranks and nations, and placed his services at the disposal of the parish priest at the then newly-erected Pro-Cathedral, Kensington, and forthwith took charge of the poor schools attached to that church. He occupied the pulpit with increasing frequency; and his fame as a fluent and forcible preacher became widely known. He still, however, continued to develop his educational schemes, first by establishing on the most modest scale, at his residence in Wright's Lane, Kensington, the nucleus of a boys' public school, which has so far increased as to number nearly fifty pupils and require adjournment to other premises in the immediate neighbourhood. His great scheme of a Catholic university has been rather forced upon him *ab extra*. Monsignor Capel favoured the view of Dr. Newman for establishing a college at Oxford; but Archbishop Manning was strong on the separate university; and, like a good obedient son of the Church, Monsignor Capel yielded. This institution, which also stands in Wright's Lane, Kensington (and a detailed account of which is given above), is only in its second term, and numbers twenty *alumni*. Indeed, the formal opening had only taken place at Eastertide last, under circumstances of great pomp. The staff is a strong and distinguished one, especially in physical science and kindred faculties; Monsignor Capel wishing to prove that Catholic teaching does not involve either the suppression of scientific research or its pursuit after the method of Huxley. In school and university Monsignor Capel has, with the acumen of a veteran educator, determined to have not only men intellectually qualified for each post, but also trained *teachers*. Monsignor Capel, be he rightly or wrongly identified with the Catesby of "Lothair," is of singularly suave and attractive demeanour, and eminently qualified for the work of proselytism, in which his success has been very great, the conversion of the Marquis of Bute being almost of the nature of a climax. He is in the plenitude of his power, and may be seen daily flitting about in purple cassock and biretta in the purlieus of Wright's Lane, where his work lies, so to say, under a blanket. A large estate recently acquired is soon to be appropriated to the purposes of a medical school and hospital; and certain arrangements are contemplated—of which it would be out of place to speak now—calculated to give additional importance and usefulness to this nascent institution. Amid all these varied labours of teaching, preaching, and propagandism, Monsignor Capel still finds time to enter vigorously into current controversy, as his recent passage-at-arms with the eloquent Canon of St. Paul's sufficiently shows. Here, of course, his former book-learning, and also his minute acquaintance with Puseyite traditions and "parsons"—as it is customary with the Romish to term the English clergy—becomes of immense advantage to him. His acquaintance, for instance, with the Anglo-Catholic manuals of devotion is so minute as to make an Evangelical or Broad Churchman stare. Monsignor has studied it as he would a science. He says—and we can well believe it, while listening to his earnest incisive speech—that he makes it a rule never to take up a subject without, as far as possible, exhausting it. He may thus be taken as the very type and embodiment of that young Romanism which, not content with being talented, is conscientiously aggressive, and, whilst Ultramontane in its principles, is largely absorbent of all those secular and social aids which men of smaller calibre consider incompatible with, or even antagonistic to, "the Faith."

The title of "Monsignor," it may be mentioned, is given to Papal chamberlains, domestic Papal chaplains, domestic prelates, and bishops. The first two are addressed "Very

Reverend;" the latter two, "Right Reverend." The chamberlains and chaplains change at the death of the Pope; but the prelates retain their office and dignity for life. The Pope conferred the dignity of prelate on Monsignor Capel about two years ago. His title in full, therefore, is "The Right Reverend Monsignor Capel, D.D., Domestic Prelate of Pope Pius IX., and Rector of the Catholic University College, Kensington."

THE GREEK CHURCH.

Marsden says:—"The most recent computations give the number of those Christians who are comprehended in the communion of the Greek Church, as 50,000,000 in Russia; 12,000,000 in Turkey; Greece, including the Montenegrians, 800,000; the Austrian dominions, 2,800,000; the patriarchate of Alexandria, 5000; Antioch, 150,000; and Jerusalem, 15,000; in all about 65,500,000.

"In doctrine, the Greek Church differs but little from the Church of Rome. It receives tradition as a joint rule of faith with Holy Scripture. But while the Pope may authorize new traditions, those of the Greeks are stationary: they include the writings of the Greek fathers to the time of John Damasciensis, early in the eighth century, and the decisions of the first seven general Councils recognised as such: the two Councils of Nice, three Councils of Constantinople, and those of Ephesus and Chalcedon. The Greek Church admits the seven sacraments of Rome; but with regard to Baptism, it teaches that the chrism, or unction with oil, is necessary to complete the sacrament; and it makes use of the chrism likewise as an extreme unction when death approaches, and to anoint the sick, that they may recover, and receive remission of sins. Baptism is performed by the immersion of the infant three times. The Lord's Supper is administered to the laity in both kinds. The doctrine of transubstantiation, which may be traced in Chrysostom's treatise on the priesthood, became soon after an accredited dogma of the Eastern Church. The Greek Church rejects the doctrine of purgatory, and that of works of supererogation; nor does it assign infallibility to its head, the Patriarch, or address him as the Vicar of Christ. It differs from the Church of Rome in rejecting image-worship, though paintings are allowed, and receive a superstitious homage; and, above all, in the absence of that intolerant and ambitious spirit which denounces all other Christian sects as heretics, and enforces submission to her authority by the sword. Besides the ancient creeds, the doctrines of the Greek Church are to be sought in her liturgies and confessions. Of the former there are four, used in various places, and substantially agreeing with each other."—*Dictionary of Christian Churches and Sects.*

PRESBYTERIAN CHURCH IN ENGLAND.

Presbyterianism derives its name from the Government of its Churches by Presbyters or Elders, chosen by the members, and ordained to the Spiritual oversight and rule of the congregations. Each church or congregation has a body of Presbyters or Elders associated with the Pastor, and known as the Church Session. Presbyteries are composed of the minister, and a representative elder from each of the Church Sessions within a given district, who meet together periodically, quarterly, or monthly, and oftener, if necessary, to consult for the interests of the churches within their bounds, exercise a general superintendence over their affairs, and decide, as a court of appeal, on cases brought before them by conflicting parties. The first Presbytery in England was formed at Wandsworth in 1572; but the intolerance of the times prevented such a development of the system as it reached in Scotland, and in all the other Reformed churches of Europe. The Presbyterians remained in the Church of England, and formed the leading Puritan element in her bosom, until the days of the Long Parliament, and Laud, and the Westminster Assembly, when. they revolutionized Church and State, and raised Presbyterianism to the position of the established religion of England. Overthrown politically at the Restoration, crushed ecclesiastically by their ejection from the National Church under the Act of Uniformity, and denied the right and liberty of such presbyterial organization as was necessary to the stability and extension of their system, a large portion of them gradually emerged into Congregationalism, and others lapsed into Arian and Socinian error (hence the name of "Presbyterian," by which Unitarians, who hold Presbyterian endowments style themselves, and are known in many parts of England). Some, however, continued to retain congregational presbytery, and adhered to the orthodoxy of the old Puritan or modern Nonconformist type. It was the collecting into one body of these scattered fragments of the old orthodox Presbyterianism of England, which in the year 1836 formed "The English Presbyterian Church," now numbering 153 Congregations, with 658 Elders, 1080 Deacons or managers, 26,856 Communicants; divided into 8 Presbyteries, meeting periodically, and combined into a general Synod, meeting annually. It is provided with a Theological College, partially endowed; it has its Home, Jewish, and Foreign Missions; with a staff of 15 European labourers, ministerial and medical; Day and Sabbath Schools, with 24,228 Scholars; a Church-building and Debt-extinction Fund; and an allowance to Aged and Infirm Ministers, and to the Widows and Orphans of deceased Pastors. 95,791*l*. were raised by this body for Church purposes in 1874.

SUMMARY OF THE PRINCIPLES OF THE UNITED PRESBYTERIAN CHURCH.

The United Presbyterian Church was formed in the year 1847 by the union of the United Secession and Relief Churches. After the union of the two portions of the Secession Church in 1820, an impression was produced on the mind both of the United Secession and Relief Churches, that though each had been greatly blessed of God as a separate denomination, yet a union between them was scriptural, desirable, and practicable—their views of doctrine, discipline, and government being found to be identical. After the subject had been long and prayerfully considered by the respective Synods, a union was consummated on 13th May, 1847, when both, according to previous arrangement, met together and adopted the following articles as the

Bases of Union.

"1. That the Word of God contained in the Scriptures of the Old and New Testaments, is the only rule of Faith and Practice.

"2. That the Westminster Confession of Faith and the Larger and Shorter Catechisms are the confession and catechisms of this Church, and contain the authorized exhibition of the sense in which we understand the Holy Scriptures; it being always understood that we do not approve of anything in these documents which teaches, or may be supposed to teach, compulsory or persecuting and intolerant principles in religion.

"3. That Presbyterian Government, without any superiority of office to that of a teaching presbyter, and in a due subordination of church courts, which is founded on, and agreeable to, the word of God, is the government of this Church.

"4. That the ordinances of worship shall be administered in the United Church as they have been in both bodies of which it is formed; and that the Westminster Directory of worship continue to be regarded as a compilation of excellent rules.

"5. That the term of membership is a credible profession of the faith of Christ as held by this Church—a profession made with intelligence, and justified by a corresponding character and deportment.

"6. That with regard to those Ministers and Sessions who may think that the 2nd section of the 26th chapter of the Confession of Faith authorizes free communion—that is, not loose or indiscriminate communion, but the occasional admission to fellowship in the Lord's Supper of persons respecting whose Christian character satisfactory evidence has been obtained, though belonging to other religious denominations— they shall enjoy in the united body what they enjoyed in their separate communions—the right of acting on their conscientious convictions.

"7. That the election of office-bearers of this Church, in its several congregations, belongs, by the authority of Christ, exclusively to the members in full communion.

"8. That this Church solemnly recognises the obligation to hold forth, as well as to hold fast, the doctrine and law of Christ, and to make exertions for the universal diffusion of the blessings of his gospel at home and abroad.

"9. That as the Lord hath ordained that they who preach the gospel should live of the gospel—that they who are taught in the word should communicate to him that teacheth in all good things—that they who are strong should help the weak—and, that having freely received, thus they should freely give the gospel to those who are destitute of it—this Church asserts the obligation and the privilege of its members, influenced by regard to the authority of Christ, to support and extend, by voluntary contribution, the ordinances of the gospel.

" 10. That the respective bodies of which this Church is composed, without requiring from each other any approval of the steps of procedure by their fathers, or interfering with the rights of private judgment in reference to these, unite in regarding as still valid the reasons on which they have hitherto maintained their state of secession and separation from the Judicatories of the Established Church, as expressed in the authorized documents of the respective bodies, and in maintaining the lawfulness and obligation of separation from ecclesiastical bodies in which dangerous error is tolerated, or the discipline of the church, or the rights of her ministers or members are disregarded."

To this basis was appended the following solemn resolution:—

" The United Church, in their present most solemn circumstances, join in expressing their grateful acknowledgment to the great Head of the Church for the measure of spiritual good which He has accomplished by them in their separate state—their deep sense of the many imperfections and sins which have marked their ecclesiastical management—and their determined resolution, in dependence on the promised grace of their Lord, to apply more faithfully the great principles of Church fellowship—to be more watchful in reference to admission and discipline, that the purity and efficiency of our congregations may be promoted, and the great end of our existence as a collective body may be answered with respect to all within its pale, and to all without it, whether members of other denominations, or the world lying in wickedness. And in fine, the United Church regard with a feeling of brotherhood all the faithful followers of Christ, and shall endeavour to maintain the unity of the whole body of Christ by a readiness to co-operate with all its members, in all things in which they are agreed."

At the time of the union, the two Synods together represented about 500 congregations.

WESLEYAN METHODIST.

The body of Christians, now known as *Wesleyan Methodists*, arose about the year 1730; their founder being the Rev. John Wesley, who with his brother Charles and other students at Oxford, being excluded from the pulpits of the Established Church, took to preaching in the fields, and to the erection of chapels. From the strict regularity of their lives they were called Methodists. Hence their present name.

The Chief Ecclesiastical Court of the Wesleyan Methodist Church is, by the Rev. John Wesley's Deed of Declaration (enrolled in Chancery, and dated February 28, 1784) defined to be "The Yearly Conference of the people called Methodists," and to consist of "Preachers and Expounders of God's Holy Word, commonly called Methodist Preachers." The number of members forming this Conference is one hundred; but besides these, there are present at its meetings other ministers, authorized by their District Meetings to attend, and who take part in the proceedings. The principal business transacted at the Conference is the reception of Probationers—the ordination of Ministers—the examination of the moral and public character of every Minister and Preacher on trial—

their appointment to Circuits, and the general supervision of the various institutions.

SOCIETY RULES.

The following Rules were written and published by Mr. Wesley, and are recommended as briefly expressing the duties enforced in the Holy Scriptures:—

1. In the latter end of the year 1739, eight or ten persons came to me in London, who appeared to be deeply convinced of sin, and earnestly groaning for redemption. They desired (as did two or three more next day) that I would spend some time with them in prayer, and advise them how to flee from the wrath to come, which they saw continually hanging over their heads. That we might have more time for this great work, I appointed a day when they might all come together; which from thenceforward they did every week, viz., on Thursday in the evening. To these, and as many more as desired to join with them (for their number increased daily), I gave those advices from time to time which I judged most needful for them; and we always concluded our Meeting with prayer suited to their several necessities.

2. This was the rise of the UNITED SOCIETY, first in London, and then in other places. Such a Society is no other than "*a company of men having the form, and seeking the power of godliness: united, in order to pray together, to receive the word of exhortation, and to watch one over another in love, that they may help each other to work out their salvation.*"

3. That it may the more easily be discerned whether they are indeed working out their own salvation, each Society is divided into smaller companies, called classes, according to their respective places of abode. There are about twelve persons in every Class; one of whom is styled *the Leader*. It is his business,

I. To see each person in his Class once a week at least, in order

To enquire how their souls prosper;

To advise, reprove, comfort, or exhort, as occasion may require;

To receive what they are willing to give, towards the support of the Gospel.

II. To meet the Ministers and the Stewards of the Society once a week, in order

To inform the Minister of any that are sick, or of any that walk disorderly, and will not be reproved;

To pay to the Stewards what they have received of their several classes in the week preceding; and

To show their account of what each person has contributed.

4. There is only one condition previously required in those who desire admission into these Societies, viz., "*a desire to flee from the wrath to come, to be saved from their sins.*" But wherever this is really fixed in the soul, it will be shown by its fruits. It is therefore expected of all who continue therein, that they should continue to evidence their desire of salvation.

First. By doing no harm, by avoiding evil in every kind: especially that which is most generally practised. Such as—

The taking the name of God in vain:

The profaning the day of the Lord, either by doing ordinary work thereon, or by buying or selling:

Drunkenness: *buying or selling spirituous liquors:* or *drinking them*, unless in cases of extreme necessity.

Fighting, quarrelling, brawling; brother *going to law with* brother: returning *evil* for *evil*, or *railing* for *railing:* the *using many words* in buying or selling.

The *buying* or *selling un-customed* (or *smuggled*) *goods:*

The *giving* or *taking things on usury*, i.e., unlawful interest.

Uncharitable or *unprofitable* Conversation: particularly speaking evil of Magistrates or of Ministers:

Doing to others as we would not they should do unto us:

Doing what we know is not for the glory of God; as

The putting on of gold or costly apparel:

The *taking such diversions* as cannot be used in the name of the Lord Jesus:

The *singing* those *songs*, or *reading* those *books*, which do not tend to the knowledge or love of God:

Softness, and needless self-indulgence:

Laying up treasure upon earth:

Borrowing without a probability of paying: or taking up goods without a probability of paying for them.

It is expected of all who continue in these Societies, that they should continue to evidence their desire of Salvation.

Secondly. By doing good, by being in every kind merciful after their power, as they have opportunity: doing good of every possible sort, and, as far as is possible, to all men:

To their Bodies, of the ability that God giveth, by giving food to the hungry, by clothing the naked, by visiting or helping them that are sick, or in prison:

To their Souls, by instructing, reproving, or exhorting all we have any intercourse with, trampling under foot that enthusiastic doctrine of Devils, that "We are not to do good, unless our hearts be free to it."

By doing good, especially to them that are of the household of Faith, or groaning so to be; employing them preferably to others, buying one of another, helping each other in business: and so much the more, because the world will love its own, and them *only*.

By all possible *diligence* and *frugality*, that the Gospel be not blamed.

By running with patience the race that is set before them,

denying themselves and taking up their cross daily ; submitting to bear the reproach of Christ: to be as the filth and offscouring of the world; and looking that men should *say all manner of evil of them falsely for the Lord's sake.*

It is expected of all who desire to continue in these Societies, that they should continue to evidence their desire of Salvation.

Thirdly. By attending on all the Ordinances of God: such are—the public worship of God:

The Ministry of the Word either read or expounded:

The Supper of the Lord: Family and private prayer:

Searching the Scriptures: and Fasting or abstinence.

These are the General Rules of our Societies; all which we are taught of God to observe, even in his written Word, the only Rule, and the sufficient Rule both of our Faith and Practice. And all these we know His Spirit writes on every truly awakened heart. If there be any among us who observe them not, and who habitually break any of them, let it be made known to them that watch over that soul, as they that must give an account. We will admonish him of the error of his ways; we will bear with him for a season. But then, if he repent not, he hath no more place among us. We have delivered our own souls.

May 1, 1743.   J. and C. WESLEY.

PRIMITIVE METHODISTS.

This enterprising section of the Christian Church is a genuine original branch of Methodism, and is neither a split nor division from any other body. It originated with ten persons who had been converted from the world by Evangelistic efforts, and who, in March, 1810, formed themselves into a Society at Stanley, in Staffordshire. The Society soon began to extend its influence for good, spreading through England, Ireland, and Scotland, to the Channel Islands, the United States, Canada, Australia, New South Wales, Tasmania, Queensland, New Zealand, Fernando Po, &c., and is now entering on operations in South Africa.

According to the statistics of the connexion recently published, the English and Canadian Conferences have associated with them 160,658 members; 1005 travelling, and 14,751 local preachers; 9997 class teachers; 6552 chapels and other preaching places; 3506 Sabbath schools, containing 296,512 scholars, taught by 48,973 teachers; and 44 day schools, with 4317 pupils.

UNITED METHODIST FREE CHURCHES.

This connexion was formed in 1857 by the amalgamation of the Wesleyan Association and the Wesleyan Reformers. It has in Great Britain 334 ministers, 3361 lay ministers, 67,648 members, 1560 chapels and preaching-rooms, and 165,528 Sunday scholars. It has missions in Wales, Ireland, Jamaica, East and West Africa, Australia, New Zealand, and China. It has 42 missionaries on foreign stations, 6112 members, and 4915 Sunday scholars. The receipts for missions during the past year amounted to 11,770*l.*

The formation of the United Methodist Free Churches was occasioned by the assumption and exercise of undue authority on the part of the Methodist Conference, composed exclusively of itinerant preachers. The Conference claims and exercises sole legislative authority in the connexion: from time to time enacting laws, which are made obligatory upon all the local officers and other members of the societies composing the body; without allowing them, by any system of representation, to participate in making the laws by which they have to be governed. In the year 1835 the Conference, in opposition to the wishes of a large portion of the members of the connexion, made new laws, which invest its itinerant preachers with ultimate sole judicial and executive authority. So that they now may, whenever they think proper, expel members from the Society (as they did in 1835 and 1849), against whom no charge has been proved to the satisfaction of any leaders' meeting, and even although the leaders' meeting has acquitted the accused member from the alleged offence.*

The general principles of this body are:—

"*First,* That this Association recognises and holds, as the only and sufficient rule of faith and practice, and also of Church government, the Holy Scriptures, especially the New Testament of our Lord and Saviour Jesus Christ; and regards as matters indifferent—so far as membership with a Christian Church is concerned—whatever is not manifestly enjoined in those infallible records.

"*Second,* That on subjects of Christian doctrine, this Association concurs in those sentiments generally taught in the theological writings of the Rev. John Wesley, and which are admitted, by the various branches of the Methodist community, as being consistent with the Holy Scriptures.

"*Third,* That each circuit in the Association has the right and power to govern itself by its local courts, without any interference as to the management of its internal affairs."— *Connexional Regulations of the United Methodist Free Churches,* 1860.

---

* See "Exposition of the Laws of Conference Methodism," by Rev. R. Eckett. Published at the Book Room of the United Methodist Free Churches.

BAPTISTS.

The first General (Arminian) Baptist Church is said to have been formed in London in 1607; the first Particular (Calvinistic) Church in 1616. The General Baptist New Connexion (Orthodox) was established in 1771. They now number 21,231 members. There are about 2400 churches in England, Wales, Ireland, and Scotland; and about 250,000 members. The Old General Baptists, Unitarian and Christian, have only about 13 churches, and 400 members. The Baptists publish two newspapers, the *Baptist* (Elliot Stock), 1*d.*, and the *Freeman*, 2*d.*

NEW JERUSALEM CHURCH
(SWEDENBORGIANS).

This body of Christians, who accept the teachings of Emanuel Swedenborg, and worship the Lord Jesus Christ as the only God, dates from about 1788, and has been steadily increasing for many years past. They now number upwards of seventy societies in England and Scotland. They possess a General Conference, which governs all general matters connected with the organization.

In America this body has spread much more rapidly than in England. In addition to adherents to be found in every town and village, 108 regularly organized church societies exist there; and in five or six of the principal cities German churches exist as well as English. All the societies, through representatives at a General Convention, held yearly, manage the business common to the whole Church.

FREE CHRISTIAN CHURCHES.

The following extracts from letters of the Rev. Robert Rodolph Suffield, addressed privately to me, or extracted from his published works, serve to place in a clearer light what is perhaps the most remarkable, as certainly the most recent, religious phenomenon alluded to in the foregoing pages :—

I.

"March 31st, Wednesday Night.

" My dear Dr. Davies,

"I have just this moment returned from Newcastle, and found your kind and interesting letter at the top of a pile; so I will answer it first, for I do really feel very anxious that your forthcoming work should direct the attention of thoughtful men to the possibility of a religious position securing public worship and religious sympathy and moral support, without being pledged thereby to any foregone conclusions.

"In America the Unitarians have, if I can trust hostile statements in the *Index*, placed themselves under the Unitarian Association of the country, and thereby committed themselves to *some* limitations, ex. gr., to the Christian name. In England, that is not the case. The Unitarian Association is pledged, *at present*, to the Christian *name*, to Christianity under *some form*, or *ideal;* but no chapel, no congregation, is under the Association. All the congregations called " Unitarian," " Free Christian," or " Presbyterian *English*" (of the original foundations) are quite independent, and quite unfettered. Individuals may be narrow or bigoted; others may, without narrowness or bigotry, hold opinions which I and others reject, and may elect their ministers with view to the opinion held by the majority; but nothing prevents the change of opinion, and the consequent change of liturgy and of ministers.

"Dean Stanley, by his public remark to me at Sion College, seemed not aware of the existence of all these unfettered congregations throughout the country; and he admitted that such might become the next phase of religious progress.

* * * * *

"R. R. S."

II.

From a letter published as Appendix to the "Vatican Decrees," and the "Expostulation."

* * * * *

"Having understood that those who are commonly called Unitarians, Free Christians, or Christian Theists, thus agree in the liberty inspired by self-diffidence, humility, and charity, to carry on the worship of God, without sectarian requirements or sectarian opposition; that they possess a simple but not vulgar worship, a high standard of virtue, intelligence, and integrity; and these after the Christian type, moulded by the Christian traditions, and edified by the sacred Scriptures; holding the spirit taught by Jesus Christ, and the great thoughts by virtue of which he built up the ruins of the moral world; and yet not enforcing the reception of complicated dogmas as a necessity, or accounting their rejection a crime: a communion of Christian worshippers, bound loosely together, and yet by the force of great principles enabled quietly to maintain their position, to exercise an influence elevating and not unimportant, and to present religion under an aspect which thoughtful men can accept without latent scepticism, and earnest men without the aberrations of superstition, or the abjectness of mental servitude to another—such approved itself to my judgment, and commended itself to my sympathy.

"I intend adhering to the pursuits of the clergyman and of the Christian teacher, and communications are in progress in another part of England which may terminate in my accepting there a duty conformable to the habits of my life, and which will not throw me into a position of hostility or embarrassment as to those honoured and loved Catholic friends with whom so greatly I should prize, if it were possible, to maintain kindly intercourse, inasmuch as I am only externally severed from them by my being unable to believe certain dogmas which a Catholic is bound to regard as essential. Thus I hope I have not only thanked you for your obliging offer, but adequately explained my position, and showed that the future you were commissioned to hold out to me in the Established Church would not be deemed possible by the authorities who have done me the honour and kindness to communicate in my regard, as soon as they are made aware that the Articles and the Athanasian Creed would be amongst the insuperable barriers to my entertaining such a proposal.

"Many write to me evidently under a grievous misapprehension. They anticipate from me reckless denunciations of that vision of beauty which I have left, simply because, like a vision, it had everything but reality. Allied as I am by relationship with some of our ancient Catholic families, allied by the ties of friendship with many more of them, I feel it is a shame to myself that any stranger could suppose one word of my lips, one thought of my mind, could cast moral reproach on those beautiful and honoured homes where old traditions received a lustre greater even than antiquity and suffering can bestow—crowned with the aureola of charity, nobleness, purity, and devotedness. Such memories print on my heart their everlasting record. To cease to believe and to worship with them was a martyrdom, which none but the Catholic can understand.

"I have ascended now to another stage of my life; to rise to it needed sufferings of the mind and of the heart, the sacrifice of everything in the world I cared for; but I perceive a work to do, and, by the blessing of God, I shall strive to perform it. Youth, strength, vigour, and hope return to me with the expectation. Truth obtained by suffering is doubly dear to the possessor.—Very sincerely yours,

"ROBERT RODOLPH SUFFIELD.
"To the Rev. —— &c. &c."

III.

From a "Note" to a sermon by the same author. Mr. Suffield heads this in MS. "My own position:"—

"From the intuitions of the human mind; from its reasonings, feelings, and aspirations; from its sense of right and wrong; from all these combined in the experiences of mankind, and presented to us in the history of humanity, we can obtain a Religion of Life and Hope, of discipline and trustful repose; such, held with diffidence, with earnestness, with reverence, with fortitude, and with tenderness, revealing itself in harmony with science, and with our highest moral and spiritual aspirations, gathering into itself from all Churches, Sects, and Scriptures, whatever is of universal application, will keep evolving itself to the soul of man, and presenting to us as much of certainty as is obtainable in the ordinary affairs of life; why demand for the future a certainty *of a kind* essentially differing from what is adequate for our daily actions and our daily hopes?

"The only theory of God's moral government which conforms to our sense of justice in presence of the various opposing beliefs held by men equally good, truth-loving, and anxious, is that what is really important is attainable by all— namely, to be truthful in word and act to whatever we think, to strive to think as correctly as we can, and to practise according to our light and means, the best to which we see our way. Such is the best and the happiest religion."

IV.

The following letter from the Rev. J. B. Heard, to his former parishioners, has been received since the publication of the article " A New Iconoclast."

"Woodridings, Pinner, July 25th, 1874.

"MY DEAR FRIENDS,

"Under any circumstances, I think the pastoral tie is one so sacred that it should not be sundered without a frank and free explanation on the part of the pastor to his flock; but especially is this the case under the peculiar circumstances which compel me to resign the charge at Woodridings. Were I leaving for promotion or for a better living, my removal would seem to some of you quite a natural and proper step to take; but as my reasons are of a very different kind, and grow out of the existence of a legal Establishment and its repressive action on the free play of spiritual forces, I feel the more bound to give you an explanation in writing, and so to clear up misunderstandings which have arisen with regard to my course in the future.

"I have for some time held the conviction that Cæsarism, or the supremacy of the civil power in spiritual things, is a national evil. Its only vindication arose from the fact that such a barrier was necessary perhaps at the time of the Reformation, and to some extent is so still against that other and worse tyranny of Clericalism. In God's moral government of the world, one form of oppression or repression of Divine truth is sometimes raised up to check another. As for myself—who was born and educated as a member of such a National Church, and who took orders heartily approving of the pure and Protestant teaching of its formularies—I have only lately felt any scruple about officiating as a minister in that Church on account of my convictions as to the general question of Establishments.

"But the opportunities which I have had, during the last four or five years, of mixing with Christians of all denominations, have taught me how small and insignificant were our differences, and how deep and real our agreements. I have asked myself with astonishment what it is that separates us still, and I can find no barrier against the reunion of Evangelical Christendom except the Establishment.

"That institution—more civil than religious, and more political even than ecclesiastical—emphasizes the class distinctions of society. It is the State Church that invests the ministers of the meek and lowly Jesus with the pride, pomp, and circumstance of a worldly hierarchy. It is this which turns Christian bishops into prelates, which makes them peers in Parliament; and, by its law of patronage, has come to regard a solemn spiritual trust as a piece of property which may be bought and sold in the open market. It has thus created a scandal for which there is not another parallel in all Christendom.

"As for myself, I have long sought for Christian union, and have laboured in my humble way to show fraternal recognition to all faithful ministers of Christ's Gospel, whatever their denomination. Now it happened on two occasions last year, when on deputation for the Religious Tract Society, that I felt called on to show that fraternal recognition by preaching in Nonconformist pulpits, and on both occasions was presented to the Bishop of London by the Incumbents of these parishes (one of them an advanced Ritualist, practising confession and other Romish ceremonies) for intruding into their parishes, and officiating without their consent. My defence of my conduct to the Bishop of London was this: that I had committed no breach whatever of the Act of Uniformity, either of its letter or of its spirit, and that my only ecclesiastical offence lay in a breach of one of those canons which are binding on the clergy but not on the laity. My real offence, however, lay in not acting on those exclusive principles of Church communion which have become the unwritten tradition of the Church since the days of the Laudian divines. Thus I came " perilously near," to use the Bishop's own expression in his letter of remonstrance to me, "doing evil that good may come." Now, as I do not agree with the Bishop that I was doing evil in this case, and do not believe that good can in any case come out of doing evil, I had to face the question, in what consisted the sin of schism, which, by implication of my Bishop, I had committed. In other words, I had to ask myself, Did I believe in apostolical succession at all, or in the Divine right of an Episcopal Church to consider herself the exclusive channel of God's grace to men? Holding, on the contrary, as I do, that all our existing forms of Church government and organization are of no more importance to the spirit athirst for the living God than the shape of the cup is to the man who is parched with thirst, I have been reluctantly compelled to decide between obeying the higher law of unity or the lower law of uniformity. I do not complain of the Bishop's interpretation of what my duty should be; it is narrow and unsympathetic, but it is the strict letter of the canon law, which regards every parish as a preserve into which no trespassers, especially of the clerical order, may intrude, under penalties which are awful exactly because they are indefinable except in a lawyer's bill of costs.

" For myself, I have resolved to obey the higher law, and have accordingly sent back my licence to the Bishop, which I shall not seek to renew until either the two Acts of

Henry VIII. and Charles II.—the one of Supremacy and the other of Uniformity—are repealed, or else until the Church is otherwise nationalized so as to open its communion to those who were ejected for conscience' sake in 1662.

"Having thus explained my own course of conduct, I wish to add a remark on one or two expressions in my farewell sermon, which may otherwise be liable to be misunderstood. I used the expression, 'That, for myself, I had learned to live above ordinances,' which might seem to weak minds to disparage the sacraments and services of the Church. Now, I should grieve to hurt the consciences of any whose 'faith is fixed in form.' But my justification for using such an expression is, that it is substantially the teaching of that great apostle, who certainly used a very disparaging expression of those who exalted the external at the expense of the internal and spiritual. He desired the Philippians to beware of the circumcision, which he called the concision, when that Divine ordinance, the Sacrament of the Old Testament Church, was set up as an exclusive channel of salvation. Now, I should speak of either or of both of the two sacraments in the same way to any who misuse them, by confounding a moral and spiritual ordinance with certain magical powers supposed to inhere in the priest as such. Moreover, if I cared for the support of human testimony, I should quote that of Dr. Frazer, the Bishop of Manchester, with whom I am almost in verbal agreement on that subject.

"Again, I said that 'I desired to be a High Churchman,' using the phrase not in the colloquial sense but the true. By this I only implied a desire, which I have long felt, to realize church communion and the fellowship of all believers in Christ, which is impossible, from the nature of the case, in a National Church. This desire may excite the ridicule of the worldly, and the scornful contempt of those who are at ease as to this world and the next, but no serious Christian of any persuasion will regard it as any other than a genuine desire of the spiritual nature, though it may always be fairly open to question whether one external community is more favourable to spiritual life than another. This question each one must judge for himself. As for myself, my convictions are that a spiritual and a National Church are a contradiction in terms; and consequently, that for those who are in a legal state of mind, conformity to an Act-of-Parliament governed Church is as natural and easy as it is difficult to those otherwise minded. I ought not, perhaps, to dwell on this topic, lest I should seem to reflect on myself and others who have long attempted to reconcile these standing contradictions by drawing distinctions between the Establishment and the Church. But compelled as I now am to decide between the two, by the act of the Bishop enforcing on me his interpretation of the Act of Uniformity, I have no hesitation in saying of myself 'we must obey God rather than men.' It is better to dissent from a law-made Church, than from truth and conscience. It is better to lay down social advantages and a worldly position of some comfort than to palter with convictions, and leave the laity under the impression that the clergy are slower than other people to see the path of duty and honour.

"I have only, then, to say to you farewell, under the conviction that life is too short to waste it in controversies with bishops as to the interpretation of musty canons enacted in the reign of James I. Again, it seems to me to be a waste of time to carry on feeble protests against Ritualism such as those of the Church Association, to agitate the country, and, as the last resort of all, to appeal to Parliament to pass a special act 'to put down the Ritualists,' as the Prime Minister described the Public Worship Bill. We shall see whether legal enactment can restrain spiritual forces of any kind. To me it seems like 'putting new wine into old bottles,' and time will tell whether our legislators, who in perfect good faith are trying to save the Establishment, are not actually hastening its overthrow.

"I may be wrong in this view of the case; but if so, I am wrong with some of the most farseeing men of the day. But, for myself, the conviction is decided that the voluntary tie is the only one under which a spiritual truth can be safely held in its purity and integrity; and I mean to act accordingly. I have only, then, to bid you farewell, and to thank you each and all for much kindness during the past, and much forbearance with my many shortcomings. May each of you be able to say, 'I know in whom I have believed;' may each of you be 'fully persuaded in your own mind;' and ever remember, as my parting word to you, that it is a very small matter hereafter what external communion you belong to on earth, provided you are joined to the Lord by faith, and are members of that Church of the firstborn whose names are written in heaven.

"Your faithful friend and late Pastor,

"JOHN B. HEARD."

THE REV. JOSEPH PARKER, D.D.

This eminent clergyman, whom it is scarcely fair to identify with any *sect*, is the author of the well-known works "Ecce Deus," "The Paraclete," "Ad Clerum" (a Book for Preachers), and "A Homiletic Analysis of the Gospel of St. Matthew." His age is forty-four, and he was born at Tyneside, Northumberland. He was eleven years in Manchester in succession to the Rev. Dr. Robert Halley.

The City Temple accommodates 2500 persons, and the total cost of land and building was 60,000*l*. It includes schoolroom, class-rooms, and every kind of convenience.

From an exhaustive article in the *British Quarterly Review*, No. 85, called "Religion in London," we gather the following particulars as to the statistics of chapel accommodation in 1865 as compared with 1851, when the census of religious bodies was taken:—

	1851. Sittings.	1865. Sittings.	Increase since 1851.
Congregationalists	100,436	130,611	30,175
Baptists	54,234	87,559	33,325
Wesleyans	44,162	52,454	8,292
U. Methodist Free Churches	4,858	13,422	8,564
Methodist New Connexion	984	6,667	5,683
Primitive Methodists	3,380	9,230	5,850
Calvinistic Methodists	800	3,790	2,990
Church of Scotland	3,886	5,116	1,250
English Presbyterians	10,065	12,952	2,887
United Presbyterians	4,280	4,860	580

	1851. Sittings.	1865. Sittings.	Increase.	Decrease.
Society of Friends	3,157	3,179	22	
Unitarians	3,300	4,440	1,140	
Plymouth Brethren	230	3,360	3,130	
Foreign Lutherans	3,002	3,502	500	
Roman Catholics	18,230	31,100	12,870	
Catholic & Apostolic Church	2,700	5,020	2,320	
Latter-Day Saints	2,640	1,530	—	1,110

PLACES OF WORSHIP IN LONDON AND THEIR ACCOMMODATION.

	No. of Places of Worship.	Sittings.	Population.	Proportion per cent. of Population accommodated.
1851	1,097	698,549	2,362,236	30·2
1865	1,316	917,895	3,015,494	30·4
Increase	219	219,346	653,258	·2

There has thus been an increase of accommodation in fourteen years of about 31 per cent. Had the increase been threefold, it would only have sufficed to meet the increase of population. Taking 52 per cent., Mr. Mann's estimate, as the maximum number to be provided for, the following result is obtained :—

DEFICIENCY OF ACCOMMODATION.

Number of persons unprovided for in London in 1851 . 669,514
Ditto in 1865 831,387

Increased deficiency 161,873

If all the persons in London who are not physically disqualified, or for any legitimate reasons, were to attend church or chapel at the same time, 52 per cent., or more than one-half the population, would be shut out for want of room.

THE END.

LONDON:
SAVILL, EDWARDS AND CO., PRINTERS, CHANDOS STREET
COVENT GARDEN.

www.ingramcontent.com/pod-product-compliance
Lightning Source LLC
Chambersburg PA
CBHW030341230426

43664CB00007BA/495